ESCAPE FROM TERROR

The five explosive worlds of air combat, capture, confinement, chaos and escape from Nazi Germany.

PAUL BURTON

Published by Looking Glass Graphics
Post Office Box K
Murfreesboro, AR 71958
(501) 285-2244

Cover Design by Branden Sharp
Document restoration by Michael Cate

Printed in the United States of America

Library of Congress Cataloging Data
Paul T. Burton
Escape from Terror
History, World War Two

ISBN # 1-886130-03-5

Library of Congress Catalog Card Number: 95-081643

1. Military History
2. Paul T. Burton (1913 -)
3. Germany
4. World War Two
5. U. S. Air Force

DEDICATION

Major Weldon K. Burton

Dedicated to the memory of my brother,
Major Weldon K. Burton,
464th Group Operations Officer, Fifteenth
Air Force, lost in action over the Northern
Adriatic.

And to my cousin,
Major Lawrence E. Jarnegin,
Anti-Submarine Patrol Pilot, killed in action
over the Bay of Biscay;
and to all the others who didn't make it back.

W.K. Burton, Magnolia Flier, reported missing

Magnolia, Ark., Nov. 13 (1944) Special-- Mr. and Mrs. E.T. Burton, of Magnolia, have received a message from the war department reporting their son, Major Weldon, K. Burton, 25, operations officer of a B-24 bomber group based in Italy, has been missing over Germany territory since Oct. 29. His brother Lt. Col. Paul Burton has been a prisoner in Germany the past six months. He was captured in Belgium when his plane was shot down last April.

Major Burton has been in foreign service about a year. He volunteered in March '41, for service in the Canadian Air Force, along with his brother, Paul, and when the U.S. entered the war they transferred to U.S. Army Air Corps. Major Burton has been awarded the Distinguished Flying Cross and the Air Medal with Oak Leaf clusters.

*****

The following named crew members, were flying together, the day they failed to return:

Major Weldon K. Burton, Pilot
Capt. Brooks Sheldon, Co-Pilot
1st Lt. Larry H. Dickason, Navigator
Major Kyle Spiller, Jr., Navigator
2nd Lt. Frank Whittemore, Jr., Navigator
Major Royal F. Cato
S/Sgt Raymond I. Boyd
S/Sgt Roscoe L. Ottinger
S/Sgt Herman O. Makey Jr.
S/Sgt Robert H. Dirnbauer
S/Sgt. John A. Czesniuk

IN GRATEFUL MEMORY OF

Major Weldon K. Burton

WHO DIED IN THE SERVICE OF HIS COUNTRY

in the Mediterranean Area.

HE STANDS IN THE UNBROKEN LINE OF PATRIOTS WHO HAVE DARED TO DIE

THAT FREEDOM MIGHT LIVE, AND GROW, AND INCREASE ITS BLESSINGS.

FREEDOM LIVES, AND THROUGH IT, HE LIVES—

IN A WAY THAT HUMBLES THE UNDERTAKINGS OF MOST MEN

Harry Truman

PRESIDENT OF THE UNITED STATES OF AMERICA

Foreword

When Paul Burton and I played together as youngsters in the Columbia County woods in Arkansas, and attended the same Boy Scout camp, I knew this second cousin by his complete name; Paul Travis Burton. Reading his riveting story of dogged survival and escape during World War ll, helped me appreciate the appropriateness of that memory.

"I will not surrender; I will not retreat."

Many of us have thrilled over those heroic words of Colonel William Barrett Travis, emblazoned over the Alamo he commanded. Paul Travis Burton is named for his illustrious distant relative.

At the infamous Stalag Luft lll in Eastern Germany in 1944, Paul's middle name proved to be prophetic. While capture and confinement became undeniable realities, surrender was never a consideration.

Hardly anything invigorates that spirit more than the pursuit of freedom.

This book proves in vivid detail just how sustaining that pursuit can be - not only in the face of physical danger, but under the smothering cloud of ridicule, boredom and hunger.

The resolute spirit -- the Travis spirit -- was rewarded! Paul Travis and officer Ken Martin, became the first and perhaps only Americans to successfully escape from a German Stalag!

Freedom as an abstract concept is one thing; repeatedly risking one's life to regain it is another altogether. *Escape from Terror* plunged me in the cold, wet, threatening fields and forests of Germany with Paul and Colonel Martin, knowing that warm, friendly American freedom was so near.

I experienced with them, a potent hunger for freedom. A vaguely familiar song-fragment kept teasing the fringes of my mind.

I again can hear those matchless words: "Oh, beautiful for heroes proved in liberating strife; Who more than self their country loved and mercy more than life!"

That "liberating strife" is what this book is largely about.

Sidney McMath
Former Governor of Arkansas
General, USMC (Retired)

Escape from Terror

Table of Contents

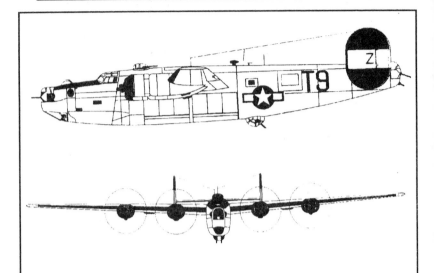

Consolidated B-24 Liberator

The B-24 J was the principal U.S. bomber used in World War II. It had a long range, high altitude capability. The B-24 was built for tough service like it's sister planes the B-17 and B-29. All were giant flying bombers, however, the B-24 had very slender wings.

This design was better for higher altitudes than other bombers could achieve. The primary drawback was added difficulty in control of the big bird when overloaded which was common during the latter part of the war in Germany.

It has safely returned with half of its tail section blown away and the fuselage peppered with holes, but because of the special wing, even a minor hit to that section of the craft often brought disaster.

The B-24 was a workhorse but not easy to control and required both mental and physical stamina from its pilots.

It weighed 36,500 pounds (empty) and could carry just under 30,000 pounds in crew and cargo including 12,800 pounds of bombs.

With a range of 2,100 miles, it flew almost a mile higher than other heavy bombers of the day. Four turbo-supercharged engines powered the airship up to 300 miles per hour.

The B-24 was 18 feet tall and 67 feet long with a wing span of 110 feet.

Part One

Combat

<u>22 April 44</u>. As we sight the flat coast of Holland ahead we can see black puffs of FLAK (antiaircraft artillery) around the bombers preceding us. This tells us that today's battle is about to begin. In my earlier combat experiences I had not been impressed by such harmless looking little puffs of smoke, apparently without any sound or substance. Now, to the contrary, I have a nauseating knowledge of their capability for damage and destruction, their jagged metal fragments tearing into human flesh.

At 20,000 feet, the three bomber divisions of the mighty Eighth Air Force make an impressive sight roaring across the North Sea toward Germany. Escorted by busy, darting fighters, B-17 and B-24 formations appear to spread to infinity as they march solidly into the enemy's homeland.

I am Command Pilot with a lead crew headed by Captain Willard P. Stotter from 567th Squadron .

Stotter's crew members are: 1st Lt. Gordon J. Baber, Jr., 1st Lt. John E. Powell, 1st Lt. Myron Gins, T/Sgt. Lewis E. Bagwell, T/Sgt. Albert A. Arndt, S/Sgt. Michael S. Sniuk, S/Sgt. Lee T. Parker, S/Sgt. Dudley A. Burr and S/Sgt. Harvey T. Belcher.

It's my nineteenth combat mission. We are in Stotter's faithful old B-24D bomber, "Round Trip Ticket." (Col. Philip Ardery, a fellow squadron commander and author of "<u>Bomber Pilot</u>" University Press of Kentucky. Lexington, Ky 40506) completed his final combat mission with this same plane and crew.) I am pleased to be with Stotter's crew and in this aircraft; I've flown with them before, and know they are as good as they come.

We are just one of the 144 bombers taking part in a bombing assault against the rail yards of Hamm,Germany,in the heavily

CONSOLIDATED B24 LIBERATOR

(ALSO BUILT BY FORD MOTOR CO. ON WEEKENDS)

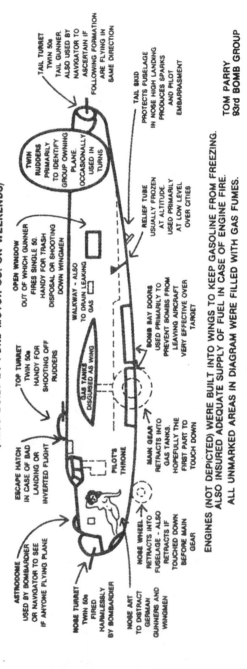

TAIL TURRET TWIN 50s TAIL GUNNER. ALSO USED BY NAVIGATOR TO ASCERTAIN IF FOLLOWING FORMATION ARE FLYING IN SAME DIRECTION

TWIN RUDDERS PRIMARILY TO IDENTIFY GROUP OWNING PLANE. OCCASIONALLY USED IN TURNS

TAIL SKID PROTECTS FUSELAGE IN NOSE HIGH LANDING PRODUCES SPARKS AND PILOT EMBARRASMENT

TOP TURRET TWIN 50s HANDY FOR SHOOTING OFF RUDDERS

OPEN WINDOW OUT OF WHICH GUNNER FIRES SINGLE 50. HANDY FOR TRASH DISPOSAL OR SHOOTING DOWN WINGMEN

WALKWAY - ALSO TO DRAIN LEAKING GAS

RELIEF TUBE USUALLY FROZEN AT ALTITUDE. USED PRIMARILY AT LOW LEVEL OVER CITIES

GAS TANKS DISGUISED AS WING

BOMB BAY DOORS USED PRIMARILY TO PREVENT BOMBS FROM LEAVING AIRCRAFT VERY EFFECTIVE OVER TARGET

ESCAPE HATCH IN CASE OF BAD LANDING OR INVERTED FLIGHT

PILOTS THRONE

MAIN GEAR RETRACTS INTO GAS TANKS. HOPEFULLY THE FIRST PART TO TOUCH DOWN

ASTRODOME USED BY BOMBARDIER OR NAVIGATOR TO SEE IF ANYONE FLYING PLANE

NOSE TURRET TWIN 50s FIRED HARMLESSLY BY BOMBARDIER

NOSE ART TO DISTRACT GERMAN GUNNERS AND WINGMEN

NOSE WHEEL RETRACTS INTO FUSELAGE - ALSO RETRACTS IF TOUCHED DOWN BEFORE MAIN GEAR

ENGINES (NOT DEPICTED) WERE BUILT INTO WINGS TO KEEP GASOLINE FROM FREEZING. ALSO INSURED ADEQUATE SUPPLY OF FUEL IN CASE OF ENGINE FIRE. ALL UNMARKED AREAS IN DIAGRAM WERE FILLED WITH GAS FUMES.

TOM PARRY
93rd BOMB GROUP

defended Ruhr Valley. We are the lead aircraft in the second section of our Wing. We are flying our section abreast and to the right of the lead section.

Seeing the coast ahead Stotter gives the order to don flak helmets and vests. The gunners have already test fired their guns. We are now ready for today's business, as ready as we know how to be.

Stotter's navigator notes that we are several miles south of our briefed route. Obviously, the navigator on the leading half of our Wing has a bad navigation error. But before crossing the coast he corrects his error by abruptly turning left and flying up the coast to a point due west of Rotterdam where we had been briefed to enter Holland. But instead of correcting his previously erroneous heading he confusingly resumes it.

This error is highly significant. At our Intelligence briefing we had been directed to stay within the boundaries of a certain narrow corridor as we fly through "Flak Alley" to avoid the heaviest concentration of the Ruhr Valley's well known flak defenses. So why are we heading straight into the thick of it? I reluctantly break radio silence and call "A" section leader, using our secret code of the day. I get a muffled reply that I can't understand.

The flak gets heavier. They are not only shooting their 88-millimeter rounds at us, but their 155's as well. The black puffs are exploding so close that we can see the red flame inside the black smoke, and hear their disturbingly close explosive sounds. Suddenly our number two engine loses power.

There's a severe drop in manifold pressure. We see a large hole in the cowling, and know that the supercharger has been knocked out by flak.

I can clearly see our target several degrees to our left. There's smoke rising from it as the bombs from our preceding groups hit. Not only are we facing fierce opposition, we're not even going in the right direction toward our target! I am extremely perplexed as to just what I should do.

I again try to inform "A" section leader that our present heading will never get us to the primary target. I get the same muffled reply as before. I am very reluctant to break wing formation but I cannot forget the axiom that maintaining the objective is the first rule of warfare. I decide to break wing formation and head my section toward the target.

But "A" section's position prevents us from turning the few necessary degrees to the left, so we must make an enormous, unwieldy right turn of more than 300 degrees.

This maneuver really confuses my section's pilots, for during the turn we are momentarily out of the flak and headed back toward friendly England. We continue the turn until we are headed for Dortmund, the briefed IP (Initial Point), where the bomb run to the target is to begin. From this point on we are committed and can take no evasive action, regardless of opposition.

During the turn the formation has become quite loose. At the IP, Stotter goes on auto pilot so that the bombardier can steer the aircraft to the target with his bombsight. We fire the flare gun signal, telling aircraft in our formation to open bomb bay doors and start the bomb run. I again break radio silence to tell my pilots to close in the formation for a good bomb run.

Immediately we hear and feel a close explosion. Stotter motions and mumbles to me (over the intercom, but calmly and quietly so as not to alarm the crew), "I think we've been hit."

I grab the copilot controls just as the aircraft noses down into a vertical dive out of formation. I don't have time to signal my deputy to take over the lead. Stotter and I quickly learn that the elevator trim control has separated, causing the elevator to jump into full nose-heavy position, as it was designed to do to prevent a deadly stall. We both put our feet on the panel and pull back on the control with all our combined strength.

The right waist gunner reports that number four engine (right outboard) is burning and the flames are extending back as far as the waist.

With great effort we are able to pull the nose up and hold it until Stotter can engage the auto-pilot's elevator control. We have lost 10,000 feet in the dive. Now the left wing is down; trying to pull it up we feel the control cable pulling apart. With full right aileron control the left wing is still down. Stotter and I push our feet against the right rudder with all our might.

We are able to skid the left wing up, not all the way but at least far enough to stop the turn. Now we skid along at an air speed barely above stall, a speed we can maintain only by descending at 200-500 feet per minute. We have no manual control over the plane. I am certain this aircraft will never get us back to England.

Stotter, on the intercom, asks me if he should ring the bailout bell. I answer yes. Stotter rings the bell. Someone asks, "Did you say bail out?" I answer, "Yes, bail out!" I add, "Engineer, shut off the fuel to number four." He answers, "Yes sir." Then Stotter calls out, "So long, boys, and good luck!" After that the interphones are quiet.

Stotter jettisons the bombs with the emergency handle. We tear off our oxygen masks, eager to wipe our dried lips. I am surprised to see an extra pair of feet between our seats. I look up and see bombardier, Myron Gins. Why hasn't he bailed out? He explains that from his position in the nose he would not leave the aircraft as long as he could see our feet on the pedals. He adds that the fire in number four engine is out. I push the feathering button and the big prop feathers itself to a stop, slightly reducing our rate of decent.

The ground below is a heavily wooded, thinly populated area, under the circumstances an ideal place to bail out and evade capture. "Let's go!" I shout, unbuckling my seat harness. "Go ahead," says Stotter, "I can get it back."

I am amazed that he doesn't seem to know that, as ranking officer, I have to be the last to leave. "I can't go before you," I explain. He replies, "You go ahead and jump if you want to; so long," and puts out his hand to shake good bye.

I feel totally frustrated. Not only am I convinced that this airplane can't possibly make it back, we now have other impelling reasons to get out immediately: we have no gunners, so we are a helpless target for enemy fighters; and we are skidding along, just barely above a stall, or possibly a fatal spin from lack of control. We're losing altitude steadily, and getting continually closer to all kinds of ground-to-air defenses. Very soon we will be too low for our chutes to open on bail out. I know that crash landing or ditching a B-24, even with full control, can be deadly; with no control it's suicidal.

My attempts to reason all this with Stotter and Gins are to no avail. Stotter keeps repeating the handshaking act and Gins says he will stay with Stotter.

A lone P-47 appears out of nowhere. Stotter calls to him on our emergency frequency. "Hi, Little Friend, this is Big Friend."

"Go ahead, Big Friend, I have you in sight."

"Stay with us, Little Friend, we got troubles."

"Sorry, Big Friend, I got troubles too. No gas. Lucky if I make it back."

"Okay, Little Friend, If you do make it call Winston Green-Yellow and say what happened to us."

"Okay, Big Friend, but I don't know yet." And he disappears into the setting sun.

We sight the Zuyderzee and see that we have a very strong headwind. Stotter realizes that we don't have the altitude to make it across the North Sea. He turns southward and heads for the Strait of Dover where the English Channel is narrowest, reasoning that if we don't make it that far, maybe we can land in occupied Holland, Belgium, possibly even France, and have a better chance of evading capture.

The flak is worse than ever for now we are within range of smaller, rapid-fire weapons. We see tracers floating up around us, and occasionally we can hear shell fragments spattering against the plane's metal skin. Gins is scurrying about the plane throwing out guns, ammunition, oxygen bottles and flak vests, trying to lighten the load and help the airplane stay up. I am in the bomb bay transferring fuel from the useless engines to number three, the remaining one, which has been devouring fuel at a very high rate.

While I am working furiously in the bomb bay, Gins comes back from the nose. "See if you can get Stotter out" I shout. "We haven't a chance."

Gins nods, crawls up to the flight deck and sits down in the copilot seat beside Stotter. I can see their heads together. In a few seconds Gins gets up and starts back toward me. I see Stotter get up and move toward me also. At last, I think, with a fleeting sense of relief in the midst of my desperation. I remove my helmet, pocket my escape kit, place my right hand over the chute's rip cord handle. I lean out over the open bomb bay and let gravity pull me out.

This is my very first parachute jump. I am totally unprepared for what I experience now. I am instantly and violently blasted by the prop wash from the one good engine, now running wide open. My body is turned and twisted in all directions. Then, just as suddenly, I am in a different world, a world of calmness and silence, with not the slightest sensation of falling.

I discover to my horror that in my initial floundering I have unconsciously pulled the chute's rip cord handle out of its holder and a few inches toward the open chute direction. How very fortunate that the pack has not opened and entangled me hopelessly in the multitude of shroud lines!

I decide to see if the chute will really open. The way things have gone today I am doubtful of everything. I pull the cord. Nothing happens! I look down at the bare wire and see that I have pulled it out about a foot. I pull again, this time with all my strength, all the way out. I hear a loud pop and feel intense pain in my groin. Am I being split in two? I am surprised to hear myself groan aloud from the pain. The forward motion of the aircraft has caused the canopy to open horizontally, and I swing back and forth, groaning from the pain in my groin.

I see Gins and Stotter a few hundred feet away. That's a relief. We wave to each other. I look westward at the sun setting over England. It crosses my mind that there'll be no medicinal whiskey for us this night.

My nerves feel tattered, and I badly need to relax, but I know my troubles are far from over. I can see that we are over the middle of the city of Antwerp, German-occupied Belgium. Near us, old "Round Trip Ticket" is spiraling down at about the same rate we are falling, and every gun in Antwerp seems to be shooting at it. Shells are exploding so close I can feel them shaking the canopy of my parachute.

There are few more naked and helpless feelings an airman can have than to be suddenly stripped of his plane. But it would be worse to also be without a parachute, and one hole in that silken canopy would certainly bring my busy day to an abrupt end. Could matters be worse?

Incredulous, I see our crashing bomber coming directly toward me. It comes so close I can't see how it could miss me. It misses, but comes at me again - misses again. I feel so numb I'm sure nothing more can happen that would bother me.

I pull down on my shroud lines, collapsing half of the canopy to speed my descent and guide the direction of fall. I want to guide myself toward the outskirts of the city so as to possibly evade capture. But I am now close enough to the ground that I have a sensation of falling fast. I manage to avoid some sharp-roofed buildings and aim for an open courtyard. I'm too late to avoid colliding with a small tree, but luckily I recall the part of a paratrooper's lecture about how to land in a tree: legs together, toes pointed down, arms close in, head on shoulder. I slide through most of the tree as the shroud lines catch onto the tree's limbs and I am gently eased down close to the ground. Wriggling around I manage to get my feet on the ground. I am trying to get untangled when I see a young man of about seventeen running out of the house in front of the courtyard. He's clad only in pants and shoes, and he's rushing at me with a bayoneted rifle pointed at my stomach. He stops when he sees I am unarmed and tangled in my parachute. (If captured, we were more likely to be shot if we carry a gun. We had therefore been advised to remain unarmed while on missions.)

Feeling drained and empty I continue disentangling myself from the parachute cords, then slowly untie a small emergency kit from the chute harness. The boy grows impatient and motions at me with the bayonet to precede him to the house. I've seldom felt more dejected. I now taste the bitter dregs of defeat.

* * *

I was born on my father's inherited cotton farm near Magnolia, Arkansas, the second of six children. Like so many others during the Depression Era my family had to struggle to make ends meet. We children were brought up as puritanical Christians, and a strong work ethic was instilled in us at an early age. My brother, Weldon, who was six years younger than me, was my closest friend throughout his life.

In 1931 I went to sea on an oil tanker, sailing out of Aransas Pass, Texas. The following year, while the tanker was in dry dock in Brooklyn, I was injured and sent to Merchant Marine Hospital on Ellis Island. When I was discharged from the hospital six weeks later my ship had sailed without me. To survive I took jobs no one else wanted before I finally landed one with the National Broadcasting Company at Rockefeller Center as an engineer's helper. When Weldon (now shortened to "Don") graduated from high school he joined me in New York. We were again a happy twosome.

My graveyard shift at NBC was not very demanding . I wanted desperately to get into aviation. NYU was then the only place in the USA that offered a degree in Aeronautical Engineering. I could not meet their stiff requirements (a State Regents diploma, two years of a foreign language, and two years each of intermediate level science and mathematics) So I worked nights, slept days, and attended Rhoades Prep evenings from seven to ten until I met NYU's entrance requirements. I continued with the same schedule while attending NYU at Washington Square, studying engineering.

On days off from work or school I spent as much time as I could as a student pilot at Floyd Bennett Airport. After I had acquired fifty hours solo flying time I got a private license. This license enabled me to carry passengers, who paid for renting the airplane. In this way I was able to build up the 200 solo hours required for a commercial-instructor rating. I gained experience as an instructor by letting my passengers hold the controls if they wished to. I passed the flight test for my commercial license on September 1, 1939, the same day Germany invaded Poland and started World War Two. England declared war two days later, but the United States remained neutral until Pearl Harbor was bombed by Japan on December 7, 1941.

With my commercial license I formed Radio City Flying Club and we bought an old open-cockpit biplane. It soon became obvious that Don and I were doing all the work, so we bought the club and agreed to pay off the club members with flying time. About that same time I decided I had rather fly as a pilot than be an engineer so I dropped out of NYU after two years.

Soon after England declared war the British formed the British Commonwealth Air Training Plan and gave Canada the job of training air crews for the whole Commonwealth. Canada desperately needed pilots and secretly started recruiting them in the USA. (This was a violation of the U.S.'s neutrality, but the Commonwealth knew they had strong support in the U.S.) I was interviewed at the Waldorf Astoria Hotel and instructed to go to Ottawa as a tourist and register at the Chateau Laurie Hotel. The RCAF contacted me there. I was told to report to Air Force Headquarters, where I was commissioned in the name of King George the Sixth as Pilot Officer, Temporary Flying Officer in the RCAF.

Don remained in New York to close out our flight school, but in a few months he, too, came to Canada and was commissioned in the RCAF. We were both assigned to Number One Bombing and Gunnery School on the north shore of Lake Erie.

I was in Bombing Flight (a unit I later commanded), and

George the Sixth, by the Grace of God of Great Britain, Ireland and the British Dominions beyond the Seas, King, Defender of the Faith, Emperor of India, &c

To Our Trusty and well beloved Paul Travis Burton Greeting:

We, reposing especial Trust and Confidence in your Loyalty, Courage and good Conduct, do, by these Presents, Constitute and Appoint you to be an Officer in Our Active Air Force of our Dominion of Canada from the Twenty-ninth day of July 1940 You are therefore carefully and diligently to discharge your Duty as such in the Rank of Pilot Officer or in such other Rank as We may from time to time hereafter be pleased to promote or appoint you to of which a notification will be made in the Canada Gazette, or in such other manner as may for the time being be prescribed by Us, in Canada, and you are in such manner and upon such occasions as may be required of you to exercise and well discipline in Arms both the superior Officers and Men serving under you and use your best endeavours to keep them in good Order and Discipline. And We do hereby Command them to Obey you as their superior Officer, and you to observe and follow such Orders and Directions as from time to time you shall receive from Us, or any your superior Officer, according to the Rules and Discipline of War, in pursuance of the Trust hereby reposed in you.

In Witness Whereof Our Governor General of Our Dominion of Canada hath hereunto set his hand and Seal at Our Government House in the City of Ottawa this Twenty-fifth day of September in the Year of Our Lord One Thousand Nine Hundred and Forty and in the Fourth Year of Our Reign

By Command of His Excellency the Governor General

Air Secretarium for Minister of National Defence for Pilot Officer Paul Travis Burton Royal Canadian Air Force Special Reserve

Paul's Appointment Certificate from the Royal Canadian Air Force

Don was in Drogue Flight, which towed targets for the gunners in Gunnery Flight to shoot at.

During our two years in the RCAF the United States entered the war against Germany and shortly afterward the Canadian-American Military Board was formed. That enabled Don and me, as American fliers, to transfer over to the United States military forces with ranks equivalent to those we had attained in Canada. Thus, as a Flight Lieutenant in the RCAF one day, I became a Captain in the USAAF that same day; transferees received two days pay for the transfer day, since we were paid by both the losing and the gaining Powers.

Don and I were immediately put to work at Greenville Basic Flying School in Greenville, Mississippi, as BT-13 Instructors. The team of Don and me became separated when I transferred to B-17 School at Hendrix Field in Sebring, Florida; and later to Tucson, where I instructed in B-24's, before I was given command of a B-24 squadron. (See illustrations on following pages.)

We new squadron commanders trained our crews for combat out of El Paso and Denver before flying our "Liberators" across to Europe to enter the war. I never saw my brother again after leaving Greenville.

My combat experience started in July 1943 in the Libyan desert, at a small air base just outside of what was left of Benghazi after the bitter North African campaign. As Squadron Commander I had accompanied my squadron flying personnel in our new B-24's from the USA to England by way of Goose Bay, Labrador, and Reykjavik, Iceland. In addition to our ten-man crews, we had brought along our Air Echelon, consisting of our aircraft maintenance people and their tools and equipment. Our Ground Echelon would arrive by surface ship and remain at our base in England.

When we arrived at our assigned base at Hethel, a tiny village near Norwich in East Anglia, we were surprised to learn that our real destination was Benghazi, Libya. Along with the two other B-24 groups stationed in England, we were to join two B-24 groups of the Ninth Air Force already stationed at Benghazi.

The idea was to unite at Benghazi all B-24's then in the European and Middle Eastern Theaters in order to provide strategic support for the upcoming invasion of Sicily.

HEADQUARTERS, CANADIAN-AMERICAN MILITARY BOARD

BELLEVILLE	ONTARIO	CANADA
(Station)	(Province)	

May 16   1942
(Date)

Special Orders   E X T R A C T
No.

     By direction of the President and under authority contained in unnumbered Circular, War Department, dated March 9, 1942, Subject: "Information governing transfer from Canadian Armed Forces to Armed Forces of the United States", the following-named officer is ordered to active duty, effective this date, and will report to the Commanding General, Canadian-American Military Board, for temporary duty until   26 ,1942, when he will proceed without delay to the United States station indicated below, reporting upon arrival to the commanding officer for temporary duty.

Name: **Paul Travis Burton**   Serial No. **O-1699162**

Grade: **Captain, AC**   A. U. S.   Rank from: **May 16, 1942**

Home address: No. & Street: **215 W. 109 St.,**
               City & State: **New York, N.Y.**

Now at: **Belleville, Ontario, Canada**

U. S. Station: **C. G., Southeast Air Force Training Center**
            C. G., Southeast Air Forces Training Center,
            Maxwell Field, Alabama.

     The travel directed is necessary in the military service.

     By command of Brigadier General HENRY:

                     s/ J. H. Lowell
                     J. H. LOWELL,
                     Major, A. G. D.
OFFICIAL: Adjutant.

               A TRUE COPY

WAR DEPARTMENT
THE ADJUTANT GENERAL'S OFFICE
WASHINGTON

AG 201 Burton,
    Paul Travis

May 16, 1942

SUBJECT: Temporary Appointment

TO: Captain Paul Travis Burton, AUS   A 01699162
    215 W. 109 Street
    New York, New York

    1. By direction of the President you are temporarily appointed and commissioned in the Army of the United States, effective this date, in the grade and section shown in address above. Your serial number is shown after A above.

    2. This commission will continue in force during the pleasure of the President of the United States for the time being, and for the duration of the present emergency and six months thereafter unless sooner terminated.

    3. There is inclosed herewith a form for oath of office which you are requested to execute and return promptly to the agency from which it was received by you. The execution and return of the required oath of office constitute an acceptance of your appointment. No other evidence of acceptance is required.

    4. This letter should be retained by you as evidence of your appointment as no commissions will be issued during the war.

By order of the Secretary of War:

Inclosure:
Form for oath of office

/s/ J. A. Ulio
    Major General
    The Adjutant General

A TRUE COPY:

JAMES K. ADSIT
1st Lt, AC

Volume 1   ARMY AIR FORCES BASIC FLYING SCHOOL, GREENVILLE, MISS., JUNE 10, 1942

They're Flying For Uncle Sam Now

Two brothers, Captain Paul T. Burton, right, and First Lieutenant Weldon, K. Burton, left, are flying planes of the United States Army Air Forces now after spending a year in the Royal Canadian Air Force. Both were in commercial avaiation flying in the New York area before joining the RCAF. They are attending the instructor school at the Greenville field. The brothers are graduates of Magnolia, Arkansas High School.

United States Army

Army Air Forces

Be it known that

Captain Paul T. Burton

has satisfactorily completed the course of instruction

prescribed for

First Pilot

at the Army Air Forces Combat Crew School
Hendricks Field

In testimony whereof and by virtue of vested authority

I do confer upon him this

DIPLOMA

Given at Sebring, Florida this   14th   day

of   August   in the year of our Lord one thousand

nine hundred and Forty-two.

Carl E. McDaniel
Colonel, Air Corps,
Commanding.

Attest

William G. Vaughan
Captain, Air Corps,
Acting Adjutant.

U. S. GOVERNMENT PRINTING OFFICE : 1942—O—446650

Lincoln, Nebraska
11 June 1943

SPECIAL ORDERS)   C-O-N-F-I-D-E-N-T-I-A-L

NO.........21)   E-X-T-R-A-C-T

    1. Under the prov of 2AF Memo 75-1, dd 30 Dec 1942 and pur to instructions contained in immediate action ltr, Hq, 2AF, sub: "Movement Orders, Flight Echelons, Shipments, 0489-FF, GG, HH, JJ, and KK," file 370.5(E-3), dd 29 May 1943 and immediate action ltr, Hq, 21st Bomb Wing, sub: "Movement Orders, Flight Echelons, Shipments, 0489-FF, GG, HH, JJ, and KK," file 370.5(E-3), dd 5 June 1943, the flight echelon of 565th Bomb Sq (H), 389th Bomb Gp (H), consisting of the following staff personnel and combat crews are reld fr atchd this Hq and WP by mil acft and/or rail to Air Transport Command Station, Presque Isle, Maine and/or such other ports of embarkation as the Commanding General, Air Transport Command may direct, reporting upon arrival to CO for further instructions and disposition preparatory to departure overseas on shipment No. 0489-HH.

CREW #1-19

CAPT KENNETH M. CALDWELL, 01699045 (P)
2D LT OTIS T. HAMILTON, 0736516 (CP)
1ST LT JOHN A FINO, 0725422 (B)
2D LT STELL MEADOR, 0795282 (N)
T sgt ARTHUR N. GREENHALGH, 39091347 (E)
T sgt BERNARD P. GREELEY, 31133130 (R)
T sgt PAUL A. SWETZ, 13040764 (AE)
S sgt LAVELL SMITH, 38190871 (AR)
S sgt HOWARD GIBSON, 18118057 (G)
S sgt WILLIAM R. NESSLER, 33293141 (AG)

CREW #1-20

1ST LT HAROLD L. JAMES, 0666209 (P)
2D LT DONALD T. NICKEY, 0704809 (CP)
2D LT CECIL D. STOUT, 0734759 (B)
2D LT CHARLES B. QUANTRELL, 0797389 (N)
T sgt HAROLD M. THOMPSON, 39092072 (E)
T sgt EARL ZIMMERMAN, 16098186 (R)
S sgt MAX C. CAVEY, 17079844 (AE)
S sgt HUGH R. McLAREN, 35370285 (AR)
S sgt ROBERT L. HAMILTON, 35385441 (G)
S sgt JOHN P. MORRIS, 13086504 (AG)

CREW #1-21

1ST LT ROY E. BRALY, 0793721 (P)
2D LT NORBERT N. GEBHARD, 0740786 (CP)
2D LT MERLIN H. VERBERG, 0734763 (B)
2D LT JAMES H. McGAHEE, 0670770 (N)
2D LT BERNARD LEIBOWITZ, 0856734
           (Sq Comm O)
T sgt VIRGIL L. HOFFMAN, 14081963 (E)
T sgt ESSMAN G. MATTHEWS, 13079143 (R)
S sgt ANDREW S. TOTH, 35333607 (AE)
S sgt GEORGE W. SCOTT, 16018506 (AR)
S sgt EDWARD M. GOODALL, 39188102 (G)
S sgt JOHN B. FILLEGER, 13109989 (AG)

CREW #1-22

1ST LT ELMER D. RODENBERG, 0661966 (P)
2D LT EDWARD J. BRECKEL, 0675270 (CP)
2D LT LOW J. BLUM, 0734307 (B)
2D LT HAROLD L. POLISKY 0736026 (N)
1ST LT BRUCE J. FRANZ, 01685490
           (Sq Med O)
T sgt GEORGE K. HOLROYD, 16053349 (E)
T sgt LESLIE W. MARTIN, 33360580 (R)
S sgt ROBERT J. CLARK, 12045050 (AE)
S sgt MARCELLUS L. OBERSTE, 37372236 (AR)
S sgt JAMES E. MORGAN, 33192700 (G)
S sgt WILLIAM C. EGGLESTON, 16097962 (AG)

CREW #1-24

1ST LT JACK M. CONNERS, 0728833
        (Asst Sq Opn O)
1ST LT ROBERT J. O'REILLY II, 0734129(P)
2D LT ERNEST L. POULSON, 0740272 (CP)
2D LT ALBERT A. ROMANO, 0735930 (B)
2D LT RICHARD W. BRITT, 0674128 (N)
T sgt FRANK J. KEES, 35501754 (E)
T sgt CLELL B. RIFFLE, 15019267 (R)
S sgt JACK R. BONKER, 18097392 (AE)
S sgt TROY O. McCRARY, 34431809 (AR)
S sgt DONALD MacLACHAN, 32383446 (G)
S sgt LOUIS MEDEIROS, 11083092 (AG)

CREW #1-25

CAPT DOYLE HICKS, 0403849 (P)
2D LT GEORGE A. BRITTAIN, 0675031 (CP)
2D LT MARVIN MOSCO, 0734818 (B)
2D LT MARVIN R. MENDELSOHN, 0796566 (N)
T sgt WILBURN TUCKER, 15090246 (E)
T sgt ALFRED P. ROSSI, 33322203, (R)
S sgt MARTIN R. VAN BUREN, 6547871 (AE)
S sgt WILLIAM J. BUDAI, 35337676 (G)
S sgt PAUL M. MILLER, 34431182 (AG)
S sgt GERALD E. MURPHY, 35166638 (AR)

(Crew #1-26)

MAJ PAUL T. BURTON, 01699162 (Sq Comdr)
1ST LT JAMES F. TOLLESON, 0666382 (P)
2D LT RICHARD A. WOOD, 0741007 (CP)
2D LT STEWARD W. MONROE JR, 0734964 (B)
2D LT LEON KLINGHOFFER, 0670759 (N)
T sgt SILAS W. EASTERLING, 35431091 (E)
T sgt JOHN DZUDYK, 33264167 (R)
S sgt JOHN J. GALINUS, 13046771 (AE)
S sgt ROBERT J. NAULE, 31032357 (AR)
S sgt LLOYD E. SHEPHERD, 37374752 (G)
S sgt MARVIN R. ELMORE, 34236035 (AG)

(Crew #1-27)

1ST LT ROBERT W. SPENCE, 0725543
(Sq Opns O (5   10
1ST LT KENNETH A. WATSON, 0793807 (P)
2D LT ALAN L. GREEN, 0740790 (CP)
2D LT RUSSELL A. FRANKLIN, 0734882 (B)
2D LT JACK B. ENGELHARDT, 0798772 (N)
T sgt OSCAR R. WHITE, 34169988 (E)
T sgt HARRY J. MICHOS, 36251303 (R)
S sgt WILLIAM R. STRASMETER, 15103012
(AE)
Cpl JAMES A. EDWARDS, 37202754 (AR)
S sgt ROBERT R. DRIVER, 16009315 (G)
S sgt WILLIAM H. CROLEY, 36342635 (AG)

Upon arrival at destination, Squadron Commander will relinquish control of squadron to Commanding General, Air Transport Command.

This is a permanent change of station. Personnel involved in this movement will not be accompanied by dependents, neither will dependents join personnel upon arrival at destination.

Combat Crew members will be equipped as prescribed in Code No. 300, dd Feb 12, 1943. Cost of transportation of troops and individuals including the shipment of things, will be governed by the prov of Sec II, WD Cir 206, 1942. Equipment and baggage of crews not carried by them in the airplane will be prepared and sent on Govt Bill of Lading to the Port of Embarkation for shipment marked as follows:

       TO: Port Transportation Officer.
           New York Port of Embarkation.
           New York, New York.
       FOR: 0489-HH.

In lieu of subsistence a flat per diem of six dollars ($6.00) is auth for travel and for periods of temporary duty when necessary enroute, for Officers and Flight Officers in accordance with existing law and regulations. Payment of mileage is not authorized. Such times as the individual is billeted and subsisted, as outlined in WD Memorandum W35-2-42, Sept 30, 1942, per diem will be suspended.

For EM a flat per diem of six dollars ($6.00) is authorized for travel by mil acft, in accordance with existing law and regulations. For travel by rail and for periods of temp duty enroute a monetary allows in lieu of rations and qrs is authorized, in accordance with Table II, AR 35-4520.

TDN. TOT. FD 33 P 433-01-02-03-07-08 A 0425-23.

Travel by air is chargeable to FD 31 P 431-02 A 0425-23.

Officers involved are reld of asgmt of qrs in BOQ Bldgs, eff on date of departure.

If movement is by air, personnel are authorized to continue journey by rail if it is impracticalbe to proceed by air.

By order of Major FORD:

L. L. SMITH
1st Lt., Air Corps,
Adjutant.

OFFICIAL:

E. E. SMITH
1st Lt., Air Corps,
Adjutant.

DISTRIBUTION: "A"
PLUS:
   30 - CG, AAF (Air Adj Gen Pub Sec)
    7 - CG, ASF (For distribution to chiefs of Sup Serv)

1 - Air Serv Com, Patterson Fld,
    Fairfield, O (air mail)
1 - Port Air Officer, New York POE
1 - Plans Div, ASF, Wash, D.C.
1 - The Adj Gen (OB-I)
2 - AAF, Dir of Pers (Attn: AFPMP-9)
5 - CG, 2AF
3 - CO, 21st BG
1 - Rets Sec, Misc Div, AGC

At that time Germany occupied or dominated most of the European continent, as well as the Bay of Biscay. Therefore, since we were carrying no guns or ammunition with which to defend ourselves, the route to Libya from England was long and complicated.

First we flew to Lands End in extreme southwest England, then out to longitude ten degrees west, then southward to Portugal, and from there eastward through the Strait of Gibraltar to Oran, Algeria, for an overnight stop.

I occupied the copilot's seat on one of my own squadron's aircraft on our departure from Hethel. Taxiing out for takeoff we slipped off the left edge of the unusually narrow taxiway. The left wheel dropped into the soft soil, causing the left wing tip and the propeller of the left outboard engine (number one) to scrape the ground, incapacitating the aircraft. I hurriedly hitched a ride on the next plane in line for takeoff. I climbed up through the bomb bay of a 567th Squadron (also 389th Group) plane, commanded by Major "Hank" Yaeger. When we landed at Port Reath at Land's End that aircraft suffered fuselage damage from a very hard landing and had to remain in England for repairs. So again I had to find a ride. From Port Reath I flew with another crew from my squadron, commanded by Lieutenant Robert J. O'Reilly. (O'Reilly's navigator, 2nd Lt. Richard W. Britt, published a book titled "The Princess and the P.O.W." Gabriel Publishing, P.O. Box 173, Comfort, Texas 78013. It details his unusual imprisonment in Rumania after they were shot down in the area of Ploesti.)

Left to right: O'Reilly, Poulson and Britt.

Approaching Portugal heavy clouds made it impossible to keep the formation together and yet be certain not to violate Portugal's neutrality.

I decided to try to descend below the clouds. We broke out at about 1,000 feet. It was raining lightly, but we had sufficient visibility to determine that we were precisely on course. We steered visually for the exact middle of Gibraltar Strait so as not to violate the neutrality of either Spain on our left or Spanish Morocco on our right.

We were at least five miles from land on either side when I saw a few small, harmless looking puffs of dark smoke. Then someone in the formation yelled out over the radio, "The sonsabitches are shooting at us!"

I looked to the right and saw a warship in Ceuta Harbor (Spain) with guns flashing. At the same time, someone shouted into the intercom that we had received a hit in the waist skin that had left a hole the size of a football. Luckily no one was injured.

I'd never been shot at before, yet there I was, flying in a flak-damaged aircraft, fired on by a neutral power! Welcome to warfare's mass madness, where everyone is trigger happy! (Later, we made three more flights to and from North Africa but we would laboriously detour well around the southern end of Spanish territory.)

We stopped at Oran, Algeria, to refuel and spend the night in a French army barracks. Our sleeping accommodations of bare wooden boards with no bedding prepared us somewhat for the less-than-luxurious conditions to come.

We arrived next day at our destination near Benghazi, on the stark, reddish Libyan desert. The Engineer Corps, in just four days, had scraped out the dirt runway we would be using to fly our missions. From that headquarters, living in tents and subsisting on "C" (combat) rations (usually pink on top from the eternally blowing pink dust) we would fly bombing missions over the next seven weeks.

Lack of proper sanitary conditions soon gave nearly everyone the "GI's" (in this case, slang for "gastroenteritis"), so new paths were quickly worn between the tents we lived in to the primitive outdoor latrines we came to know so well.

For our first combat mission we pilots visited the two neighboring groups that were permanently stationed near

Benghazi. We rode along with experienced crews as observers. I flew with another former RCAF pilot, Lieutenant Slough, whom I had met in Canada. We flew to Gerbini, Sicily, and bombed a military air base there.

We encountered no opposition over the Mediterranean and very little flak over Sicily.

The biggest problem of our mission was landing back at Benghazi after dark. There were no lights to tell us exactly when we had crossed the coast, and the runway lights were nothing more than primitive kerosene pots. Slough said he had made almost no night landings in a B-24. Since I had experience as a B-24 instructor under all kinds of conditions, I assured him, "You find the landing strip and I'll make the landing." So went my very first, and probably easiest, of all combat missions.

Three days later my own group, the 389th, made a short trip to bomb an enemy airport at Maleme, on the island of Crete. Two events stand out vividly in my memory of that trip, even today. Over Crete we were attacked by Italian fighters. One passed in front of me so close I could actually hear his guns firing and see them recoiling in and out of his wing. I called the top turret gunner to ask why the hell he hadn't fired, how could he miss! No answer. The poor guy had passed out from lack of oxygen, and the enemy fighter could easily see that our top turret was neither tracking nor firing.

Leaving Crete, we were able to revive the gunner.

The other event also involved a top turret gunner from another group in our formation whose plane had been shot down. The top turret gunner's primary job was flight engineer. He usually sat between the pilot and copilot and watched the engine instruments, hoping to catch and remedy any engine problems before they became serious. Of course, like everyone else, he had to wear a seat-type parachute. But when under attack his position was in the top turret located directly behind and above the pilots. But to squeeze himself into the turret he had to unbuckle his leg straps. All too often, in the extreme excitement of an emergency bailout, a top turret gunner would forget to re-buckle those leg straps. So when his parachute opened he would tragically slip out of his harness and fall the rest of the way to his death.

That is what I saw happen on the Crete mission.

That type of accident was partially remedied when chest pack parachutes came into use; the parachute harness could be worn, but the pack itself was stored close by, allowing freedom of movement for crew members who needed to move about the aircraft. In an emergency they could quickly snap on the chest pack.

Nevertheless, there were cases in which a crew member would reach for his chest pack and it would be gone, or he would grab it by the rip cord and find himself covered by expanding silk. Miraculously, some victims of both those kinds of horrors have survived.

While at Benghazi my job as a squadron commander was comparatively simple. We had no ground echelon nor any paperwork to worry about. We couldn't even get paid! But that didn't matter; there was nowhere to spend money anyway.

All of North Africa had just been evacuated by the enemy after heavy fighting and pursuit by our forces. Many abandoned trucks, tanks, guns and much ammunition were scattered around Benghazi and all along the Mediterranean coast. Benghazi itself was in shambles and was nearly deserted. A few of its residents were slowly wandering back, often with donkeys, camels and wives in tow. There was nothing to prevent them from wandering right through our base, for we had no barriers or guards. One day, John Fino, my squadron bombardier, surprised a native inside his tent groping through John's possessions. John pulled out his pistol, thinking the Arab would flee. But the man simply continued searching, ignoring John and his pistol, then calmly sauntered away when he was finished.

Frequently we would see and hear enemy land mines exploding nearby; we assumed that they had been stepped on by returning natives or their animals.

About the only wildlife on our base was scorpions. They could be found hiding under rocks or any other shelter they could find. All of us slept on army cots in army pyramidal tents. The first thing we did every morning was religiously invert and shake our shoes, because scorpions were often to be found inside them. Our cots had mosquito netting suspended on all four sides and over the top, and the bottom was tucked under our mattresses so that nothing could surprise us while we slept. Nevertheless, one morning Hank Yaeger awakened to find a scorpion halfway up the inside of his netting. Our group's nickname then became "Sky Scorpions." (Later

(Above) Major John Fino

(Below) Part of the crew... Gebhardt shown third from left, Caldwell-fifth from left, Stell Meadow-fourth from right and Fino-second from right.

changed to "Green Dragons")

The missions out of Benghazi were comparatively free of opposition. The weather was usually mild and clear. Our routes were largely over water and we were almost never attacked. Our targets were either on islands or short distances inside the mainland. After dropping our bombs we would soon be back over the ocean far enough to be able to descend confidently. Only then, finally, we could remove those very uncomfortable oxygen masks. (This, remember, was before the development of pressurized cabins.) What a relief to be able to rub out dry lips and itching noses, eat our "K" (emergency) rations and smoke cigarettes! The water in our canteens would be refreshingly cold because of the low outside temperature at bombing altitude (usually 20,000 feet or better).

There were some outstanding exceptions to those almost luxurious missions. By far the one most costly in every way was the low-level attack on 1 August 1943 against the oil refineries near Ploesti, Romania. That mission has been so well publicized that I don't have anything to add to it except to say I still feel very proud of my squadron and group's performance during that raid. (See "Bomber Pilot" by Col. Philip Ardery for details of this and other missions flown by our Group.)

Two other rather unique missions out of Benghazi deserve mention. Just ten days prior to the Ploesti attack, we bombed Rome, Italy, for the first time. The significance of that attack was its two objectives. One was to deepen the political wedge between Italy and Germany.

The other objective was not to offend American Christians among us whose religion regarded Rome as Holy City. During the usual pre-mission briefing all Christians were offered the choice to refuse to participate in the Rome mission, and assured that their decision would not be held against them in any way. Not a single man refused to go. One convincing factor was that our target was a totally industrialized part of Rome, almost completely surrounded by the Tiber River, so it would be extremely unlikely for us to accidentally bomb any churches, or the Vatican itself. (Nevertheless, Mussolini screamed afterward that we had bombed Christian Churches.)

We'd been briefed that we would be escorted by P-40's from the Twelfth Air Force out of North Africa. As an example of warfare confusion our fighter "escorts" were too slow to keep

The Curtis P-40 Tomahawk had an unbelievable record of performance in World War II primarily due to the determination of its pilots and ground crews. First produced after WWI, its speed, range and ability to fly at higher altitudes was stretched to the extreme in the new war. Whether fighting the Japanese over China or challenging the Luftwaffe over Russia and Egypt, the P-40 bought time for America's technology to perfect high-performance aircraft which later defeated the Axis air power.

During routine assignments as an escort craft, the P-40 found it difficult to keep up with the powerful new air bombers like the B-24, especially at higher altitudes.

This sometimes created more of a hazard to the big airships than the escort defense was worth, since a very large, low flying bomber was more vulnerable to air and ground flak.

The P-40 had a single engine and was rated at 352 miles per hour at 15,000 feet. The craft was armed with six guns and had a normal range of 730 miles.

In general, the P-40 was completely obsolete at the war's beginning but served freedom with all their might until they were replaced by more modern fighters near the end of the war. Bomber escorts over Italy were probably among the last for the P-40.

up with us! We went right off and left them as we were passing the toe of the Italian boot.

While approaching our target on the final bomb run I could see straight ahead what looked like sheets of shiny metal. I thought the enemy was firing a new kind of flak at us. Then a sheet came straight at my windshield, so close that I could see it was not metal, but a printed leaflet. Later I learned that propaganda leaflets had been dropped from a higher altitude; the fact that they glistened like metal was due to the extremely bright light at that altitude.

Shortly after the famous low-level bombing of refineries in Romania we were rewarded with three-day passes. We were allowed to use two B-24's, each going to a different destination, one Alexandria, Egypt, the other Tel Aviv (then Palestine).

I chose Tel Aviv. I mention it here because of the unforgettable contrasts and historical significance of that trip.

First, there was the extreme contrast between the barren, red Libyan desert, and then, suddenly, the dark, fertile Nile Valley.

Next, to another sudden contrast, the Sinai Desert, so sandy and infertile looking it was hard to believe that even an insect could survive there. Then up the Mediterranean coast and directly over the full length of that controversial, poor-appearing Gaza Strip; And finally, into prosperous and modern-looking Tel Aviv. What looked best of all, there was no evidence of any kind of war going on.

We were astonished to find that Tel Aviv was really two distinct cities, divided only by a street. Modern Tel Aviv was almost totally Jewish, and there were all kinds of delicious foods everywhere. But right across the street was Jaffa, almost totally Arabic. That was truly the greatest contrast of the contrast-filled trip. It seemed like we were stepping across the street from modern into Biblical times.

Another memorable mission out of Benghazi was the bombing of a Messerschmidt factory at Wiener Neustadt, Austria. What stood out about that raid was the extreme distance to and from the target, the return route, and the weakness of enemy opposition.

To provide sufficient fuel for the distance, in addition to using our extra wing tanks we had to carry a full bomb bay tank in one of our two bomb bays. The route was northward across the Mediterranean to the Adriatic, then to the north end of the

This was the leaflet dropped on Rome, 19 July, 1943
The English translation is found on the following page.

Servizio della R.A.F. e dell'aviazione americana

Testo di un Messaggio
DIRETTO AL POPOLO ITALIANO DAL PRIMO MINISTRO BRITANNICO CHURCHILL E DAL PRESIDENTE ROOSEVELT

IN QUESTO momento le forze armate associate degli Stati Uniti, della Gran Bretagna e del Canada, sotto il comando del Generale Eisenhower e del suo Vice-Comandante, Generale Alexander, stanno portando la guerra nel cuore del vostro paese.

Questo è il risultato diretto della politica vergognosa che Mussolini ed il Regime fascista vi hanno imposto. Mussolini vi ha trascinato in questa guerra come nazione satellite di un distruttore brutale di popoli e di libertà. Mussolini vi ha gettato in una guerra che egli credeva essere stata già vinta da Hitler.

Malgrado l'Italia sia estremamente vulnerabile dal cielo e dal mare, i vostri Capi fascisti hanno mandato i vostri figli, le vostre navi ed i vostri aeroplani in zone di operazioni lontane ad aiutare la Germania, a conquistare l'Inghilterra, la Russia ed il mondo intero.

L'adesione dell'Italia ai piani della Germania nazista era indegna delle antiche tradizioni di libertà e di cultura del popolo italiano; tradizioni alle quali tanto devono i popoli dell'America e della Gran Bretagna. I vostri soldati non hanno combattuto affatto per gli interessi d'Italia, ma solo per quelli della Germania nazista. Essi hanno combattuto con coraggio, ma sono stati traditi ed abbandonati dai tedeschi sul fronte russo e su ogni campo di battaglia in Africa, da El Alamein al Capo Bon.

Oggi, le speranze che nutrivono la Germania di dominare il mondo sono state frantumate su tutti i fronti. I cieli dell'Italia sono dominati dalle vaste flotte aeree degli Stati Uniti e della Gran Bretagna; le coste dell'Italia vengono minacciate dal più grande ammassamento di forze navali che la Gran Bretagna e gli alleati abbiano mai concentrato nel Mediterraneo.

Le forze che ora vi stano di fronte sono impegnate a distruggere la potenza della Germania nazista, la quale ha spietatamente inflitto schiavitù, distruzione e morte a tutti coloro che rifiutano di riconoscere nei tedeschi la razza dominante.

L'unica speranza che l'Italia ha di sopravvivere sta in una capitolazione che non sarebbe disonorevole data la potenza soverchiante delle forze militari delle Nazioni Unite. Se continuate a sostenere il Regime fascista asservito alla potenza criminale dei nazisti, voi dovete subire le conseguenze della vostra scelta.

A noi non fa piacere di invadere il suolo d'Italia e portare la devastazione tragica della guerra in seno al popolo italiano. Noi siamo decisi ad eliminare i capi falsi e le loro dottrine che hanno ridotto l'Italia al suo stato attuale. Ogni momento che resistete alle forze associate delle Nazioni Unite, ogni goccia di sangue che versate non può servire che ad uno scopo: a dare ai capi nazisti e fascisti un altro margine di tempo per sfuggire alle conseguenze inevitabili dei loro delitti.

Tutti i vostri interessi e tutte le vostre tradizioni sono state tradite dalla Germania nazista e dai vostri capi falsi e corrotti. Solo abbandonando la Germania nazista ed i capi fascisti, un'Italia rinnovata può sperare di acquistare un posto rispettato nella famiglia delle Nazioni europee.

E' venuto il momento, per voi italiani, di considerare la vostra dignità, i vostri interessi ed il vostro desiderio in una restaurazione del decoro nazionale e di una pace sicura. E' venuto il momento per voi di decidere se gli italiani debbono morire per Mussolini e per Hitler o vivere per l'Italia e per la civiltà.

1/63

English translation of leaflet dropped over Rome is as follows:

Service of the R.A.F. and American Aviation

DIRECTED TO THE ITALIAN PEOPLE FROM THE BRITISH PRIME MINISTER CHURCHILL AND PRESIDENT ROOSEVELT.

In this moment the associated Armed Forces of The United States, Great Britain and Canada, under the command of General Eisenhower and his vice commander General Alexander, are bringing the war to the heart of your country.

This is the direct result of the embarrassing politics that Mussolini and the Fascist Regime have imposed on you. Mussolini has dragged you into this war as a satellite nation of a brutal destroyer of people and liberty. Mussolini has thrown you into a war that he believes was already won by Hitler.

Despite Italy's extreme vulnerability by air and by sea, your Fascist leaders have sent your sons, your ships, and your planes in far away operations to help Germany, and to conquer England, Russia and the entire world.

Italy's adhesion to Nazi Germany's plans was a shameful act contrary to the age-old traditions of liberty and culture of the Italian people; traditions that you owe to the people of America and Great Britain. Your soldiers haven't battled for Italian interests at all, but only for those of Nazi Germany. They have battled with courage, but they have been betrayed and abandoned by the Germans on the Russian front and on every battle field in Africa from El Alamein to Cape Bone Annaba).

Today, the hopes that nourished Germany to dominate the world have been shattered on all fronts. The Italian skies are dominated by the vast air fleets of the United States and Great Britain. The Italian coasts are being threatened by the largest accumulation of forces Great Britain and the allied forces have ever concentrated in the Mediterranean.

The forces that are now confronting you have undertaken to destroy the power of Nazi Germany, who has ruthlessly inflicted slavery, destruction and death to all who refuse to recognize the Germans as the dominant race.

The only hope that Italy has to survive is in a capitulation that would not be dishonorable given the overwhelming power of the United Nations' military forces. If you continue to give in to the Fascist Regime, having been won over by the criminal power of the Nazis, you will have to suffer the consequences of your choice.

It does not give us pleasure to invade Italian soil and to bring the tragic devastation of the war into the bosom of Italy. We have decided to eliminate false leaders and their doctrines that have reduced Italy to its present state. Every moment that you resist the associated forces of the United Nations, every drop of blood that you spill can only serve one purpose: to give the Nazi Fascist leaders another margin of time to escape the inevitable consequences of their offences

All of your interests and all of your traditions have been betrayed by Nazi Germany and by your false and corrupt leaders. Only by abandoning Nazi Germany and its false leaders can a renewed Italy hope to gain a respected place in the family of European nations.

The moment has arrived all Italians to consider your dignity, your interests and your desire in a restoration of national decorum and of secure peace. The moment has arrived for you to decide if Italians need to die for Mussolini or Hitler, or live for Italy and for a civilized society.

The Egyptian Gazette

64th. Year, No. 18,961   Sunday, August 15, 1943   Four Pages P.T. I

Hedy Lamarr Found Fame In Bombed Works

As American airmen released their bombs on the Wiener Neustadt war plants, they probably did not realise that they were destroying factories that once provided the setting for "Ecstasy", the film that launched glamorous Hedy Lamarr on her career as the world's "Oomph Girl No. 1".

For the smoking ruins that, once were Austria's industrial centre, belonged in days gone by to Hedy°s former husband. the armaments king, Fritz Mandl.

It was while shots were being taken, in his factories that he came to know Hedy Kiessler the daughter of a modest official.

She later became Mandl's wife and the leader of Vienna's gay society.

ALREADY SOLD

"Ecstasy" however, had already been released and bought up by foreign film companies. It was shown in picture houses all over the world.

But it did not suit the rich armaments king that people could view his wife in the nude by buying a sixpenny cinema ticket.

He instructed his agents everywhere to buy up all coples of the film at any price. Millions of Austrian Schillings finally withdrew the film from the market.

NOT OBTAINABLE

One copy, however, was unobtainable at any price, it was owned by Mussolini, and it was theis copy which circulated widely.

Today, Frizt Mandl, with Prince von Strahremberg, can reflect on the destruction of Vienna's war plants at some lonely little South American ranch.

*A newsclipping detailing the bombing of the
factory where Lamarr was filmed years earlier.*

"We Made A J Out Of The U"

Liberators made a 'J', as one pilot put it, of the U-shaped Messerschmitt aircraft Works at Weiner Neustadt yesterday when they dropped 350,000 pounds of bombs on their target.

Scores of bursts were observed among some 400 newly assembled aircraft parked in neat rows in the parking area. The enemy defences were caught entirely by surprise and only slight anti-aircraft and fighter opposition was encountered.

Bomb bursts completely blanketed the great factory, the machine shops and assembly plants which cover an area of 1,339,000 square feet.

The Weiner Neustadt Airframe Works is one of the Axis largest assembly plants, accounting for 400 planes per month or approximately one third of the entire Messerschmitt output. Its destruction would strike a crippling blow to the Axis' already waning air power.

2500-Mile Trip

The Liberators which carried out the raid travelled a round trip distance of nearly 2,300 miles.

Several of the returning airmen said that red and yellow flames rose to a height of 500 feet with clouds of black smoke rolling thousands of feet higher.

Of some 15 enemy fighters which half-heartedly attacked the strong force of Liberators, one ME-109 was shot down. None of our aircraft was lost.—Reuter.

Adriatic, and from there across Yugoslavia to the target in Eastern Austria. After bombing the target the return trip brought us straight across the middle of enemy-occupied Italy.

We were very surprised to receive no attacks over mainland Italy. In fact I saw only one aircraft and that one ducked quickly into a cloud.

After crossing Italy we headed southward toward Africa via the Strait of Messina for a refueling stop at Tunis, Tunisia.

It was in the vicinity of the Strait of Messina, which separates Sicily from Italy, that we received our only determined attack. Fighters, apparently German, dived straight down through our formation, but without inflicting any damage.

We continued on to Tunis where we landed, refueled, and spent the night trying to sleep on the bare desert under the wings of our airplanes. Next morning we flew the remaining five-and-a-half hours of that eighteen-hour mission back "home" to "dear old Benghazi".

On 25 August 43 we returned to Hethel by way of Oran, Algeria; Marrakech, Morocco; and Fort Mawgan, England. At Hethel, we were happily united with our ground personnel who had arrived and set up our permanent headquarters there. (See Illustrations on following pages.)

On 16 September 43 we again departed Hethel for North Africa, this time for Tunis, Tunisia to support the invasion of mainland Italy.

While at Tunis we shared the base at Masicualt with a B-17 group already stationed there. When we had a mission they would "stand down" staying completely out of our way, and vice versa. Our stay in Tunis was short, about two weeks, because the ground invasion of central Italy appeared secure enough that our strategic support was not required. So after three missions we again returned to our home base at Hethel.

Flying missions out of England over enemy-dominated Europe was quite different to what we had become accustomed in the Mediterranean area. First, the U.K. weather, both on the ground and in the air, was difficult to say the least. On the ground there was a constant, bone-chilling dampness, and mud everywhere. In addition, there was frequent fog that sometimes completely covered the runway, requiring us to make tense and scary instrument takeoffs in our always overloaded bombers.

HEADQUARTERS
IX BOMBER COMMAND
NINTH U. S. AIR FORCE

APO 683, c/o Postmaster,
New York, New York,
20 July 1943.

SUBJECT: Commendation.

TO: Commanding Officer, 389th Bomb Group and attached Units.

1. I wish to commend you and the members of your command for the splendid work you have done during the preparations for and the invasion of Sicily.

2. You have proven how rapidly a new group can enter into active combat. I feel that you hold the record in this respect. The records of sorties initiated and those reaching the target, the maintenance of aircraft and the high morale of combat and ground personnel are equal to those of the older and more experienced groups and bombing accuracy has improved with each mission.

3. These results reflect great credit upon your ability as a leader and upon the training and ability of every officer and enlisted man assigned or attached to your Group. You have made a fine contribution to the success of this campaign.

U. G. ENT,
Brig. Gen., USA,
Commanding.

1st Ind.   JWW/mms
Hq, 389th Bomb Gp (H) AAF, APO 634, c/o Postmaster, New York, New York, July 23, 1943.

TO: All Personnel of this Command.
1. The undersigned wishes to express his sincere appreciation for the superior work done by the combat crews and ground personnel of this command.

2. The excellent results which have been obtained in spite of numerous hardships and difficulties are a definite proof of the high standard of training and moral of all units based at this airdrome.

JACK W. WOOD,
Colonel, Air Corps,
Commanding.

On the backdrop of a B-24, Paul (wearing sunglasses) reunites with his ground personnel in England after time spent in Lybia.

Reunion Time...

Paul, (kneeling at right in group photo) poses in front of a B-24 with a group of flying personnel and his dog "Brownie" after returning to England.

Brownie accompanied Paul in England and Lybia. Soon after this photo was made, Paul was shot down.

Brownie desperately searched the airbase for his owner, making a circuit trek between Paul's office and the other points at the base where Brownie expected to find him.

After weeks of relentless pacing and searching, Brownie was getting on everybody's nerves. He was sent back to The United States. When Paul returned to the states after his escape from German prison, he was greeted by an excited Brownie in New York.

ADDRESS REPLY TO
HEADQUARTERS OF THE ARMY AIR FORCES
WAR DEPARTMENT
WASHINGTON, D. C.

WAR DEPARTMENT
HEADQUARTERS OF THE ARMY AIR FORCES
WASHINGTON

20 August 1943

TO OFFICERS AND MEN OF THE 201st COMBAT WING OF THE EIGHTH AIR FORCE:

I have listened with greatest interest to the stirring accounts brought back to me of the details of the attack on the Roumanian oil refineries by heavy bombers of the Eighth and Ninth U. S. Air Forces. The destruction of these oil wells will be far reaching in its effect upon the German ability to carry on their operations. In fact, it might well be the "straw that broke the camel's back" and cause the dislocation of the German war effort. The dogged determination to reach and destroy each of those vital installations; and an utter disregard for personal safety, characterized the action of officers and men of your striking force and evokes my profound admiration.

The heroic accomplishments of the combat crews, and the splendid efforts of the members of the ground echelons who made the mission possible, are all deserving of the highest praise.

You were assigned the tremendous task of destroying in one day a target that could have been reached by surface forces only after many months of combat involving great losses both of men and materiel, and you carried your attack home in spite of the strongest kind of opposition built up by the Axis forces. Some of your comrades fell in the attack - others are now held as prisoners of war. Those of you who return to fight again must realize, as I do, that those who gave their lives did so that others might live. The officers and men of the U. S. Army Air Forces all over the world take pride in your achievement.

H. H. ARNOLD
General, U. S. Army
Commanding General, Army Air Forces.

In the air it was common to have to climb through several layers of clouds, hoping our weather forecasters had accurately predicted the top layer, and the level to stay beneath because of prohibitive icing conditions. (In our B-24's we were not able to stay together in clouds, nor could we maintain a formation above 25,000 feet. A tight formation was essential for mutual protection against enemy fighters. In addition, we had removed the de-icing boots from the wings to improve lift. So that, also, forced us to avoid clouds above the freezing level.) Also, Germany's defenses were then very intense, and sickeningly close to our English bases.

Returning from a mission and letting down through the clouds over the English Channel it was not uncommon to break out over a warship that would immediately open up on us with antiaircraft fire. Further, on crossing the English coast it was all too usual for the coastal defenses to throw up a barrage, even though we persistently fired the top secret colors of the day with our flare pistols (or "biscuit guns") that was supposed to identify us as friendly.

***

During my earlier combat experience in Libya I had been optimistic about eventually completing my combat tour of twenty-five missions. And on the April day I was shot down I would have logged my nineteenth mission toward that goal. (Later, in a German prison, I learned from a survey of other American airmen that the average number of missions they'd flown before being downed, was five!)

By early 1944, I had become increasingly doubtful that I would manage to complete my twenty-five missions. There were two simply-stated requirements we had to meet to get credit for a completed mission. One was: drop your bombs on the target; the other was: be attacked by the enemy. Certain hazardous flights such as diversions, that were meant to confuse the enemy about our actual objective, didn't meet both of these requirements and so didn't count as credit for a completed mission.

My squadron's losses were so heavy that replacement crews would sometimes be gone before I met them. And fifty-percent of my aircraft returning from missions had sustained Class A battle damage, meaning that they had to go to a repair depot for work that could not be done on our base, and I wouldn't see them again.

The last three missions I flew were increasingly difficult.

(See Illustrations on following pages.)

I had the visceral feeling that not only had my time come, but I was actually overdue.

R E S T R I C T E D

HEADQUARTERS EIGHTH AIR FORCE
Office of the Commanding General
APO   634

15 April 1944

GENERAL ORDERS)

NUMBER   280)

E X T R A C T

*   *   *   *

AWARDS OF THE DISTINGUISHED FLYING CROSS..........................SECTION II

*   *   *   *

II.   Under the provisions of Army Regulations 600-45, 22 September 1943, and pursuant to authority contained in Restricted TT Message #2139, Hq USSAFE, 11 January 1944, the DISTINGUISHED FLYING CROSS is awarded to the following named Officers and Enlisted Men:

*   *   *   *

PAUL T. BURTON, O-1699162, Major, Army Air Forces, United States Army. For extraordinary achievement, while on a heavy bombardment mission over Germany, 20 February 1944. Flying as Command Pilot, Major Burton led a Group of B-24 airplanes. Though briefed for an instrument bombing attack, he quickly ordered a visual bombing run to be made when he observed a break in the clouds. In spite of savage assaults by hostile fighters, Major Burton maneuvered his unit over the assigned target and bombed it with devastating results. The high degree of success acheved by the Group is largely attributable to the courage, initiative and skilful leadership of Major Burton. His actions on this occasion reflect great credit upon himself and the Armed Forces of the United States. Entered military service from Arkansas.

*   *   *   *

By command of Lieutenant General DOOLITTLE:

JOHN A. SAMFORD,
Brigadier General, U. S. A.,
Chief of Staff.

OFFICIAL:

/s/ Edward E. Toro
EDWARD E. TORO
Colonel, A.G.D.,
Adjutant General

A TRUE EXTRACT COPY

RICHARD G. WINTERS,
Major,   Air Corps,
Assistant Adjutant.

Burton's key personnel as photographed around the first of April, 1944. Within three weeks of this photo, almost everyone in this group was either dead or missing.

Success made the papers, but the good news was intermingled with bad as numerous Allied planes made a one way trip into enemy territory.

Plants Deep in Reich Hit In 4th Day of Huge Raids

London, Apr. 11 (AP) -- Nearly 1,000 American bombers, with an equal number of escorting fighters, carried the onslaught against German air defenses through its fourth day today with massive attacks against plane factories as Oschersleben and Bernburg and other objectives deep in Germany.

The latest daylight blows, in a new series of attacks intended to smash the Luftwaffe ahead of the Allied invasion, followed night assaults by 900 bombers -- the greatest force ever dispatched by the RAF against occupied territory.

The German radio told of terrific air battles over the Reich today. At oschersleben the 8th Air Force lost 60 bombers Jan. 11. Both it and Bernburg had been hit Feb. 20 in the Americans' first big series of assaults on the German air force.

The first crews back from today's attack said they obtained good results, bombing mostly in clear weather.

"It looked to me as if the Germans had their first team -- the Goering boys -- up today," said Lt. Col. Paul T. Burton of 215 W. 109th St., New York, who flew as a Liberator co-pilot. "They were good -- but not good enough, and there were not enough of them to stop us."

7,000 Tons in 60 Hours

In the last 60 hours, more than 7,000 tons of bombs have been dropped on at least 23 German railroad centers, aircraft factories and airfields.

A final tabulation of yesterday's U.S. air victories showed 15 enemy planes downed and many others destroyed or damaged on the ground. Three bombers and four fighters were lost in the attack upon for airfields, three repair works and an assembly plant.

The main targets of the RAF night raiders, an Air Ministry communique said, were railway yards at Ghent, Tours, Tergnier, Aulnoye and Laon in northern France and Belgium.

Mosquito squadrons thrust into western Germany to bomb Hanover and the Ruhr. Twenty-two planes failed to return from the night operations.

HEADQUARTERS EIGHTH AIR FORCE
Office of the Commanding General
APO 634

30 April 1944.

GENERAL ORDERS)
:
NUMBER   327)   E X T R A C T

*   *   *   *   *

AWARDS OF THE OAK LEAF CLUSTER TO THE DISTINGUISHED FLYING CROSS..II

*   *   *   *   *

II. Under the provisions of Army Regulations 600-45, 22
September 1943, and pursuant to authority contained in Letter,
Hq USSTAF, AG 200.6, Subject, "Awards and Decorations", 3 April
1944, the OAK LEAF CLUSTER to the DISTINGUISHED FLYING CROSS is
awarded to the following named Officers:

*   *   *   *   *

PAUL T. BURTON, O-1699162, Lieutenant Colonel, Army Air
Forces, United States Army. For extraordinary achievement,
while serving as Command Pilot on a successful bombing mission
into Germany 11 April 1944   As the Combat Wing I.P. was reached
Colonel Burton's compact formation was disrupted by enemy fighter
attacks, causing the loss of several aircraft. Remaining calm
and disregarding the imminent danger, Colonel Burton cooly rallied
his Group and prepared for a steady bomb run without fighter protection. Despite concentration of intense flak and persistent
fighter attacks during the bomb run itself, so determined was
Colonel Burton's leadership that an excellent bombing pattern was
laid, effectively blanketing the target area. The courage, cool-
ness under fire, and inspiring leadership demonstrated by Colonel
Burton on this occasion materially contributed to the successful
completion of the assigned mission. These qualities as displayed
by Colonel Burton are an inspiration to all members of the United
States Army Air Forces. Entered military service from New York.

*   *   *   *   *

By command of Lieutenant General DOOLITTLE:

JOHN A. SAMFORD,
Brigadier General, USA,
Chief of Staff.

OFFICIAL:
/s/EDWARD E. TORO
/t/EDWARD E. TORO,
   Colonel,   AGD,
   Adjutant General.

A TRUE EXTRACT COPY

RICHARD G. WINTERS,
Major, Air Corps,
Personnel Officer.

DISTRIBUTION: Special Awards.

Paul T. Burton Is Promoted To Lieutenant Colonel

Editor's Note—The following story on Lt. Col. Paul T. Burton was dispatched from an Eighth AAF Liberator Station in England to the Banner-News on April 19, just four days before he was reported "missing in action over Germany". Since May 10 when his family was officially notified no further word has been received concerning the young squadron leader.

AN EIGHTH AAF LIBERATOR STATION, ENGLAND—The promotion of Paul T. Burton of Magnolia, and 215 West 109th St., New York City, from Major to Lieutenant Colonel was announced by Brigadier General James P. Hodges, commanding general of a Liberator bomb division.

Commanding officer of a Liberator squadron that has seen service in three theaters of operations, North Africa, the Middle East and England, Col. Burton learned of his promotion a few minutes after he had brought his Liberator, "Round Trip Ticket" back to its station from an aerial battle over targets in Germany.

"This is a swell piece of news," the New York man said, after he had been informed of his promotion by Col. Robert L. Miller of Clinton, Ill.,

7 Apr 1944

11 APR 1944

RESTRICTED

Hq ETOUSA

EXTRACT

SO 98

1. Announcement is made of the temp promotion of the following C, AC, Eighth AF, to the gr indicated in AUS w/rank fr date of this order:

Maj to Lt Col

PAUL T. BURTON, 01699162

Capture

I had thought of getting shot down, maybe even killed. But I had had confidence in my ability to evade capture. I had never envisioned myself as a prisoner so I was quite unprepared for what followed.

My captor was a young *Luftwaffe* soldier. He took me upstairs in the house in front of the courtyard where I had landed. I was quickly surrounded by dozens of curious enemy soldiers who were billeted there. My luck was holding; I had parachuted into the back yard of a *Luftwaffe* billet!

In about five minutes they brought in Myron Gins. He had landed in a street nearby and started running. Belgian civilians had cheered him on while German soldiers chased him. He'd come to the end of a dead-end street where the soldiers quickly caught up with him.

A few minutes later they brought in Bill Stotter. He had landed on the roof of a warehouse and had crashed through it. His shroud lines got caught on the roof, leaving Bill dangling six feet above the floor. He'd managed to get out a concealed razor blade and had started cutting himself down. He'd cut through one of the two tough parachute risers and was almost through the other when he was found. His fingers were cut and bleeding from the double-edged blade.

The three of us were goofy from shock, addled from the exhilaration of having survived, and very hungry. It was then about 8 p.m. and we had not eaten since early that morning. We opened the candy we'd been given at the base to eat on our way home and passed it around. All the Germans refused, but they were clearly tempted to accept.

A medic was brought in. He examined us for wounds and doctored our scratches. I didn't know any German. It appeared at the time that neither Bill nor Myron understood the language either. We and the Germans, apparently none of whom knew English, sat and gaped at each other. I'm sure most of us thinking, "So this is the enemy!"

At about 9 p.m. we were loaded onto the back of a truck

driven by green-uniformed soldiers of the *Heer*, or German army. As we proceeded through Antwerp's streets we stopped from time to time to pick up more *Heer* soldiers. We stopped at many barricades also, where the driver had to identify himself each time. Antwerp seemed very much on the alert, perhaps in expectation of the upcoming allied invasion.

The soldiers at the billets where we were captured had not searched us or confiscated our possessions so we still had our escape kits. I was on the floor of the truck trying to remove something from my kit without attracting attention when I received my second wound due to enemy action (the first being my scratches and bruises from landing in the tree.)

I was concentrating on hiding a 200 franc note from the money pouch of my escape kit in the finger of my glove when the truck came to a sudden stop. One of the soldiers fell forward. Good-soldier-like, he didn't let go of his rifle to catch himself. Instead, he held onto the rifle with both hands, one hand at each end, and came down on me with his full weight, slamming the rifle across my shin. I thought my leg was broken.

We were taken to Antwerp Municipal Airport on the southeast edge of town and shoved into what appeared to be a guard house. Two young soldiers were assigned to guard us. They were our first contact with the fanatical Hitler *Jugend*, or Hitler Youth. Extremely conscientious about keeping the muzzle of their machine pistols pointed directly at our heads they didn't take their eyes off us for an instant. Neat, clean and often handsome, we learned later that they were waiting to take pilot training. We heard several times during the night the query which amused us: "*Machine kaput?*" (I learned later that this simple question was asked of nearly all personnel captured away from their downed aircraft. The words were so similar to American slang that they were understandable even to those of us who knew no German.)

At the airport I discovered with dismay that I had some secret information in my pocket: the frequency and identification letters of our assembly beacon in England printed on a small square of rice paper. I managed to mouth and swallow it without detection.

An officer came in and ordered us to empty our pockets on the counter. There was a good looking girl with him who translated for him. They seemed very interested in our paraphernalia, especially our escape kits, which contained maps, money (both American dollars and currencies of the countries we flew over), compasses, hack saw blades, and other useful items. We hated giving those up. Although they searched us rather thoroughly they didn't find my 200 francs.

I protested when the officer confiscated my fountain pen, since that was my personal property. He responded that it was for the *Vaterland*. That, of course, was the last I saw of my pen.

I protested again as forcefully as I dared when they tried to take our dog tags. I explained to the girl that without those we could be shot as spies. Both the officer and the girl laughed, and assured us that that was absurd. Nevertheless, we each were allowed to keep one of our two tags.

The officer suddenly flew into a tirade of German. He interrogated us in German and became more incensed when we didn't seem to understand.

His angry exhibition was something we would soon become unpleasantly familiar with. Bill and Myron explained to me later that the officer had become enraged when he noticed that their dog tags showed "J" for their Jewish religion; not only did the officer hate all Jews but he expected them to understand German because of it's similarity to Yiddish.

I had not been aware of their religion before. Jew-hating, we soon discovered firsthand, was very big in the Nazi party, and was a major factor in uniting that aggressively negative group of bigots.

That night we were kept in a guarded room in the same building. We slept on a huge "bed," actually a bare wooden shelf across one entire end of the room that could probably accommodate twenty men. The head of the mass bed was slightly higher than the foot, which pointed toward the center of the room.

Our guards were the same alert, eager young Nazi types who would have loved having a reason to use their guns on us. One young guard spoke English. He asked why we were fighting them. That was a difficult question for us to answer. Another guard posed the same question and persisted until he got an answer. I replied that the best answer to his question could be found in Hitler's *"Mein Kampf."* ("My Struggle," Hitler's autobiography and presumed basis for NAZI philosophy.)

His startling reply was, "Hitler did <u>not</u> write *Mein Kampf.*"

We slept very little. People came and went throughout the night. Guards changed shifts, and other soldiers came by to gape at the *Amerikanisch Terrorflieger* out of curiosity.

When early morning came we watched a guard having his breakfast. He tucked a loaf of black bread under his arm and sliced off a piece with his bayonet. He then took a plastic container of margarine from his pack and smeared some on the bread. He seemed to enjoy it thoroughly, and his performance started our mouths watering. We gestured to him that we were hungry too. It was now more than twenty-four hours since we'd eaten anything except a few pieces of candy from our escape kits. He wouldn't share his bread, but offered us some cold "coffee" from his canteen. It had such a strangely vile taste we couldn't drink it.

Later that morning we were taken across the street and into a hangar to wash up. But there was no soap. How could one wash without soap? We learned soon enough that soap was only one of many small "luxuries" we had previously thought of as essentials that we would now have to do without.

We observed some excellent and clever camouflage around the airport. The tell-tale shape of the hangars had been given steep roofs to make them appear to be residences.

Soon after we'd washed up we were loaded into an armored car and driven into the city to a very old, fortress-like structure which was probably the former Antwerp municipal jail. It's atmosphere was gloomy and depressing. Once again, our guards were green-uniformed *Heer*. We three wondered privately if we would ever get out of that place alive, but none of us revealed our gloomy thoughts to the other two.

While being booked we got another taste of Nazi Jew-hating. One particularly sadistic NCO asked us some questions through an interpreter. After we gave our names, ranks and serial numbers we refused to answer any more questions. The NCO became infuriated. He ranted and raved for several minutes in high, screeching, insulting tones. We soon became quite accustomed to hearing those inflections, as they appeared to be among the prime requisites for German leadership. That Nazi manner of addressing subordinates was roughly equivalent to the tones a high-strung farmer might use in addressing a stubborn mule: a high volume half-scream, half-snarl, clearly intended to terrorize subordinates into submission. That demoralizing noise seemed to ring in our ears twenty-four hours a day during the next few days. That particular NCO repeated the word *Jude* frequently in his tirades. I didn't need to know German to know what that word meant to him.

Eventually we were taken down a long corridor that was lined on both sides with cells. It was a duplex structure with a second tier of cells above. The turnkey selected a cell, shoved us in and slammed the heavy door shut. It resounded with a loud bang. We looked at each other, smiled, then laughed. We were happy to be still alive and away from our captors, even if only for a short while.

We inspected the cell. It was about eight feet long and six feet wide. There was one heavily barred window. Our "toilet" was a metal pail. The cell had no bunks. There was a bag of straw on the floor with three blankets folded on top. A shelf in one corner held a water pitcher, three aluminum bowls, and three metal spoons.

At noon the door opened. A small, scared looking Belgian civilian came in with a pot of soup. He said, *"Essen, essen."*

That word, meaning food, was the second word in our German vocabulary. We caught on quickly and handed over our bowls and he ladled them full of soup. The man left and we sat down to enjoy our first food in thirty-six hours.

Just as we started eating the door opened again and two NCO's strode in. When we didn't get up and come to attention they went into an insane rage and ranted in German with gestures that we should be more respectful. I could not understand how they could show so much anger without flying into a real rage and killing us, or at least beating us up. They stood us in a brace and proceeded to "eat us out" in true German fashion. We fully expected to be beaten or shot. The now familiar *Jude* rang out in nearly every breath. I noticed that their tirades were directed at Bill and Myron more than at me. I was beginning to learn first-hand about anti-semitism, Nazi-style.

Finally they left. We went back to our now-cold soup, and found that our ravenous appetites had disappeared.

Bill and Myron then told me, "Colonel, we're Jews. That's why they are picking on us. That's why we didn't want to bail out yesterday. That's why the officer got so mad yesterday when he read our religion on our dog tags. He expected us to know enough Yiddish to understand German. He thought we were lying when we couldn't understand him. They hate Jews like poison; they have killed thousands."

Knowing that their survival in prison was less likely than mine would be, they asked me to memorize their home addresses and parents' names back in Cleveland. "You have a much better chance of getting through this than we do," Myron said. "If anything should happen, you know, and you get back, tell the folks about us."

I, of course, agreed. They checked my memory periodically throughout the day until I had everything memorized.

I hadn't known Gins and Stotter well back on the base, except at their jobs. After our recently shared experiences I felt a bond with them. The NCO's actions made it clear they were in significantly greater danger than I, and I worried about them.

That evening another Belgian brought us each a box of *knickebrot* (miser bread, a thin wafer resembling rye-krisp), a one-inch portion of link sausage, a loaf of black bread, a lump of margarine, and a pitcher of water. Our spirits soared as our stomachs filled. We expected to live another few days at least; we figured they would never give us that much food if they were going to kill us. When we finally stretched out on our straw sacks on the floor and covered ourselves with the dirty blankets we slept the sleep of the completely exhausted.

We were awakened at daybreak the next morning with the command, "*Herauf!*" A guard handed us a broom, mop, pail, a rag and some powder that resembled sand soap without the soap. He made it clear that we were to clean the cell and our eating utensils until they were bright enough to shave by. We willingly undertook our chores, glad to have something to do. The sudden change from the extreme activity to jailed inactivity was hard on us, so we continually sought things to occupy our hyperactive minds.

We cleaned the cell as well as we could, then sat down to a breakfast of *knickebrot*, margarine and sausage. I gulped my little sausage down greedily. My cell mates bit off tiny pieces of theirs, and let them slowly melt in their mouths. I had to admire their willpower.

I still had a half-package of cigarettes, and Myron had a whole pack, but our matches had been confiscated. I craved a smoke madly. The more I looked at the cigarettes the more I wanted to smoke; I couldn't get it off my mind. I went so far as to take a chair rung and wind the electric cord from my heated suit (Our flight suits could be electrically heated by plugging into our aircraft's electrical system) around it, and tried all day to make a fire, boy-scout fashion. My efforts were to no avail. I went the day without smoking.

The interminable Jew-bashing continued throughout the day. Soldiers would barge in, bring us to a stiff brace, strut around and leer awhile, then let go with a verbal storm against Jews until they were out of breath. I greatly admired Bill's and Myron's poise during those tirades. They would stand unflinchingly at attention and give back stare for stare with no sign of fear or intimidation. "Valorous under fire" is a weak description of those two. I appreciated their bravery even more now. As Jewish airmen they were convinced that capture in Nazi Germany was tantamount to death for them. Yet there they were, perfectly calm. The Germans continued their oral torture of my cell mates (and me to a lesser extent, because I was with them) until it seemed every NCO in the area had had his turn at that sadistic pastime.

Every day air raid alarms blasted. Antwerp's alarms were set off by every group of allied planes that flew over, both to and from targets, since the city was near a direct lane from England to Germany. There would be loud orders barked, then the clatter of many feet double-timing to shelters. The place would become eerily quiet. When the all-clear sounded we'd hear them clattering back. That happened several times a day. We liked to imagine that happening in every town in Germany and German-occupied Europe that was near the paths of our planes. We felt proud and amused to think of the great loss of energy and productivity our planes were causing, just by flying over. (We knew, of course, there was nothing amusing about actual bombing and strafing, or the fear that the mere sight of those bombers must have caused. But those things were unavoidable aspects of the warfare of the times.)

I discovered that by standing on tiptoe on a pipe I could open the window slightly by pulling it upward from the top. That allowed us to peek into a courtyard outside, thereby providing a break in the monotony. Our window gave us a chance to observe the Germans and local civilians from an interesting angle.

The soldiers were truly magnificent specimens: tall, lean, clean-cut, neat and very military; Hollywood had not exaggerated their impressive appearance.

Most of the people we saw in the courtyard were Belgian and Dutch laborers wearing plain white clothes and wooden shoes. Some were employed at digging potatoes from a storage pit.

My mind was still obsessed with the need for a smoke. I tried for hours to get their attention. Occasionally I would catch the eye of one of the diggers and signal that I wanted a light by pointing to the cigarette in my mouth. Usually he would roll his eyes toward the guard, then look at me and point to his own eyes to indicate that the guard was watching.

At last I connected with a lively little fellow with a twinkle in his eyes, the irrepressible sort who can never be totally subdued. He kept darting looks at me, then at the guards. Finally, after a few quick glances, he took the half-smoked cigarette out of his mouth and tossed it onto the ledge just below our window. Stretching myself to the limit I reached over the top of the window and down to the ledge. I felt around until I found and retrieved the butt. What a thrill of achievement swept through me! Myron and I chain-smoked until we were dizzy.

We were clad in our regulation, electrically-heated flying suits. They were purposely designed to resemble inconspicuous civilian clothes when the inner lining was removed, to facilitate evasion and escape. Yet the color and texture were almost like that of our dress uniforms, so as to be regarded as a military uniform under international law. I appreciated that small, yet important detail, which showed that our high command was capable of some really superior brainwork.

Our suits and shoes had separate inner linings containing wires for heating them electrically. By removing the suit linings we could use them as extra blankets. The inner linings of the shoes could be laced up with wire and worn without the cumbersome outer shoes. In that way our one outfit gave us a complete change of clothing.

During the week we spent in Antwerp the Germans began their subtle, but sometimes obvious interrogations. One day we were taken out of the cell and to the office of the prison *Sanitäter* (medical orderly), supposedly for a physical checkup.

The *Sanitäter* turned out to be a mild-mannered, English-speaking fellow in his early twenties.

One of our earliest observations after being captured was that English-speaking Germans appeared to be mild mannered and lacking in hostility.

The "physical examination" soon appeared in its true light: interrogation. The man's tactic was to first throw me off guard, assuring me, "You three have nothing to worry about. You were captured in uniform. You are automatically classified as prisoners of war and your rights under the Geneva Convention will be respected." Then he would chat awhile before suddenly coming out with questions like, "How many were in your crew?" or "Where are the rest of your boys?" He wasn't persistent and his questions were easily evaded, but he was dogmatic overall. He visited us daily. But that man was clearly a novice at interrogation. His job evidently was to pick up a thread or two of information to pass along for the main interrogation center to use later.

Another man, disguised as a Red Cross social worker, brought some forms for us to fill out. We balked after giving name, rank and serial number. He argued, threatened and cajoled, but to no avail. We had been warned about that ploy. Finally he asked us to sign the bottom of the form. We refused, knowing that they could type in anything they chose over our signatures.

One day *Sanitäter* took me into his office alone. He appeared worried. "Colonel Burton," he said, "We have a sad case here. Four of your boys were caught in civilian clothes. As you know, they will be shot as spies. We don't want to do that. We want to send them to a POW camp with you. But they won't tell us where they got their civilian clothes. We have to know who helped them. Won't you please tell them to cooperate with us so that we might cooperate with them?"

I was amused by his naivete'. I thought of what would surely happen to the Belgians or Frenchmen, or whoever managed to help them, if they were caught-certain death at least.

Then I became angry at being caught in such a frustrating position of responsibility. I could only stare at him and say what I believed: "Any American soldier would die before he would betray the ones who helped him." I had no more trouble from *Sanitäter* on that subject.

Another time he came to me excitedly, "Come and see if

you can help one of your boys." I followed him to the upper tier and into a cell. Standing at rigid attention was a lone little fellow in a grimy fighter pilot's jacket with Second Lieutenant's bars. The cell was a mess. Everything that could be broken or torn up was strewn about. He had taken his spoon and scooped the plaster off the walls as high up as he could reach.

I asked the prisoner what the trouble was. He stood rigidly, stared straight ahead and recited, "My name is William C. Ingram, my rank is Second Lieutenant, my serial number is ..."

I introduced myself and tried a little small talk, hoping to get him to relax. He repeated, "My name is William C. Ingram, my rank is Second Lieutenant, my serial number is ..."

I said, "Listen Bill, I'm not a stooge. I'm on your side. I'm proud of you for not talking and for being suspicious of me. Don't tell me anything. Just sit down and relax and let me talk."

I sat down. He remained standing. "Sir, I prefer to remain standing," he stated.

"OK," I said, "but listen. You're not furthering the war effort one bit by acting like that. You're only making it hard on yourself."

"What's the difference. They're going to shoot me anyway!"

He obviously thought sincerely that his young life would soon be over. He was determined to die as he had lived, fighting with every ounce of his strength for what he believed in. I thought, there are many others like him; how can we lose? I felt a lump in my throat from my pride in him. I knew I had won the lieutenant's confidence when he'd say "they" instead of "you." I couldn't think of anything more to say except to mumble, "I don't think so," slap him on the back and walk out.

I hadn't accomplished much that day, but when we eventually left Antwerp I was glad to see Second Lieutenant Ingram in the train with us.

Sanitäter came to me another time. "Colonel, as senior officer you will take all Americans and march them out for exercise." That, if not a trick, was a welcome break. After being in a cramped cell for five days the opportunity to move about would be most welcome by everyone. I walked out into the corridor.

"All Americans downstairs!" I shouted.

I had expected possibly twenty Americans besides us three.

The scene that followed almost floored me. Over a hundred men of every description filled the corridor and started streaming down the stairs. There were men in every allied uniform, and many in civilian clothes. I spotted the four that *Sanitäter* had mentioned. They wore ill-fitting, grimy European clothes and had convict, chili-bowl haircuts; their faces had a sickly prison pallor. Others wore filthy, ragged clothing. Most were unshaven. Some were obviously wounded.

Several immaculate German officers looked on. I was determined to give them as good a show as possible under the circumstances. I lined up the rabble and ordered them to count off. They counted off until about the middle, then the count suddenly stopped. I looked at three husky men in civvies. *Sanitäter* explained they were Russian merchant seamen. Then one of the Americans saved the situation by continuing the count, patting the Russians on the back as he counted them.

I ordered odd numbers to take two paces forward, closed ranks with a right dress, then right-faced them; We marched out into an open courtyard into sweet, fresh air. We double-timed round and round the courtyard, getting faster and faster in our zest, causing the Germans to get nervous and start fingering their pistols. They called *Sanitäter* over and spoke to him. He came over and told me, "Stop them and do something else."

We opened ranks and did side-straddle hops, and arm exercises, then started a game of tag which was just getting going when the *Fliegeralarm* sounded. We formed ranks and double-timed back in.

"Too bad your comrades interrupted your exercises," *Sanitäter* said with a smirk, pointing upward toward the familiar drone of a bomber formation.

"Oh, that's all right," I answered with a smirk of my own.

A few days later we were taken through the streets of Antwerp for a short train ride to an unknown destination. I remember the picture Bill Ingram presented when we left the jail. He still maintained his aloof military attitude, marching stiffly erect, squaring every corner, with eyes frozen dead ahead. His physical appearance made a strange contrast to his military bearing. His uncombed hair was standing up, his jacket and trousers were caked with mud, a week's growth of fuzz grew on his young freckled face. He had a half-loaf of black bread clutched tightly under one arm and a precious square of margarine perched on top.

As our guards herded us through the streets they stiff-armed any civilian in our way, knocking them right and left. The Belgians were unintimidated, however, and open in their friendliness and acclaim for us. We saw friendly looks, admiration, smiles, "V" signs, waves, and hands clasped over heads.

During a short train ride to Brussels we had the opportunity to view one gratifying result of our precision bombing: a Renault factory had been blasted neatly out of a community and reduced to rubble, yet not a single dwelling had been damaged. We felt very proud.

While at the Brussels station we were joined by three RAF sergeants who had been shot down only the night before. One young man, curly-haired, good-looking, had a compound fracture of the right arm; the bone was sticking through, and I think infection was setting in. He clearly was in intense pain, but tried hard not to show it. His pale face maintained a forced smile all the way.

Spring had arrived in Belgium. There were fruit trees covered with lovely blossoms, a small bit of beauty in that saddened, war-torn land.

Our destination, the prison called Brussels-Saint Giles, was outside of town. A tremendous structure, it was laid out like a wheel with long, triple-decked cell blocks forming the spokes.

All watches, rings, and other personal items were confiscated there, but we were given receipts in a very businesslike way.

I kept calling for a doctor for the RAF sergeant, but was ignored.

For a time we were in an office where an officious little German was reading off numbers to a Belgian who was copying them down. The German's little Hitler-type mustache bounced up and down crazily as he pronounced the numbers 444 and 555 in German. It was all we could do to keep from laughing at him. When his back was turned the Belgian tossed us a package of cigarettes.

Ingram, Stotter, Gins and I were placed in the same cell. It was slightly larger, but had the same general arrangement as the one in Antwerp. The RAF men were next door. We talked through a hole where a pipe went through, being careful not to talk shop. We were certain there were microphones.

The RAF sergeant's arm continued to get worse and it began to smell. There was a lever inside my cell that triggered a flag outside to signal a guard to the cell. I pulled the trigger repeatedly to ask a guard for a doctor, but no guard would answer. I wondered what became of the sergeant; We never saw him after that day.

There were two obvious attempts at interrogation at Brussels-Saint Giles. Over the steam pipes there was a rattle of Morse code in English. We could make out Yank, USA, RAF, Air Corps, etc. We never answered.

The other was in the person of a very talkative, so-called Englishman who was shoved in with us during one exercise period. We didn't trust him because he talked shop continuously, telling us all about himself and his former companions and occupation. I ignored him as long as I could, but when he began asking direct and pointed questions I asked him if he didn't think it better that we not discuss those things. He said he had never been alone so long before and he was anxious to talk to anyone. The end of the exercise period settled that, as we were separated again.

Most of the ordinary prison personnel seemed to be Belgians. Although in German uniforms, it was easy to see they were not German loyalists. The question on everyone's lips was, "When is the invasion coming?" It was clear that invasion jitters was taking its toll along the Belgium coast. Some of the Belgians told us that as soon as it came they would kill every German in sight.

As Ingram warmed up to us we became a congenial foursome. We passed the time playing "three thirds of a ghost," using home-made cards Stotter had made out of *knickebrot* boxes and marked with a pencil stub he'd managed to keep. The cards were our most valuable possession until a guard saw them, and with the worn-out phrase, "*nichts, verboten,*" confiscated them.

During one of our exercise periods I tried to get some matches from a Belgian guard. He crossed his arms as though they were tied and rolled his eyes; those actions spoke louder than words.

I remembered the 200 francs I still had hidden. I began trying to buy something-anything-with the money. I started by trying to buy a pack of cigarettes. I came down to one cigarette. I ended trying to buy a match. I wound up having the money confiscated later at *Dulag*.

The food at Brussels was almost sufficient. We had no physical activity and therefore required little nutrition. The diet lacked protein and sugar and contained synthetics. Most meals included or consisted of potatoes, boiled skin and all. We didn't mind the skins; however, many had sprouts as well. We never could eat those sprouts, with their quinine-bitter taste; we'd carefully dig out the sprouts and eat the remainder.

One day while eating an unusually tasty bowl of soup Myron dug out a piece of white meat; "Chicken!" he shouted excitedly. The rest of us examined the few squares of meat in our own bowls. It was tripe.

After a week in Brussels-Saint Giles we again boarded a train for an unknown destination. We saw the same friendly looks on the faces of civilians in the streets. If we had then realized how completely opposite an attitude our presence would evoke among civilians within a few hours, I know we would have clung appreciatively to those friendly glances.

When we sat down in the small compartment, a young Jew in a Canadian flight sergeant's uniform joined us. "Whoopee!" he cried, "Goldberg rides again." (Of course this was before the actress by this name was known and probably before she was even born.)

Each compartment contained six allied prisoners and one guard, armed with machine pistol. At each end of the car was a guard armed with bayoneted rifle, pistol and "potato masher" (slang for German hand-grenade with long handle). All guards wore the blue uniform of the *Luftwaffe*. An NCO-in-command, carrying only a pistol, walked back and forth checking each compartment.

Our guard was another Hitler *Jugend* who spoke some English. He started off announcing, "The *Luftwaffe* destroyed 4,300 of your four-engine bombers in the last week!" We were amused, but alert enough not to reply. We knew enough not to be tricked into revealing anything about our bombers. The *Jugend* kept repeating his platitudes, parrot-like, as though carefully schooled to make such pronouncements.

We returned his Nazi propaganda with American propaganda. Interestingly, he was receptive, and soon became engrossed in conversation with us. Before long we were smoking his cigarettes. He became so relaxed that he forgot about his weapons and duty to guard us, and slept soundly through part of our journey.

Though our destination was kept from us no effort was made to prevent us from looking out the window. Stotter still had his compass so we could tell we were following a northwesterly course. At one point we were surprised to find ourselves back in Holland, but assumed that a circuitous route was necessary because of the damages done to the railroads by our bombers.

Sometime during the night we came to the lower Rhine Valley and turned southward on the main line tracks which follow that picturesque valley all the way to Switzerland.

After dawn we enjoyed the scenery along that famous and historical river, with its innumerable vineyards on shelves and its ancient castles. We enjoyed the unique experience, too, of observing the enemy and his country at close range.

Most of us were bomber personnel so we amused ourselves by picking out "fat, juicy targets." My favorites were the hundreds of barges floating down the river loaded with everything imaginable. What a well-placed load of bombs could have done to all that! The sunken barges would block that vital traffic artery.

Escape was constantly on my mind. I studied the possibilities from every angle. First, obviously, we'd have to overpower the guards. We could pass instructions through to each prisoner to grab the weapon nearest him and use it at a given signal. That idea appealed to me greatly, and for a while I stood with my foot not two inches from the butt of a submachine gun balanced loosely at the barrel by a dozing guard. I contemplated kicking it out of his hands before he knew what was going on.

I weighed other possibilities. In confiscating a strange weapon everyone would have to know how to use it immediately. Where was the safety? How was ammunition pushed into the chamber? Many of us were barely acquainted with our own small arms, much less those of the enemy. If we were successful in overpowering the guards, could we get out of Germany? Would the others go along with me on such a desperate venture? What about the wounded who couldn't participate? Would they be massacred by the guards after we left? An escape plan had to be carefully planned, briefed, and precisely executed to have any chance of success. Needless to say, I decided against it. But the mental activity of planning escape kept me busy through much of the train ride.

At length we arrived at the bombed-out city of Cologne. Here was our first close-up view of the results of our bombing of Germany's cities. The impression was almost sickening. The only building we saw undamaged was the famous Cologne Cathedral with its twin spires dominating all else. I hadn't dreamed our bombs had done such damage. The whole city resembled a pile of rubble with only an occasional shell of a building still standing.

The people looked pale and dazed. Many had the glassy-eyed look of shock and moved with the listless gait of apathy.

Our guards were impressed too. Some of them, we learned, had been given the duty of guarding us as an excuse for a brief furlough. But there before them were the remains of their shelled-out homes. Some of them hadn't even heard that their homes had been bombed, and didn't know whether or not their families were still alive. And they were guarding us, the ones who had done this. We felt very uncomfortable.

One American surveyed the ruins and laughed, the hollow, hysterical laugh of a psychotic. His companions quickly quieted him. The angry guards glared at him.

When we changed trains at Cologne station German civilians crowded around us. No friendly smiles here. We saw angry stares of hate. Those people had lost homes and families, and we were the ones who had destroyed them. They hated us with all the pent-up venom they had accumulated from years under Hitler. Gone was our elation, our bravado. In the face of that hate we felt fear-sickening, demoralizing, awful fear. It didn't matter who had started the war, or who was right or wrong. We felt the hatred emanating from those Germans as strongly as we had ever felt anything in our lives.

We were relieved to finally leave Cologne, glad again about just being alive. Our shock was wearing off; in its place was depression.

We continued up the Rhine and arrived late that afternoon in the bombed-out city of Frankfort-am-Main. Cologne had been badly bombed but Frankfort looked worse, if that was possible. The once-beautiful station had been almost solid glass; now hardly a pane remained.

On the trip from Cologne we had noticed the sidings were

cluttered with gutted cars. Here in Frankfort we saw hundreds more of those skeletons. The interior of the station was scorched and black. We wondered how the railroads managed to operate at all.

An angry mob gathered around us, glaring their hate. Some made signs by moving their fingers across their throats. Others raised clenched fists at us. It was terrible to search through those pale, gaunt, angry faces and see only hostility of the worst sort. One man raised his fist and screamed, "bastards, bastards!" I could now understand what it was like to be the victim of a mob. Up to now we hadn't been too worried. But the crowd started muttering and edging closer. The guards became nervous and their anxiety was instantly transmitted to us and amplified many times. Something had to be done in a hurry. Of course we were helpless to do anything except wait to be torn apart by the mob.

Fortunately our guards started jabbering as only German soldiers can, and herded us along with another group of prisoners, mostly British, who'd just come in on another train. We were taken into the central part of the station and down a dark, scorched stairway. At the bottom of the stairway was a black, burned-out windowless room, and no doors except the one which we were streaming through. The room was fifteen feet square at most, and about fifty men were already crowded in it. And there were about that many more of us yet to pack in. The room was lighted only by flashes from the electric torches of the guards. Packed and jammed as it was with dirty, unshaven, sweating men, many with wounds festering and stinking, it was one of the gloomiest sights I have ever seen.

Someone remarked, "Perfect place for a quick massacre." A Britisher sized up the situation perfectly: "Cripes," he said, "The black hole of Calcutta!"

Half of us never made it to the bottom of the stairs, but remained jam-packed on the stairway when the little room reached its saturation point. We were too close together for anyone to sit down. About a third of us were wounded, and many of those wounds were stinking from infections and must have been unbearably sore as they were bumped and jostled. My heart went out to the wounded.

Fortunately, our stay in that hell hole didn't last long. I leaned against the wall and must have dozed off a few minutes. When

I awoke I was flowing back upstairs with the stream of bedraggled humanity.

We were hurriedly loaded onto another train. The usual crowd of curious stared through windows at us, cold-blooded murder in their every glance.

Soon we were clacking along on a dim, single-track line. After just a few miles we pulled into a small station which, we were relieved to see, was almost deserted.

We unloaded and formed up two abreast in the street. We were led slowly through the neat, peaceful-looking streets of the quiet town. It reminded me of small towns I'd seen in Texas, Colorado, New York.

We at the head of the column had to slow down several times to allow the ones in the rear with leg wounds to catch up. Several of those unfortunates were being half-carried, half-dragged by their comrades. As we proceeded at our snail's pace people would stop tending their gardens and lawns to heap verbal and visual abuse upon us.

Finally we turned onto a straight road and I could see the whole column. I thought, what a sad, miserable-looking outfit we were. Most of us had gone down in flames, and few had escaped the facial burns accompanying that ordeal. Most burns had scabbed over and had ugly stubbles of beard sticking through them. Some were dripping. All of us were ragged and filthy. Some men's uniforms had been almost completely torn off. A few Americans were clad only in their blue heat suits, which looked like long-handle underwear. Nearly everyone limped. Many arms were in slings. All of us were stooped from hunger, fatigue or pain. I reflected that that sorry scene was probably being enacted all over Germany and German-occupied Europe.

But as bad off as we were, I later learned that we were much better off than many prisoners. Similar columns of allied prisoners in other parts of the *Reich* reported being stoned, beaten, spat on, and some were killed.

Word was passed up and down the column that we were approaching *Dulag Luft*, the Interrogation Center. We approached with dread. I'd noticed during my previous two weeks as a captive that Germans respect force and despise signs of weakness. I was determined to present a hard-boiled front to them, regardless of how fearful I felt. That decision stood me in good stead during my constant bickerings with my captors while in *Deutschland*. (Unfortunately, my hard attitude became so ingrained into my personality during my ordeal that I had difficulty throwing it off even in friendly relationships when I got back home.)

We were kept standing in formation at *Dulag*, endlessly it seemed, before anyone took notice of us. We used some of our time surreptitiously looking over our surroundings.

Dulag Luft consisted of many temporary wooden buildings, much like those at our station hospitals in the States. The main differences were that the windows were heavily barred and there were barb-wire fences surrounding the place, interspersed here and there with guard towers, and everyone who was not a prisoner was armed. Apparently all German military personnel carried arms at all times.

At last a *Feldwebel* (sergeant) approached us and asked for the senior officer. Before I could answer, someone called my name and pointed me out. The *Feldwebel* told me to follow him.

I followed him inside a building and into a small office where he motioned me to sit down. I was glad to sit. I felt weak from hunger and thirst, having had only half a loaf of black bread and no water in thirty-six hours.

The *Feldwebel* appeared to be courteous and affable.

"I am Sergeant so-and-so," he introduced himself. "Are you alone?"

"What do you mean?" I asked.

"We want to know whether or not your crew is with you. You see, we realize that combat crewmen like to stick together, so we keep them together as much as we can."

I knew that was his method of finding out whether I was a fighter pilot or from a bomber crew. "I can't answer that question," I said.

He looked hurt, then said in a pleading way, "You see, Colonel Burton, we have to account for every allied airman shot down over Europe. We can't have enemy personnel running around loose all over the continent. If you have any of your boys loose it would be to their advantage for you to tell us about them so we can round them up before they get into serious trouble."

I hadn't thought about it in that way before, but I could see through his line of reasoning enough to realize it was a clever trap.

"Let's get this straight, Sergeant," I said, "If you expect me to give you that or any other information you're wasting your time. Furthermore, I think it's a disgrace the way you people are treating prisoners of war. Don't you make any attempt to uphold the obligations of the Geneva Convention? We treat Germans a darn sight better than this. You not only starve us, you don't even give us a chance to clean up." My scruffy two-weeks beard bore silent testimony.

He didn't answer, but shuffled through a pile of papers on his desk and selected one. Then, looking relieved, looked up at me.

"Oh yes," he said. "Here you are. Burton, Stotter and Gins. Shot down over Antwerp in view of the whole town on April 22nd. We have you all typed already. We make an effort to type all prisoners before they get here so we will know how to deal with them."

I was vain enough to wonder what type they thought I was, and curious as to how I would be dealt with, but I remained silent when he paused and waited for me to take the bait.

He started telling me about himself, that he had lived in Canada, and some other stuff I don't remember. When he saw I wasn't interested he got up abruptly.

"You'll get your shave and bath," he said. "If you need anything else just ask for me."

Fat chance! I could imagine the implications involved in asking for him.

A guard beckoned me to follow him. We went into another small room furnished with a table and a chair. Two bored looking, middle-aged enlisted men were inside. In German-American English they ordered me to strip to the skin. They examined every inch of my clothing. They then removed the warm inner liner from my shoes and flying suit. That devastated me as I was already cold, and felt shaky from hunger. I knew one thin layer of clothing would not be enough. I also figured the cells would be unheated. My protests met a stone wall. I shrugged and dressed in what clothing they left me.

They gave me a safety razor and a blade sharpener and escorted me to the shower room. When I asked for soap one of the men looked at me with disbelief. When he left I searched the room carefully and found a piece of soap about the size of a quarter. "Better save that to shave with" I thought.

A happy surprise-the shower had hot water! I turned on the luxuriously hot water and let the heat warm my chilled body. How little it takes to make a person blissfully happy!

I was beginning to think captivity might not be so bad after all when the water suddenly went cold. That shocked me back to reality and I sprang out of the shower. "Everything has its price," I thought, as I remembered what the *Feldwebel* had told me about asking for him if I needed anything.

Shaving a week's growth of beard is bad enough with a sharp razor and plenty of good shaving cream. With my dull blade and pitifully small spot of soap it was torture. By shaving a few whiskers at a time, then sharpening awhile, I finally managed to get the beard off; well, most of it anyway. Notwithstanding the torture, trouble and skin it had cost, I got a lift out of getting the itchy beard off.

After returning the razor and sharpener, as I had been so carefully directed, I was led down a long corridor past innumerable branch corridors and to my own little cell. I had noticed small letters and numerals of different colors on each door. When I asked what those were for, I got only a shrug and mumble in reply.

I thought surely they would bring some food then, but I was wrong. When I asked, my escort assured me that I would get plenty to eat in the morning. I felt really hungry then. I didn't think for a minute that my interrogation was completed, but now that the preliminaries were over and I was all checked in and bedded down I could think about nothing but food.

I tried to turn my attention to my surroundings. The cell was the size of a small bathroom, with a wooden bunk on the side. The bunk had wooden slats topped with a six-foot burlap bag filled with excelsior. There was one small, dirty blanket. There was a small electric radiator beneath the heavily barred and shuttered window. To my surprise it was warm. I literally wrapped myself around the radiator and spent the next hour absorbing every calorie of its puny heat. Finally, exhausted, I fell on my bunk, wrapped the four-foot blanket around my six-foot frame, and slept.

Daybreak came; breakfast, I thought. It was getting to be an obsession with me. If I didn't eat soon I thought I would go mad.

I signaled for a guard to escort me to the toilet. While he was with me it occurred to me that a cigarette might ease the hunger pangs. I communicated that to him in the very understandable way people do when they have no spoken language in common. Like most of the guards, that one was middle-aged, tired, bored, apathetic. "*Nein, nein, nein; verboten!*" (No, no, no; forbidden) he answered.

I washed my face and hands without soap, then wet my hair, combing it with my fingers. When the guard returned me to my cell and locked the door I looked around for something to use for a towel. My eyes rested on the small blanket. I realized then why it was so small. I thought, what the hell, and tore off a piece.

There came the familiar banging of cell doors and pots and pans. My heart leapt for joy. Food at last! It was now forty-eight hours since I'd eaten my half-loaf of black bread.

It seemed they would never get to me. I was literally drooling when they finally opened my door. A thin sandwich and a quart decanter of yellowish liquid was thrust into my hands. "Tay," shouted the German in answer to my questioning look at the stuff.

I stood in the doorway waiting for the rest of my breakfast. The door banged shut in my face. That was it? That was the hearty meal I had been anticipating for so long? I was furious. Oh, well, a condemned man always eats a hearty breakfast, so perhaps that meant I would live another day.

I sat down on the bunk and looked at the sandwich. Two thin slices of black bread, the thinnest spot of margarine I had ever seen, an even thinner layer of ersatz jam. The "tea", I later learned, was made from the leaves of the linden tree and sweetened with saccharine. It tasted like nothing I had ever tasted before. At least it was warm.

I wouldn't have minded solitary confinement if I could have had something to read or write or smoke, or someone to talk to. But all of those were *verboten*. I could only lie on my sack and think of food, food, food.

When the sun was out I could tell by the shadows approximately when a "meal" was due.

The black German bread tasted absolutely delicious when I'd finally get my two thin slices at sunset. I'd nibble at it for hours, never allowing a single crumb to fall to the floor. Every little swallow was ecstasy. I would look sorrowfully at the ever-diminishing size of it. Finally, when the last crumb was gone I'd heave a deep, philosophical sigh, and start sweating it out waiting for the next two slices.

The noon-day bowl of soup was a feast. The guard would carelessly ladle out enough to bring my bowl up to a half-inch from the top. I'd look at him pleadingly, hoping that he would respond to my silent plea, while my mind screamed, "Why in hell don't you fill it up!" I would gulp down the soup, then while away the hours by making spoon marks and erasing them. Each drop picked up that way was another minute, heavenly swallow. A bowl could be cleaned as thoroughly that way as if it had been washed.

There was no logic to the length of time prisoners were kept in solitary. I believe the average was about a week. After three days you would quit taking exercise, and after five days, you would lie in a mildly pleasant stupor. I don't know how long one could last under such conditions but I knew men who were kept in solitary for as long as six months. Most prisoners, after a few days of solitary, would be extremely uncomfortable, confused, lonely, hungry, bored and worried. They would then be ripe for interrogation, by German reasoning. However, I believe they overlooked a very important angle. Hunger is soothing to the nerves. Starvation, if it didn't take so long, might be a comparatively pleasant death. One drifts into a sort of drugged lethargy that eases pain and tempers anxiety. One can achieve a state of mind in which he doesn't particularly care what happens. His resistance to temptation becomes greater while, on the other hand, his reasoning power and thought processes become reduced and retarded.

At first I tried to keep my mind occupied. I searched every inch of the cell for something with which to open the shuttered window. I found a loose screw in the radiator bracket, took it out and started working on the shutter catch. Engrossed in that puzzle the time flew by. The time between morning sandwich and noon soup was shortened by hours it seemed. That afternoon, to my surprise, I succeeded in opening the catch. I opened the window a crack and looked out upon what would have been a drab scene under normal conditions. I spent that entire afternoon studying the yard, fascinated by that small break in the monotony.

I sat up a daily routine of pacing the tiny cell to keep my feet in good condition. I made mental calculations to determine the length of my step in centimeters, then how many steps it would take to cover a kilometer. I then took pieces of excelsior from my bed to use as counters. I would transfer a piece from one pocket to the other after each hundred meters. Between that diversion and looking out the window I was beginning to feel more at home in my cell.

My preoccupation with escaping was enhanced by my ability to see out. On the second day I had discovered a loose ceiling panel in the prefabricated structure of my cell. I found that by removing a slat from my bunk and pushing it against the ceiling with all my strength I could raise the heavy panel about an inch. Terrifically excited by my discovery I quickly replaced the slat and lay down to see if the noise I had made would bring a guard. I lay still for fully twenty minutes, my heart pounding from exertion and excitement. The corridor remained quiet so I tried again, this time lifting the panel a little higher. Life had taken on a new importance. Now, I thought, I had three very interesting and possibly fruitful preoccupations: fighting hunger, exercising, escaping.

I spent that day and part of the night working on and planning my escape. In my imagination I would pry up the panel far enough to get through, prop it up with the slat, pull my bunk over to stand on, and climb into the loft. I would climb up during early evening and make my way through the loft to one of the ventilators that were built along the roof at intervals. Then I would remove some of the wooden louvers from the ventilators and climb out onto the roof. From there, at night, I would be able to see without being seen. I felt confident that with most of the night ahead of me I would be able to formulate some kind of plan to get through the gate with a reasonable chance of success. If some insurmountable problem should arise when I was on the roof I could retreat to my cell to think it over. I barely closed my eyes that night, so exhilarating was the prospect of getting out.

After morning ablutions on the third day I devoured my sandwich and gulped down my decanter of tea, eager to get to work. I paced up and down until I figured by counting the pieces of excelsior that I had covered four kilometers. I was surprised and dismayed to find myself fatigued by the exertion. I spent the rest of the morning looking out the window.

I gulped down the noonday cup of soup hoping that would replenish my energy, then reached under the bunk, got a slat and pushed upward against the loose panel. I pushed again with all my strength. The panel raised infinitesimally. I felt faint and my muscles quivered from the exertion. I sat on the bunk discouraged, and so tired I soon stretched out.

Lying there it dawned on me that hunger was taking its toll. I fell asleep. When I woke I had no desire to try again. All I wanted to do was just lie flat and stare. It felt so comfortable. I didn't even have that intense yearning for food.

It had already occurred to me that the worst part of starvation was that period immediately following a "meal" when one realized it was gone, and was now faced with the long period before there would be more.

I had been worried about being interrogated and imagined my limitations might be reached by force or by cunning. I believed that for an officer to talk out of mere human weakness was not acceptable, at least. Now in my comfortable stupor I was confident that I could withstand enemy interrogation no matter what the cost. Death had no particular horror. If that was the price of remaining silent I could pay.

I dozed awhile, then spent some time staring through the peep hole in my door. I could see guards carrying paper and pencils, cigarettes and books. The books were in English. I remembered the *Feldwebel's* last remark, "If you need anything, just ask for me." How I would have enjoyed a cigarette, a book -any book-a pencil and paper. I could have them, I thought, but at what a price!

On the fifth day, a soldier came in dressed like a Red Cross worker. He used almost the same routine as the other one had used on us in Antwerp. When I refused to fill in the blanks and sign, he became indignant. I matched his indignation, telling him in no uncertain terms what I thought of his insult to my intelligence, thinking I would fall for such an obvious trick. I went on to condemn the *Luftwaffe* for their inhuman treatment of American prisoners of war, and wound up by informing him that German prisoners of war in America were living in comparative luxury. He replied that I probably could get better treatment, too, if I would ask to see an officer.

When he had gone I expected the worst, but didn't particularly care.

That afternoon a guard beckoned me to come out of the cell and follow him. I was weak, dizzy and confused as I followed the middle-aged, apathetic guard through what seemed like miles of passageways. When I asked where we were going, he answered, simply, "*Offizier*." I figured that this was the long-awaited interrogation. I was not mistaken.

We stopped before a glass-paneled door marked *Hauptmann* something-or-other. The guard knocked, we entered, he saluted and left.

The *Hauptmann* was a tall, thin, middle-aged officer with red hair, a ruddy complexion and buck teeth. I saluted, he returned the salute, called me by rank and name and invited me to sit down. His English was very good with a slight accent that was more British than German. Immaculately dressed, he had the air and manner of a cultured nobleman without the arrogance and hauteur usually associated with German officers.

He offered me a cigarette. I greedily accepted and he took one for himself. The cigarette tasted like straw, as foreign brands taste to Americans, but I inhaled it deeply and was soon so dizzy I could hardly see.

I had dreaded that occasion for a long time, and knew that in my weakened state I could be outwitted so I started trying to forestall the inevitable questions by criticizing German treatment of American prisoners again. I could tell immediately by his amused expression that I'd made a mistake by talking at all. I realized then that to talk about anything, no matter what, was to play right into their hands. For the first time I fully appreciated our army indoctrination, to give name, rank, serial number, nothing more.

When I stopped abruptly he asked me which cell I was in. I answered, "B-6." He replied that "B" block was truly rough. He then asked if I wanted to see where I was. When I didn't answer he motioned me over to a large map of Europe on the wall. I tried to hide my eagerness as my eyes scanned the map. I was disappointed that the printing was in German-Gothic type, making the place names difficult for me to read.

He pointed to the map and said, "Here is where we are now, here is the Rhine, and the Ruhr, and here is where you were shot down, over the city of Dortmund."

Until now I had not known the exact place where we had gone down. I reasoned later that all that courteous talk was to win my confidence and throw me off guard.

"Where did you drop your bombs?" he asked abruptly.

"I haven't the slightest idea," I answered, truthfully.

"Did you order your crew to bail out to lighten the load so that you, Stotter and Gins could get back to England?"

The question was very clever. Its subtle insult was designed to make me lose my temper. Anger would place me at a decided disadvantage and perhaps cause me to blurt out the information he wanted. And, indeed, I did almost fall for that one, so angry did I become. But I maintained my control and managed to reply, "I can't answer that question."

"I see you had two Jewish officers in your crew. Is it customary for you Americans to commission Jews?"

I couldn't resist giving him a shot of American propaganda.

"In our army we don't question a man's color, race or creed; all we ask is that he be a good soldier," I said, as firmly as I could, looking at him very hard.

"And are those Jews good soldiers?" he asked, incredulous.

"The best!" I replied.

That was the end of that.

He returned to his desk and I to my chair. My heart was pounding. I expected him to pick up his phone and order my immediate execution, knowing as I knew by then, how sincerely Germans hated all Jews. I wondered if Stotter and Gins were still alive, and if so, what tortures they were going through.

But my interrogator remained suave, scholarly. He asked me a few more pointed, technical questions. After hearing my, "I can't answer that question," time after time, he finally raised his hands in exasperation. He said absently, "It really doesn't matter. We know all about you and your mission. Look, here is the complete report."

He showed me a four-page mimeographed booklet. He pointed to a formation diagram on the last page. Here is your formation, and here is where you were flying." The diagram was inaccurate, but I said nothing.

"You are in 567th Squadron of 389th Group, based at Hethel." That statement was correct except for the squadron number. Although I was flying with a 567th Squadron crew in a 567th airplane, my own squadron was the 565th. I remained silent, amazed at the amount of information he had. I wondered where he had gotten it but was content to let him do all the talking. "You were flying in a B-24D type aircraft called 'Round Trip Ticket,' bearing serial number 38435." He continued reading from the booklet, "This was to have been the last mission for the aircraft before being retired from combat."

Every word was true.

"Is this correct?" he demanded.

That method of interrogation was their favorite. They would demoralize a prisoner by appearing to know everything about him. Most men would feel let down that someone else had talked, and would likely think, "Oh well, they know it all anyway," and blurt out important information that the Germans did not have, the connecting links, and often the very information they were seeking.

"I cannot answer that question," I replied firmly.

He raised his hands again in exasperation. "It doesn't really matter," he said again. "Your case is complete. You will go now to your permanent camp where you will get Red Cross parcels and cigarettes and see movies and play games."

I wasn't impressed. Another trick, I thought, and said nothing. When he picked up his phone and started talking in German I was certain he was ordering my execution.

Another bored guard came in, saluted, and motioned for me to precede him out of the room. I can't remember thinking anything for the next few minutes. Perhaps I was too nervous and confused.

The guard ushered me out of the building and toward a barbed-wire-enclosed compound. Another guard opened the gate and pushed me into the open enclosure. I waited while he locked the gate behind me.

When he seemed to have no further interest in me I was at a loss as to what to do next. I looked around the compound.

American and British officers and enlisted men were sitting, lying and standing all about. A lieutenant approached and offered me a cigarette, an American cigarette. I asked him what happened next. I couldn't believe my interrogation was over and I could now breathe the sweet, fresh air, talk to people, and smoke. Yet the others around me were doing those things, and seemed relaxed about being in the barbed-wire-enclosed compound.

The lieutenant assured me that nothing in particular happened next.

"We do as we please in here," he said. "Come in and pick out a bunk for yourself, any bunk. If somebody is already in it rank him out. We get five cigarettes a day and you can take a shower, all the hot water you want. Pretty soon we'll have chow, real American food. We get Red Cross parcels here. The interrogation is over. They just keep us here till they get a train load, then send us to a *Stalag*."

As his words slowly sank into my befuddled brain I began to feel excited, and tremendously happy. I had made it! I was alive! Best of all I had managed to get through the dreaded interrogation without revealing anything. I had a strong impulse to run madly through the compound, yelling, "I made it! I made it! I got through without telling the bastards a thing!" But a sobering thought dampened my jubilation. Yes, you made it, I reflected, but only by the grace of God. I wondered how many others had not been so fortunate.

I selected a bunk, then immediately dashed for the shower. Hallelujah, there was plenty of hot water! I soaked in luxurious warmth for a full hour. I washed my long-handle underwear which, after almost three weeks of continuous wear, was in a shameful state. There was even a large hunk of GI soap. I had not appreciated the stuff before, but now it was a supreme luxury just to have real soap!

Mealtime arrived. We formed a chow line where we were issued a handout of the now-familiar black bread and margarine, supplemented by a soup made from liver paté and kidney beans. There was even a dessert made from prunes, raisins, powdered milk and sugar. All that was topped off by a delicious cup of real American coffee. The bread, margarine and beans were German-issue; everything else was from Red Cross parcels, direct from the good old USA. We were also issued five American cigarettes a day.

The *Dulag* comprised perhaps two acres. It was surrounded by two substantial-looking barbed-wire fences, with a six-foot space in between filled with barbed-wire entanglements. At each corner of the compound was a high tower, equipped with searchlight and machine gun, and manned by a guard with a rifle. There were three buildings in the compound: officers' barracks, enlisted men's barracks and mess hall. (Under the

Geneva Convention, officer POW'S had to be separated from enlisted POW'S. However, enlisted POW'S could volunteer to serve as orderlies in officers' camps. Their incentive was that they would be paid by the officers after returning home, an amount agreed to between them.)

At least a third of the prisoners had wounds, some of them serious. In spite of that, morale was extremely high. There was a kind of rejoicing, almost to the point of hysteria. Everyone wanted to talk, talk, talk, especially to tell his own story about his recent close brush with death. It was hard to prevent indiscriminate discussion of military matters. The mad elation that pervaded the atmosphere overcame caution. If the Germans didn't pick up lots of information through microphones and stooges placed in the compound at *Dulag*, they certainly missed a good chance.

Some of the wounded were pathetic. One sergeant had a heavy cast on his head. He staggered around without equilibrium.

Most wounds were burns around faces and hands. Facial burns showed a definite pattern. If the injury had occurred at high altitude, burns were confined to a neat pattern around the eyes, the rest of the face having been protected by helmet and mask. At lower altitudes, burns included nose, mouth and chin, with neat lines around the face to the point where the helmet had come.

In some cases where the helmet had been discarded preparatory to bailing out entire faces would be raw and red; and sometimes the ears would be burned off around the edges.

Other common injuries were sprains, lacerations and broken bones suffered during parachuting. There were few gunshot or shell wounds in the compound; presumably men who'd been shot had either been killed or wounded seriously enough to be confined to hospitals. From the looks of some of the quite serious wounds here one would have had to be practically dead to be hospitalized.

Although the quarters at *Dulag* were warm and fairly comfortable, very few slept; we were too excited. We bubbled over with the elation of having a new lease on life and seemed to want to grasp and hold on to every second of that blessed time. Even if we had tried to sleep, the ones who insisted on talking all night would have prevented it.

My bunk was in a room in the most popular spot in the compound. The walls had been decorated with comic murals. There were beautifully colored, life-sized paintings of women in various enticing poses. There were paintings of airplanes, and a caricature of an RAF officer arriving at *Dulag* with baggage, tennis racquet and golf clubs. Those cheerful decorations accounted for the popularity of the room to a large extent.

On sunny afternoons we would sit in the sun and sing. Our arrogance was boundless as we sang sassy American and patriotic songs. When a formation of German soldiers passed by, singing their beautiful old marching songs, we would try to drown them out.

As stated in "Part I, Combat," my brother Weldon and I had been commissioned by the Army Air Corps when we'd transferred to it from the RCAF in 1942. We had been assigned as BT-13 instructors together, but our careers went in separate directions after I was reassigned to B-17 school, and from there to B-24 instructing at another base. I'd eventually been assigned as Squadron Commander of 565th Squadron, 389th Group. Weldon wound up in the 464th B-24 Group in Italy as Group Operations Officer.

While at *Dulag* I ran into the Group Executive Officer from my brother's group in Italy who had been captured on his first mission. It was only the second mission for their group. He assured me my brother was in the best of health. Later we were assigned to the same compound. That officer, Lieutenant Colonel Hand, continued to keep me informed about Weldon right up until the last by screening new prisoners as they arrived.

Another pleasant surprise was seeing Lieutenant Colonel Bob Sears from my own combat wing. When he saw me, he shouted, "Hey, boy, we thought you was drownded!" using the easy, lack-of-pretense manner so treasured by the Air Corps.

Bob's story about how he'd gotten there was unusual. Let me begin by saying, there are two things few flying people live to tell about: one is getting blown up, and the other is going through a bomber's top hatch. Yet there was Bob, without a scratch, as calm as if he was in the officers club in England, telling about how he'd gotten blown up and out of the top hatch of a B-24! Miraculous happenings were becoming so commonplace that I was beginning to accept them without so much as a, "You don't say."

The *Dulag* compound was managed by two Air Corps lieutenants. Those two maintained all necessary liaison with the Germans. There was very little contact between most prisoners and the Germans. That was obviously a desirable situation for both sides.

I managed to acquire a new pair of British shoes, a pair of socks and a suit of G.I. long-handles from the limited stocks of Red Cross clothing at the camp. The extra suit of underwear gave me a welcome barrier against the chilly spring wind, in addition to providing a spare suit when one was being washed. I felt adequately dressed now that I could discard the cumbersome, felt outer-shoes from my heat suit and replace them with a pair of real shoes. Getting the shoes was a piece of luck. The only reason I was able to get them was because no one else could fill them; they were size twelve. Otherwise I would have had to be bare footed to obtain them.

I also acquired a tiny compass from one of our Air Corps escape kits which, to my delight, I found I could hide inside my ear.

We were allowed to fill in brief information on a few postcards to be mailed to our next-of-kin back home.

I was relieved to see Stotter and Gins on my second day in the compound. (As senior officer I was frequently sought out by our captors. Stotter and Gins, as company grade officers - captains and lieutenants, as were most POW'S - could remain inconspicuous.) Both were thin and pale, and had spots of long beard left over from where they had tried to chew off two-weeks growth with a dull blade, but they were otherwise OK.

On the third day in the compound word spread that a group would leave the next day for one of the *Stalags*. I was to be senior officer of the group. The German who brought my instructions was known as "Halitosis" throughout the camp because of his foul breath. In his obnoxious manner he sought me out, stuck his face close to mine, and said, "Ah, Co-lo-nel, I have been looking for you. Tomorrow you will go with your comrades to your permanent camp. You, as zeenior officer, will be in command, zee? It will be a long, hard trip. Your shoes and belts will be taken from you. Your windows will be blinded-all dark-unnerstand? No one will leave his zeat, zee?

A terrible long trip, *nicht*? Now, Co-lo-nel, if you will sign this paper it will be all different, unnerstand? You will ride in zecond class coach, shades up. You keep your shoes and belts. You can walk around and visit, zee? A comfortable trip, unnerstand?"

I was flabbergasted by the proposition and well-nigh asphyxiated by his breath. I studied the paper, or parole. It was an agreement not to escape or make any plan for future escape during the trip from Oberursel to Sagan, under penalty of death. I was to sign the parole on behalf of the entire group of 112 British and American officers.

I was unprepared to make such a decision on the spot. My first impulse was to tell him to shove it. Then I thought of our thirty-odd cripples who didn't have a chance of escaping, and who could use all the comfort they could get. I told Halitosis I would think it over and let him know.

Halitosis used all the salesmanship he could muster to get me to sign the parole. One of the American lieutenants interjected that all former purge commanders had signed the agreement. (Purge was the term for a group of prisoners being transferred from a transient camp to a permanent prison camp.)

When Halitosis left I sought out Bob Sears. Bob was a West Pointer and I had confidence in his judgment.

"What's the date of your rank, Bob?" I asked.

"April twelfth," he replied. "Why?"

From his answer I outranked him by a week, but I decided to try to put it off on him anyway.

"Hey, you outrank me, then. Besides, you're a West Pointer. This job is yours."

"Oh, no you don't! You outrank me a week, thank God. This is your headache."

Realizing I was stuck with the job I asked for his advice. He suggested we call the group together and talk it over. A splendid idea, I thought. We got the men together and Bob and I explained the proposition.

Someone remarked that an escape attempt by a few might cause the annihilation of all without a coordinated plan to include everyone. Yet no plan could include everyone because of the wounded. I told them that if a single man voted against signing, the parole would not be signed. Then we asked all who were against signing to raise their hands. There were four or five hands raised. "That settles it," I said. I was about to dismiss the group when I noticed that the "for's" were trying to convince the "against's". After a brief pow-wow some of the men wanted another vote. That time not a hand was raised against signing.

Halitosis was very happy. He had sold another bill of goods. (See the restored document below.)

Early next morning we were grouped along a road outside the compound. A white-haired, fat Prussian major called me out of the group to stand alongside him on a bank while he delivered a long, monotonous oration on discipline in a blood-curdling screech.

He screamed out at the group, "Although this man is your zenior officer his orders can be countermanded by the lowest German *Gefreidter* (Private)! You will obey! You will obey! You will obey!"

I stood beside him feeling mortified and helpless. With my bushy hair flying around my bare head and my sloppy clothes flapping in the breeze I felt very un-military. At length the major

---

We give our word of honour as British and American Officers that we will not:

      /. make any attempt to escape————————.
      2. get in touch with the civilian Population or—.
      3. other P'sOW not belonging to this transport—.
      4. make any preparations for future escape———.
during our trip from Oberursel to Stalag Luft 3 Sagan.
This is signed by....Lt/Col. Paul T. Burton................
as Senior American...Officer of the transport for all P'sOW who take part in this trip.
Any man who will break his parole will be put to death.

Oberursel, May 12th, 1944.

Lt.Col. AC

---

ended his boring tirade and put out his hand to me in farewell. I looked at the little pistol on his belt, wishing I could use it on him, and returned his handshake weakly. I called the group to attention and we marched off down the road, escorted by four armed Germans and a dog.

At the train station we were loaded onto two typically European day coaches. We sat three in a seat, six to a compartment. Our guards for the trip had arrived before us and had brought and loaded our Red Cross parcels. The NCO in charge of the four guards informed me there would be one-fourth parcel per man for the trip, and that I should see that the parcels were distributed evenly. I delivered one parcel to each compartment, and an extra one to every other compartment so that the two extra men in one compartment could share the extra parcel with the two extra men in another compartment.

The guards brought in a large can of drinking water and soon we were chugging our way through *Deutschland*. Our bellies were full, bodies clean, morale high. We talked, ate, laughed, sang, as though we didn't have a worry in the world.

As we journeyed deeper into Germany we saw many industrial plants. I automatically made mental notes of those fat, juicy targets - as if I would ever get a chance to use the information.

One of the men in my compartment was a young giant, Second Lieutenant Herbert Mosebach, a bombardier from Paige, Texas.

Herb was a third-generation German-American and had been raised in a German-speaking settlement. Although he had spoken German at home he wasn't sure he would be able to converse in Germany.

He asked if I thought it would be OK for him to let the guards know he spoke the language. He was surprised and delighted to find that he could carry on a perfectly normal conversation with them. It was amusing to listen to Herb chatting fluently with the guards in his soft pleasant accent, and hear their strong guttural replies. It sounded as though they were speaking two entirely different languages. Yet Herb and the guards obviously understood each other perfectly.

I immediately saw the value of having Mosebach around me all the time. As senior officer, I had been at a disadvantage when dealing with our captors, because of my ignorance of their language. I decided to appoint Herb as my adjutant. Although he seemed overawed by my rank, he accepted and quickly learned to relax around me.

How lucky I was finding Herb! Beside his knowledge of German, he was remarkable in many other ways. Perhaps his best attribute was his easy-going, often comical nature. He could get a laugh out of me at times when a good laugh seemed worth a fortune. But behind Mosebach's good-natured clowning facade was a brilliant mind. Here is his story, in his own words:

We were about fifteen minutes from our target, which was Berlin, at an altitude of 18,000 feet, when our number four engine was lost. It had been throwing oil for some time and when the engine finally cut out, the pilots were unable to feather it. Just then the formation began climbing and we were unable to keep up. The pilot decided to turn back and head for home.

I had been trying to release the bombs but could not, nor could they be salvoed from the pilot's compartment. Due to the wind-milling prop we were steadily losing altitude so I decided to go back and trip the bombs out manually. I picked up a nearby oxygen "walk-around" bottle, noticed that the gauge registered 400 pounds, fastened it to my clothing and plugged my mask into it. I then went to the radio room to get the crank for cranking open the bomb bay doors. That was necessary since the electrical system was out and the doors would not open electrically. I cranked open the doors and began tripping out the bombs, one by one.

Apparently the gauge on the oxygen bottle was broken because, although it registered a supply of oxygen I was having trouble breathing. We were then at 16,000 feet and by the time I had all the bombs kicked out I was breathing on a vacuum.

After getting rid of all the bombs I started back to the nose. In order to get air I tried to unplug the connection from the oxygen bottle but was unable to do so. Desperately needing air I tore the mask from my face, and in so doing slipped and fell down between the pilot's and copilot's seats. As I hit the floor my right arm hit the escape door handle and knocked open the hatch. The engineer and navigator had both seen me tear off my mask and fall and they thought I was getting ready to jump. The engineer jumped down on my legs in order to hold me in the ship, and the navigator caught me around the throat, and in trying to hold me in was choking me. I was already short of air and as I struggled to break his hold I was nearly thrown out of the hatch without a parachute. In fact, my right arm and shoulder were out of the hatch. I reached down and caught hold of the escape handle and pulled the hatch shut, pulling the handle off in doing so.

We had been flying in an overcast for protection but the overcast was decreasing in altitude as we neared the coast. We encountered no flak or fighter opposition. Soon we noticed the Zuyderzee and made an estimate as to our position. Just as we reached the coast there was a complete break in the cloud bank and we sailed out into the clear at an altitude of 5,000 feet. As we crossed the coast the coastal batteries opened up on us, riddling our plane with holes.

Our remaining three engines were hit and a shell came through the cockpit, knocking the pilot's helmet off and removing a tuft of his hair. Luckily he was not injured in the least.

Losing power rapidly the pilot headed the ship for a cloud bank, but by the time it was reached all four engines were gone and the ship was losing altitude at a fast rate. I was in the nose and noticing the great loss of altitude, pushed my interphone button. Calling the pilot, I said, "Say, Bob, what are we going to do?" The pilot said, "I don't know, guess we're going to have to ditch." I then said, "What's the matter, did they get any more of the engines?" The pilot came back with, "Yes, they got all four of them." I then heard a gunner say, "Well, we'd better get rid of this ammunition." I cut in on him and said, "To hell with the ammunition, check your Mae West!" (life preserver)

When I got back to the radio room all the gunners were there watching the engineer and navigator picking at the safety wire on the radio compartment escape hatch. I glanced out the window and noticed that the ship was just about to hit the water.

Everybody was still standing around unready for the ditching. I estimated that the ship would hit the water in about ten seconds and almost became frantic because the escape hatch was still unopened. I reached up, grasped the safety wire with my hand, broke it and lifted the hatch out. I had just set it on the floor when we hit the water. There were two distinct impacts.

The radio room was immediately filled with water and that

helped absorb the shock of the crash on the unprepared crew. Everyone tried to get out of the hatch at the same time and as a result none were getting out. The tail of the ship had broken off just at the ball turret and the ship was sinking rapidly. The navigator had pulled the dinghy release just after the crash and they were ready for use.

After crawling out of the hatch I stood up on the fuselage just as the dinghies began to float away from the ship.

I made a dive for one and landed right in the middle of it, nearly knocking some of the men out of the raft. The sea was very rough and the waves seemed to be about fifteen feet high. The waves covered the men with water and the rafts were full of water all the time. One large wave caught us and turned the raft over.

It was very difficult to get back in the raft. It seemed like every time I got my head out of the water another wave would cover me. I finally caught the raft and held on. At that time I noticed that I had forgotten to discharge the carbon dioxide cylinder in my life vest.

After awhile, we decided we were getting nowhere, so the copilot and I put up a sail and we sailed toward the coast of Holland.

The Germans were waiting for us when we reached the shore. We had been in the water six hours. In the group of Germans who picked us up there was a lieutenant who took it upon himself to interrogate us immediately. In interrogating the pilot he kept asking him whether he was flying a Fortress Number One or Number Two. The pilot, not understanding what he meant, just laughed, so the lieutenant slapped him in the face.

We were in our wet clothes from eleven o'clock the morning of May 7th until two o'clock the following morning. They put us in a large motor bus and took us into Amsterdam where we were put in prison. From there we were taken to Dulag. *Thus ended my crew's first mission.*

On the train, seated as we were with six men squeezed into each tiny compartment, sleep was out of the question. We could only doze or nod. After a day and night of dozing and nodding we became obsessed with the desire to stretch out for a real nap. We seized on the idea of taking turns sleeping in the small, overhead baggage compartment. Those were about four-feet long, but were divided into three parts by high partitions (probably put there to prevent passengers from sleeping in them). When my turn came I managed to cram my six-foot frame into one of them and enjoyed the best sleep I had had in a week.

We passed a town with an airport on the outskirts that some of us had bombed only a few weeks previously. The mission had been the deepest penetration into Germany up to that time. We were pleased to see our target had been thoroughly plastered.

Our destination was Sagan in Lower Silesia (*Nieder Schlesien*) in German-occupied Poland. I was both relieved and dismayed when we finally arrived there. It was a relief to leave the confinement of the train, but discouraging to realize how far removed we were from the nearest friendly forces.

The town of Sagan was small. It was located near the geographical center of the (then) German Empire, which included almost all of Western Europe. Westward there were no allied forces on the European continent, and eastward we were separated from our Russian allies by German-occupied Poland and Czechoslovakia. The nearest possible exit for a would-be escapee appeared to be the Baltic Sea north of Stettin, 200 miles away. But the Baltic would be a risky route because of its domination by the Germans. Getting away from our guards would be only the beginning in any escape attempt. Getting out of Germany would be quite a feat, since Germany, under Nazi dictatorship, was a huge prison in itself.

I don't remember seeing Sagan when we arrived there, for we were taken a short distance from the train directly to the prison, *Stalag Luft III*. (See Illustrations on following pages.)

There we were processed in by German prison personnel. We'd noticed how the notoriously efficient Germans often stumbled over their own efficiency. As an example I managed to get through the search without them finding the little compass that I'd obtained from a fellow prisoner who had managed to save it from his escape kit. It was the size of a pencil eraser and I'd hidden it in my ear. I was delighted they didn't find it.

After we were searched we were lined up to be photographed. Standing at attention, our ragged group was coldly eyed up and down by a group of senior German officers, resplendent in

PAUL BURTON

Map above shows the location of prisons and camps across Germany.

Below is the prison identification issued for Paul Burton.

Name:	Burton
Vorname:	Paul T.
Dienstgrad:	Lt. col.
Erk.-Marke:	4583 OFLAG LUFT 8
Serv.-Nr.:	o - 1 699 162
Nationalität:	U.S.A.

Baracke:

Raum:

K. Liebig, Sagan

Location of German Camps and Hospitals Where American Prisoners of War and Civilian Internees Are Held

(Based on information received to December 31, 1944).

PRISONER OF WAR CAMPS

CAMP	NEAREST TOWN	MAP SQUARE
Stalag II A	Neubrandenburg	B 2
Stalag II B	Hammerstein	C 1-2
Stalag III A	Luckenwalde	B 2
Stalag III B	Fürstenberg/Oder	C 2
Stalag III C	Altdrewitz	C 2
Stalag III D	Berlin-Steglitz	B 2
Stalag IV A	Hohnstein	B-C 3
Stalag IV B	Mühlberg	B 2
Stalag IV C	Wistritz	B 3
Stalag IV D	Torgau	B 2
Stalag IV D/Z	Annaburg	B 2
Stalag IV F	Hartmannsdorf	B 3
Stalag IV G	Oschatz	B 2
Stalag V A	Ludwigsburg	A-B 3
Stalag V B	Villingen	A 4
Stalag VI G	Bergisch-Neustadt	A 2
Stalag VI J	Krefeld	A 2
Stalag VII A	Moosburg	B 3
Stalag VII B	Memmingen	B 4
Stalag VIII B	Teschen	D 3
Stalag 344	Lamsdorf	C 3
Stalag VIII C	Sagan	C 2
Stalag IX B	Bad Orb	A-B 3
Stalag IX C	Bad Sulza	B 2
Stalag X B	Bremervörde	A-B 2
Stalag X C	Nienburg	A 2
Stalag XI A	Altengrabow	B 2
Stalag XI B	Fallingbostel	B 2
Stalag XII A	Limburg	A 3
Stalag XII D	Wahlbreitbach	A 3
Stalag XII F	Freinsheim	A 3
Stalag XIII C	Hammelburg	B 3
Stalag XIII D	Nürnberg-Langwasser	B 3
Stalag 383	Hohenfels	B 3
Stalag XVII A	Kaisersteinbruch	C 4
Stalag 398	Pupping	B-C 4
Stalag XVIII A	Wolfsberg	C 4
Stalag XVIII C(317)	Markt-Pongau	B-C 4
Stalag 357	Oerbke	A 2
Stalag XX A	Tórun	D 2
Stalag XX B	Marienburg	D 1
WK 8—BAB 21	Blechhammer	D 3

CAMPS FOR AIRMEN

Luft I	Barth	B 1
Luft III	Sagan	C 2
Luft IV	Grosstychow	C 1
Luft VII	Bankau	C-D 2
Stalag XVII B	Krems/Gneixendorf	C 3
Dulag Luft	Wetzlar	A 3

NAVAL AND MERCHANT MARINE CAMPS

Marlag-Milag	Tarmstedt	A-B 2

GROUND FORCE OFFICERS' CAMPS

Oflag IV C	Colditz	B 2
Oflag VII B	Eichstätt	B 3
Oflag IX A/H	Spangenburg	B 2
Oflag IX A/Z	Rotenburg	B 2-3
Oflag X B	Nienburg	A 2
Oflag XI (79)	Brunswick	B 2
Oflag 64	Altburgund	C 2

LAZARETTS (Hospitals)

	NEAREST TOWN	MAP SQUARE
IV A	Res. Laz. Elsterhorst (Hohnstein)	C 3
IV G	Leipzig	B 2
V B	Rottenmunster	A 4
VI C	Res. Laz. Lingen	A 2
VI G	Res. Laz. Gerresheim	A 2
VII A	Freising	B 2-3
IX B	Bad Soden/Salmünster	A 3
IX C	Obermassfeld	B 2-3
IX C	Meiningen	B 3
IX C	Hildburghausen	B 3
X A	Res. Laz. II, Schleswig	B 1
X B	Sandbostel	A-B 2
XIII D	Nürnberg-Langwasser	B 3
XVIII A/Z	Spittal/Drau	B-C 4
Marine Lazarett Cuxhaven		A 1
Luftwaffen Lazarett 4/11 Wismar		B 1
Res. Laz. II Vienna		C 3-4
Res. Laz. Graz		C 4
Res. Laz. Bilin		B-C 3
Res. Laz. Wollstein		C 2
Res. Laz. II Stargard		C 2
Res. Laz. Schmorkau		C 2
Res. Laz. Königswartha		C 2
Res. Laz. Ebelsbach		B 3

CIVILIAN INTERNEE CAMPS

Ilag Biberach		B 4
Ilag Liebenau		B 4
Ilag VII/H Laufen		B 4

Key

■ Prisoner of War Camps

Ⓘ Camps for Airmen

◉ Officer's Camps

✚ Civilian Internee Camps

✜ Hospitals (Lazaretts)

⊠ Marlag and Milag

Scale: 72 miles per inch.

Published by

THE AMERICAN
NATIONAL RED CROSS

their gleaming uniforms.

We were then herded into a building and stripped to the skin. While our clothes were being deloused we were sent for a hot shower. But the hot water was shut off abruptly after five minutes and we were left shivering in our birthday suits for the next two hours while we waited for our clothes to be returned. When our clothes were finally returned I found that my woolen shirt and heavy underwear were missing.

Next we went past a window where some Americans were giving out clothing. We were each given a suit and an overcoat of G.I. OD's (government-issue olive drabs, the standard uniform for U.S. Army enlisted personnel) that had been supplied by the American Red Cross. My pants, shirt and blouse fit fairly well, but my overcoat came well above my knees, and a deep breath would have split it down the back. No head gear was issued.

About fifty yards away we could see hundreds of prisoners inside a fence. They had gathered to enjoy one of the few high points of prison life: the arrival of a new purge. They waved and shouted wisecracks at us and conducted themselves in what seemed to us to be an odd manner. Little did we realize that very soon we would be behaving in much the same way.

As we passed through the gates of West Camp (one of five separated sections of *Stalag Luft III*), we were crowded on both sides by solid walls of prisoners eager to find old buddies in our midst. All around we heard the happy greetings of pals reunited: Joe Blow, you old so-and-so, well, I'm a son of a gun, how are you, I thought you were dead, what's new?

How are so-and-so and so? You remember the day, the week, etc., etc.

Lieutenant Colonel Wilbur Aring, West Camp Prison Adjutant, addressed us when we had gathered in front of the kitchen to get a cup of coffee and a sandwich. He briefly explained the prison setup, what we could expect from Germans and Americans, and what to be particularly careful about. Later he invited me to his room for more coffee and talk.

It was May 10, 1944. Truly, we were prisoners of war now. Over the past few days we had heard from Germans the phrase, "For you, der var iss offer." (For you, the war is over) I could see that for us it had at least taken on a very different form.

(See Illustrations on following pages.)

WESTERN UNION

CLASS OF SERVICE

This is a full-rate Telegram or Cablegram unless its deferred character is indicated by a suitable symbol above or preceding the address.

A. N. WILLIAMS, PRESIDENT

NEWCOMB CARLTON CHAIRMAN OF THE BOARD

J. C. WILLEVER FIRST VICE-PRESIDENT

1201

SYMBOLS

DL=Day Letter

NL=Night Letter

LC=Deferred Cable

NLT=Cable Night Letter

Ship Radiogram

The filing time shown in the date line on telegrams and day letters is STANDARD TIME at point of origin. Time of receipt is STANDARD TIME at point of destination

NB Z4 51 45 GOVT=WUX WASHINGTON DC 8 1138P

1944 MAY 8 PM 11 58

MRS KATHERINE R BURTON=

4215 WEST 109 ST=

=THE SECRETARY OF WAR DESIRES ME TO EXPRESS HIS DEEP REGRET
THAT YOUR HUSBAND LIEUTENANT COLONEL PAUL T BURTON HAS BEEN
REPORTED MISSING IN ACTION SINCE TWENTY TWO APRIL OVER
GERMANY PERIOD IF FURTHER DETAILS OR OTHER INFORMATION ARE
RECEIVED YOU WILL BE PROMPTLY NOTIFIED==

:DUNOP ACTING THE ADJUTANT GENERAL.

News clippings collected by the Burton family.

GAZETTE, LITTLE ROCK, SUN.

Missing After Flight Over Europe.

LT. COL. PAUL T. BURTON.

Magnolia, May 13 (Spl).—Lt. Col. Paul T. Burton, aged 30, son of Mr. and Mrs. Elmer T. Burton of Magnolia, who was reported missing over Europe April 22, has been promoted to lieutenant colonel from major, and was scheduled to be home on furlough in June. The family had planned many festivities for his homecoming. They are hoping he may be a prisoner.

Colonel Burton joined the Canadian Air Force in August, 1940. After Pearl Harbor he was transferred to the United States Army Air Force. He had been across 16 months and was stationed in England. He had made nearly 30 missions over Europe. He was graduated from Magnolia High School and later worked his way two years in New York University while supporting his wife and one child. He was a model athlete and sold his pictures to sport magazines and sold blood for medical purposes to pay expenses. His wife and two children are in New York where he was stationed before going across. Colonel Burton has a brother, Maj. Weldon Burton, in Italy. A cousin, Capt. Lawrence Jarnigan of Stamps and Magnolia, was lost a few months ago in the North Atlantic.

Col. Burton Lost In Bomb Raid Over Germany

Veteran Pilot Had Been on More Than 20 Missions; Instructed Canadians

Lieutenant Colonel Paul T. Burton, thirty-year-old Army bomber pilot and squadron commander, of 215 West 109th Street, who preferred to fly nothing smaller than Flying Fortresses, and who helped organize the first bombing and gunnery school in Canada, was reported missing in action by the War Department yesterday.

Colonel Burton, an aviation enthusiast since his boyhood on an Arkansas farm and before the war the proprietor of a flying school at the Flushing Airport, Queens, held the Distinguished Flying Cross and the Air Medal, both with clusters. He was a veteran of more than twenty bombing massions over Europe, his wife, Mrs. Katherine R. Burton, said yesterday, and was flying over Germany when he was shot down.

One of the group of younger high-ranking United States Army Air Forces officers, Colonel Burton was among the first Americans to volunteer as an instructor with the Royal Canadian Air Force, becoming a flying officer in the R. C. A. F. in the summer of 1940. He was an ardent proponent of the art of bombing. The bombing and gunnery school he helped form was at Jarvis, Ontario.

Having transferred to the U. S. A. A. F. shortly after the bombing of Pearl Harbor, and commissioned a captain, Colonel Burton was first detailed to fly planes smaller than Flying Fortresses. But he thought it was a backward step to be flying smaller ships, Mrs. Burton said, and his request to be attached to a bombing squadron was granted.

Colonel Burton became a major and a squadron commander early in 1943, while still in the United States. He was promoted to lieutenant colonel about three months ago.

Born on a farm near Magnolia, Ark., Colonel Burton came to New York when he was eighteen years old to study aeronautical engineering at New York University. He learned to fly after completing three years at the university and left shortly thereafter to open the flying school which bore his name.

In his last letter to Mrs. Burton, the former Katherine O'Shea, of New York, whom he married in 1934, Colonel Burton disclosed that he had participated in raids "on two-thirds of the capitals of Europe" and speculated as to whether he "would ever hit Tokyo."

Paul T. Burton Reported Missing Over Germany

Lt. Col. Paul T Burton has been missing in action over Germany since April 22, his parents, Mr. and Mrs. E. T. Burton of 716 West Monroe, were notified by the war department today.

The 30-year-old pilot of a B-24 had been overseas for 16 months. He was based in England. He was a squadron commander and had received the Air Medal and two Oakleaf Clusters. His family expected him to return home in June.

He is married to the former Rene O'Shea of New York City and they have two sons eight and one year old.

Lt. Col. Burton attended Magnolia high school where he was an all-state football player and New York university.

Before he joined the Royal Air Force in August, 1940, he and his brother, Weldon, now a captain in the air forces and stationed in the Mediterranean area, operated their own flying school in New York.

Lt. Col. Burton and his brother, who joined the RAF in February, 1941 were transferred to the U. S. air forces after Pearl Harbor. His cousin, Major Lawrence Jarnigan, pilot of a B-24, has been missing over Africa since 1943.

Besides the brother in the Mediterranean area, Paul has two other brothers, Lynn and Ben Burton, and two sisters, Mrs. Walter Baird and Mrs. W. M. Robinson.

Col. Burton Lost in Action

Lt. Col. Paul T. Burton, 30, Squadron Commander in the American Air Forces, has been listed missing in action in England.

Col. Burton has been overseas 11 months after being transferred from the RCAF which he joined in 1939. He was credited with 20 missions over enemy territory including raids on Berlin and Rome. He also took part in the North African and Sicilian campaigns.

Prior to the war, Col. Burton operated a flying school in Flushing. His wife and two small sons live at 41 W. 94th st.

n.j

WAR DEPARTMENT

THE ADJUTANT GENERAL'S OFFICE

WASHINGTON 25, D. C.

IN REPLY REFER TO:

AG 201 Burton, Paul T.
PC-N ET0054

11 May 1944.

Mrs. Katherine R. Burton,
215 West 109th Street,
New York, New York.

Dear Mrs. Burton:

This letter is to confirm my recent telegram in which you were regretfully informed that your husband, Lieutenant Colonel Paul T. Burton, O-1,699,162, Air Corps, has been reported missing in action over Germany since 22 April 1944.

I know that added distress is caused by failure to receive more information or details. Therefore, I wish to assure you that at any time additional information is received it will be transmitted to you without delay, and, if in the meantime no additional information is received, I will again communicate with you at the expiration of three months. Also, it is the policy of the Commanding General of the Army Air Forces upon receipt of the "Missing Air Crew Report" to convey to you any details that might be contained in that report.

The term "missing in action" is used only to indicate that the whereabouts or status of an individual is not immediately known. It is not intended to convey the impression that the case is closed. I wish to emphasize that every effort is exerted continuously to clear up the status of our personnel. Under war conditions this is a difficult task as you must readily realize. Experience has shown that many persons reported missing in action are subsequently reported as prisoners of war, but as this information is furnished by countries with which we are at war, the War Department is helpless to expedite such reports. However, in order to relieve financial worry, Congress has enacted legislation which continues in force the pay, allowances and allotments to dependents of personnel being carried in a missing status.

Permit me to extend to you my heartfelt sympathy during this period of uncertainty.

Sincerely yours,

Robert H. Dunlop

ROBERT H. DUNLOP
Brigadier General,
Acting The Adjutant General.

HEADQUARTERS ARMY SERVICE FORCES
OFFICE OF THE PROVOST MARSHAL GENERAL
WASHINGTON 25, D. C.

30 June 1944

RE: Lt. Col. Paul T. Burton,
United States Prisoner of War,
Camp Unstated, Germany.

Mrs. Katherine R. Burton,
215 West 109 treet,
New York City, New York.

Dear Mrs. Burton:

The Provost Marshal General has directed me to supplement the information you received recently concerning the above-named prisoner of war.

Information has been received which indicates that he is now interned as a prisoner of war as indicated above. The report received did not give the place of his internment. Past experience indicates that one to three months is the normal time required for this office to receive that information.

Until the exact place of his internment is known, it is impossible to direct letters and parcels to him. Mailing instructions and parcel labels will be forwarded, without application on your part, when his internment address is received.

Sincerely yours,

Howard F. Bresee,
Colonel, C.M.P.,
Assistant Director,
Prisoner of War Division.

Incl.
Information Circular

HEADQUARTERS ARMY SERVICE FORCES

OFFICE OF THE PROVOST MARSHAL GENERAL

WASHINGTON 25, D.C.   mfw

12 July 1944

RE: Lt. Col. F C T. Burton,
United States Prisoner of War,
Stalag Luft 3, Germany,

Mrs. Katherine H. Burton,
215 East 109 Street,
New York City, New York.

Dear Mrs. Burton;

The Provost Marshal General has directed me to inform you of the transfer of the above-named prisoner of war to the camp indicated.

You may communicate with him by following instructions in the inclosed mailing circular.

One parcel label and two tobacco labels will be forwarded to you every sixty days without application on your part. Labels for the current period will be forwarded under separate cover.

Further information will be forwarded as soon as it is received.

Sincerely yours,

Howard F. Breaee,
Colonel, C.M.P.,
Assistant Director,
Prisoner of War Division.

Incl.
  Mailing Circular
  Information Circular

Part 3

Confinement

After a few days of relaxation I was interviewed by Colonel Darr H. Alkire, Senior American Officer (SAO) of West Camp, Stalag Luft III. He gave me the job of Camp A-I officer (Personnel) and granted me permission to keep a diary. (During wartime no one engaged in combat was allowed to keep a diary without official permission.) This allowed me to record the events of the previous section, "Part II, Capture" while they were still fresh in my mind. In addition, I was able to write the following description of West Camp, Plus subsequent events almost as they occurred:

Westlager (West Camp) is the newest and largest of all *Stalag Luft III* compounds. It is also reputed to be the most escape-proof, since it has evolved out of the experience gained from its forerunners.

Located on the west side of the *Stalag Luft III* group, it joins North and South compounds, and is separated from them by a narrow road and two double fences running north and south. Communication between camps is forbidden.

The camp is bordered on the north by a secondary highway and a small forest, on the west by a dirt road and a German army camp, and on the south by a dirt road and a large pine forest. South and west of the army camp are pistol and rifle ranges, and a POW camp known as *Stalag VIII-C*. Another camp called Belaria is six kilometers northeast of here.

I can hear almost constant firing from the pistol and rifle range. Its close proximity is said to be intended to discourage thoughts of escape by occupants of this camp.

All nationalities of allied ground troops are believed to be held in VIII-C and in Belaria; however, these camps are quite small. They were originally designed as *Truppenlagers* (troop quarters). There is also a very large Russian camp nearby.

The secondary road on the north leads westward to a French Hospital and to the main Sagan Highway.

On entering the compound from the north, through its only gate, one must first go through the *Vorlager*. This is a section of the camp partitioned off for use by German administrative and supply personnel. There is a shed for storing coal, a clothing storage barracks, and a parcel storage warehouse. These buildings are of the same type and size as our living quarters. There is one other building in the *Vorlager*, evidently used for the storage of beds, bowls, pitchers, cutlery and other *Reich* (German government) property.

The fence that surrounds West Camp is ten feet high and five feet thick. That is, there are really two fences with a thick barbed wire entanglement between. This entanglement rises to a height of about two-feet above the ground. The posts are cedar-like poles averaging five inches in diameter and spaced five feet apart. At the top of each post is a two-foot board nailed on at a forty-five degree angle. Stretched along this board are three additional strands of barbed wire.

The main fencing is of eight-by-eighteen-inch mesh, galvanized barbed wire, with barbs spaced four inches apart. Concentric with the main fence and some fifty feet inside it there is a low guard rail. A sign on the guard rail reminds prisoners that guards are ordered to shoot anyone who touches or gets outside this rail. Therefore, prisoners are never allowed closer than fifty feet to the main fence.

Guard towers are located at each corner of this compound, and are also spaced along the long sides. There are nine of these towers, which prisoners call goon towers or goon boxes. They are placed at intervals to give the guards a maximum range of vision between the barracks, and so that they can completely sweep the area with their searchlights at night. Goon towers can be entered only from outside the compound, although the platform itself extends inside across the top of the fence.

Tower guards are equipped with rifle, machine-gun, searchlight, field glasses, and telephone. Guards also walk outside along the fence between the towers. These guards are called strollers. In addition to strollers, there are *Hundführers*, who walk around and between the barracks after we are locked in at night; they are accompanied by hungry-looking, but well-trained and well-disciplined German Shepherd dogs.

Last year there was a dense pine forest where West Camp now stands. Now the ground is crowded with stumps.

The soil is very sandy, resembling that of central Florida.

Many years' accumulation of pine needles has left a layer of decaying organic matter several inches thick. This material, when dry, is quite inflammable and can be used as fuel. We have to be careful where we throw our cigarettes to avoid igniting it.

On entering the compound (or camp, or *Lager*), one sees a dirt road stretching the length of the compound, with rows of dark green or black barracks (called blocks) on each side. There are seventeen barracks, numbered left to right from 157 to 173. The compound is divided in the center by the cookhouse-theater area into North and South. In the South there are two rows of four barracks each, and one row of three. In the North, there are two rows of three barracks each.

Quartered in these seventeen barracks are 2,326 officers and men of the United States Army Air Corps, two officers of the United States Navy, and two chaplains from the British Army.

Each building holds 140 persons. There are twelve to fourteen NCO's who have volunteered to serve as orderlies, in each barracks. These barracks are 150 feet long and fifty feet wide. They are built of prefabricated wood panels four feet by ten feet long, and lined with a sheet-rock material inside.

The floors are about three feet above the ground to allow the "ferrets" (German security personnel, or *Abwehr*) room to crawl around beneath the barracks and search for tunnels or listen to conversations.

A hall runs the full length of the barracks, and opening onto this hall are sixteen rooms.

There are three nine-man rooms, seven fifteen-man rooms, three three-man rooms, plus one each: kitchen, washroom, and night *Abort* (latrine) in each barracks. The fifteen-man rooms are the most crowded, being only twenty-one feet by sixteen-feet. However, they are only half as crowded as the Germans claim they safely could be; their "safe" minimum is 2.5 cubic meters of air space per man.

The washroom is almost adequate in size and contains six

bowls. But the kitchen is far from adequate for 140 men. It is about the size of a small family kitchen. The coal-burning stove is the small-family type. The 140 men have to do all their cooking in this tiny kitchen. This means that stove time has to be carefully allotted throughout the afternoon and evening by an officially designated kitchen officer, whose full-time job is preventing arguments.

The night *Abort* has two seats and a four-foot urinal. The toilets were originally the flush type but the plumbing has long since failed, so we have to haul in buckets of water for flushing by hand.

The equipment in a fifteen-man room is four stools, two benches, two tables, two water pitchers, and a locker. Each man has a cup, bowl, knife, fork, spoon and small dish towel.

The small, three-man end rooms are used by field grade officers (majors, lt. colonels, colonels), block commanders, and camp staff personnel.

Colonel Alkire, the Senior American Officer (SAO), and the two Padres each has a private room.

There are three outdoor *Aborts*. Each of these has to accommodate about 800 men. These latrines are the old-fashioned type. Divided into three sections, each section has a separate entrance, fifteen seats, and a urinal. They are always filled faster than the goons (Germans) can, or will, empty them. Consequently, we have to close one periodically. During the summer, flies from these latrines swarm over everything. With no screens on the windows, everyone soon develops a case of the GI's, or gastroenteritis.

The main kitchen is a large, rambling building. Besides the kitchen itself it houses the adjutant's office, a carpenter's shop, reference library, senior officers' mess, wash room, two *Aborts*, and three rooms for storing goon rations. It is centrally located and serves as camp headquarters.

Our all-important "radio" is located in the kitchen building. This radio consists simply of a loudspeaker swung from the rafters. Propaganda-filled programs of the *Reich Rundfunk* (German Broadcasting System) are piped through the loudspeaker.

It is a crime for Germans to listen to foreign broadcasts, so the radio itself is located in the *Kommandantur* (German Headquarters), where it may be tuned only by those officials, who see that only Nazi programs are broadcast.

We have several German-speaking kriegies (prisoners of war) whose duty it is to translate the daily *OKW* (German Supreme Command) communiqué every afternoon at four o'clock.

The translation is then posted in the news room in the theater building, where home-made situation maps are kept up-to-date from the information contained in the communiqués. Kriegies spend more time poring over those maps and communiqués, trying to forecast future moves and "G-2-ing" the war situation in general, than in any other activity. A second favorite activity is studying the books in the reference library.

The biggest job in the main kitchen is heating water. Three times a day kriegies line up for their hot water ration. This water must be stretched out to be used for cooking, dish washing, and shaving. The kitchen also boils German-issue potatoes and does whatever baking may be requested by individual rooms, or combines. Some kriegies have become expert cooks. Some of the cakes and pies brought into the main kitchen to be baked show real ingenuity.

Another big job in the kitchen is receiving and issuing goon rations. These include bread, potatoes, and some vegetables.

Block (barracks) orderlies pick up the daily rations for their respective blocks and distribute them to the combines under the supervision of the block goon rations officer.

Facing eastward from the kitchen one can see the theater, laundry, shower room and shoe shop in the same central area.

The laundry is simply a place where you can hand wash your clothes. It has two long concrete troughs with flared-out sides for scrubbing. At one end of the laundry room are five concrete tubs for rinsing.

The shower room is a small building partitioned into dressing room, shower room, and boiler room. The shower room itself is equipped with twenty-four spray-nozzles. At a rate of two men under each shower all day long, each man in the camp can get one shower per week. This rate is reduced in the winter when the days are shorter, because we are forbidden to use the shower room after dark.

Our shoe shop is a cubbyhole off the shower building and is run entirely by kriegies, as are all our facilities.

Tools and materials are supplied by the Red Cross and the YMCA. There is an acute shortage of leather, so the work of the cobblers is mainly nailing on steel plates, or hobnailing them to prevent wear.

In all the buildings in this area there is only one German on duty. He is the *Zahlmeister*, or man who supervises distribution of goon rations in the kitchen.

The theater was donated by the Swedish YMCA. It is one of our most valuable assets, but like everything else in the camp, it is much too small. Its seating capacity of 350 accommodates only one-seventh of the compound's population. Built on a concrete foundation, it has an orchestra pit, a raised floor and a basement. There is a projection booth in the rear and dressing rooms backstage. Adjacent to the dressing rooms are four classrooms. Only one of these rooms is actually used for the intended purpose. The other three have been converted to fiction library, first-aid room, and news room.

The theater was furnished and decorated entirely by kriegies from materials donated by the YMCA. The lowly tin can, a vital object in kriegie life, played a large part in the decor. The ingenuity of kriegies in furnishing their theater and in putting on shows is astounding. The theater's comfortable seats were built out of Red Cross parcel cases. The indirect lighting was accomplished by making elaborate shades and reflectors out of flattened tin cans. The walls and ceiling were tastefully painted in pastel shades in a modernistic pattern. The lighting effects would put some outside theaters to shame. To a great extent all this was achieved as a result of the genius of Lieutenant Stahl, who expended much effort installing and furnishing the theater.

The Germans loaned out a few tools with the threat of death to anyone using them to try to escape. They also allow us to rent costumes from a firm in Berlin. The money for all this comes from a canteen fund accumulated from our "salaries."

(Under the terms of the Geneva Convention the "Detaining Power," Germany, was obligated to pay prisoners of war a salary equal to that of their own personnel of equivalent rank and duties. This amounted to only a token sum. Long before my arrival in prison an agreement had been reached whereby this money would not be paid directly to prisoners. We had no possible way to spend it, even if there had been anything to buy. Instead, the money was accumulated in a central fund and controlled by a designated purchasing officer. He would buy anything he could find available on Germany's barren market that didn't require ration coupons.)

Success of the theater project can be attributed to American ingenuity and kriegie sweat. All props and sets are built out of junk lumber and painted with calcimine. Many costumes are G.I. uniforms painted with calcimine. Musical instruments and the public address system were also donated by the YMCA. The first curtain was made by kriegies from German blankets sent in from East Camp. We now have a beautiful new maroon silk curtain.

It could be assumed that our shows are amateurish. On the contrary, our presentations, under the supervision of theater officer, Major Houston, are better than many by so-called professionals. True, we are entertainment-starved and would probably enjoy any kind of diversion. On the other hand, our lives are so completely devoid of amusement that we have become severe critics. The shows have to be good to be favorably critiqued. Under Lieutenant Wally Steck, the orchestra has steadily improved, until now it could compete with many high-salaried bands. Some of our musicians have studied most of their lives.

Our sleeping accommodations are plain triple-decked bunks built by kriegies out of unpainted wood. The bed boards, or slats, are counted frequently by the ferrets because they have been used for bracing tunnels in escape attempts. They also make good kindling wood.

The mattresses are burlap sacks filled with wood shavings or excelsior. Pillows are of the same materials. Sheets, mattress covers and pillow cases are some kind of synthetic material resembling linen. The materials are blue and white checkered, and when freshly laundered add a very cheerful touch to our otherwise drab rooms. We can exchange linens every two weeks for fresh ones. Bed linens are special issue to officers only. Our orderlies are denied use of them by the Germans.

After stuffing the mattress three or four times and sleeping on it a few times between each stuffing, the lumps can be smoothed out and holes pressed into the right places. After this treatment, the sacks (beds) are fairly comfortable. With little else to do, the average kriegie spends a great deal of his time in the sack. I heard one fellow eulogizing his sack as follows: "Good afternoon, you poor, lonely little sack; I've neglected you all morning."

Pillows are satisfactory for awhile, but the excelsior soon breaks up into short pieces and falls out through the coarse weave of the burlap. The pillow then has to be re-stuffed.

Mattress covers were at first to be used to prevent escaping excelsior from an upper bunk from falling all over the bed and into the eyes of the higher-ranking occupant of a lower bunk. But the Germans decided that the friction of mattress covers on bed boards was "destruction of *Reich* property," and clamped a *verboten* on the practice. Now, we must insert our two blankets into the mattress cover, German-style, and use the whole thing as a comforter. By laying an overcoat and a jacket over this and keeping a fire burning, it is possible to keep warm when the temperature doesn't drop too low. When it does, the only thing to do is dress in all the clothes you have, go back to bed, and think about Florida.

The Senior Officers' Mess at West Camp was started by Colonel Alkire to gain better coordination among senior officers and to spare us the drudgery of cooking and doing K.P. in our own little combines. This also enabled us to devote some of our time to helping him shape camp policies. Some officers were not in favor of our segregating ourselves like this, because junior officers might imagine us taking more than our share of food or other handouts. Also it could disorganize their carefully organized Mess setups, and throw their lower-ranking roommates out to look for another "home." I highly favored the Senior Officers' Mess because I felt there was an urgent need for coordination and organization among us. The Mess was started during the summer shortly after my arrival. It quickly became an institution.

Lieutenant C. H. Pearson was hired as Mess Officer, and an enlisted man as cook. We agreed to pay those two a certain amount out of our own pockets when and if we ever got home. Pearson quickly demonstrated outstanding ability for his job. He was a genius at making much out of little, for camouflaging such things as kohlrabi and dehydrated vegetables and making them edible, for decorating the walls and inventing table cloths, for getting flatware and dishes out of thin air, and for running, according to General Vanaman, the best Mess in all *Stalag Luft III*.

The Mess room was located in the kitchen building. The

room's small size dictated that members of the Mess be limited to nine senior officers, plus Pearson, with two seats reserved for guests. Those were Colonels Alkire and Jenkins, Lieutenant Colonels Clark, Hendrix, Aring, Szaniawski, and Burton (author); Major Ingenhut; Captain McVeigh (the British chaplain), and Lieutenant Pearson.

Lieutenant Colonel Aring left the Senior Officer's Mess for reasons of his own, creating a vacancy. Colonel Alkire asked me to make up a seniority list so that he could determine, without hurting anyone's feelings, who to invite to join in Aring's place. Only three wished to join us: Lieutenant Colonels Darling, Hand and Tiller. Hand had much more commissioned service than the others, but Darling outranked him in the regular army. Tiller and Hand were both senior in the camp, although Tiller had no regular army commission. To solve the dilemma, Colonel Alkire invited all three to join. All three accepted, and now everyone is happy. Every senior officer who wanted to join the Colonel's Mess is now in.

I wish I had recordings of some of the discussions that took place in our Mess. We would often start one at breakfast, and it would run through the noon hour, and sometimes far into the afternoon if the weather was bad. Those conversations were particularly interesting when the Old Man, Colonel Alkire, would get started. He was a wonderful talker, with a strong voice. His words were smooth-flowing and well chosen, and he had perfect diction. He would hold us spellbound with his boundless tales of the Air Corps, its growing pains and the people who overcame its early difficulties. On other subjects, he was so well read and knowledgeable that just listening to him was not only entertaining, but educational as well.

Another terrific talker was Padre McVeigh. Most of us looked upon him as an oracle, and he had more formal education than anyone else in the camp. He was a graduate of two Universities, and deeply interested in sociology and economics. Sometimes he would expound on his favorite theory for solving the world's ills: abolish all businessmen (whom he considered nonproductive parasites) and set up a government based on the ancient guild system in which the guilds would elect leaders to form a governing body.

Padre McVeigh (British Army) was violently anti-Communist. He was the first of us to recognize what he called the Great Russian Menace. He saw that threat even at that early date when the rest of us looked upon Russia as a friendly and powerful ally who, of all the nations of the world, would be able to force the eternally squabbling peoples of Europe into a single, peaceful mass.

Padre McVeigh believed that communism was bent upon the destruction of Christianity and enslavement of the world. His convictions were so strong on this topic that we were suspicious for awhile that he might be pro-German. The Germans would try almost anything then to cause a split among the allies, and we suspected that Padre McVeigh was playing right into their hands.

When the Red Army broke through across the Vistula and shattered the German eastern defenses from the Baltic to the Adriatic, even while we cheered them on as our liberators and comrades-in-arms, Padre McVeigh was sad. While we jubilantly prepared to be liberated, he requested to be sent to Breslau where he could "throw himself at the great Red juggernaut rather than witness its destruction of Western Civilization."

He also predicted that England was in for a violent, though bloodless revolution right after the war was over.

With the reticence of wisdom he was usually hard to get going on a subject. Once started though, and fired by our interest, he would continue indefinitely. We would give him our rapt attention although some of his topics were beyond our comprehension.

In time McVeigh became Americanized to a great extent, and rapidly picked up our Air Corps slang and many of our kriegie words. He'd studied yoga, or mind-over-matter theories, with the Hindus in India, and he half-seriously threatened to start a yoga class in the camp. He said it would be a good thing to know when we go on goon rations.

When a plate of food went all around our table and there was anything left on it we would "throw fingers" to see who got the remainder. Throwing fingers is sort of a juvenile method of gambling. All would raise clenched fists overhead and then swing them downward and forward three times, counting to keep together. On the third swing each would stick out either one or two fingers. Whichever group was in the minority, either the ones or the twos, was eliminated. This procedure continued until there were only two contestants left. Then, one matched the other in the same way as with coins.

It was a very undignified pastime for senior officers to indulge in, but it was a fair, quick method of distributing a commodity when demand exceeded supply.

To enforce the camp's rigid blackout regulations the guards in the towers would simply shoot into any room that showed light. One colonel was shot through both legs in this way while innocently playing bridge. Needless to say, we were conscientious about complying with blackout regulations.

The German department emphasized most by our captors was the *Abwehr*. It was their responsibility to constantly intermingle with us, poking through our rooms, crawling through the lofts and beneath floors, eavesdropping everywhere. They would poke long rods into the ground to discover tunnels and discourage any escape plans as early as possible. It was the *Abwehr* who caused us the most frustration, yet provided us the most amusement. We were continually in a battle of wits with them and we openly nicknamed them "ferrets."

Incidentally, the word "ferret," along with the word "goon," was researched by the *OKW* to determine their suitability for our use; "ferret" was approved, but "goon" was disapproved.

Head ferret for West Camp was *Unteroffizier* Griese (pronounced Greaser). He was the overly-conscientious, sadistic type we all abhorred. We called Griese "Rubberneck" because he had the uncanny ability to suddenly appear where he was least expected. One would be engrossed in a conversation, a card game, or a big trading deal; looking up there would be Rubberneck, listening intently to every word. He seemed to be everywhere, peeking into windows, snooping through corridors, or craning his neck around corners. He was indefatigable in his search for tunnels, escape materials, subversive plots or contraband.

Griese attended our boxing matches religiously. His cruel eyes would gleam sadistically at each sign of injury or bleeding. Rumor had it that his home had been destroyed and his family killed by our bombs.

Other departments with whom we were in direct contact were Administration and Quartermaster. Those departments were also under *Oberst* (Colonel) Braun, *Stalag Luft III Kommandant*. Administration was the one we had most direct contact with, since it was their job to run the camp. *Hauptmann*

(Captain) Eilers was *Lagerführer* (Camp Commander); his assistant was *Oberfeldwebel* (Technical Sergeant) Eidmann. Other Administration personnel were *Unteroffizier* (Corporal) Fischer and *Obergefreidter* (Private First Class) Gambietz. Those four Germans spoke English and seemed friendly.

They appeared to have been chosen for their tolerant, patient, courteous attitudes.

At first we were suspicious of them, but after associating with them day in and day out, month after month, we actually became fond of them. I venture to say that not one of us today would fail to greet those four Germans as long-lost friends if we should encounter them.

Lagerführer Eilers was a little man, about 50 years old, whose very large hands and feet gave him a grotesque appearance. His eyes were soft brown and they twinkled when he was amused, but became sad when he was in difficulty, which was often.

Once, Eilers received a minor but provocative order from Berlin. In response to my objection, he put his big hands together and said with a twinkle, "We have a saying in Germany: food is never eaten as hot as it is cooked." He reminded us of a harassed schoolteacher. Though mild-mannered, Eilers' inefficiency and lack of forcefulness caused us many inconveniences in our incessant negotiations with the *Kommandantur*, since all our complaints had to be transmitted through him to the *Kommandant*. Colonel Alkire often became exasperated with Eilers, but instead of becoming furious he would usually wind up laughing. At one such time Colonel Alkire said, when we were alone: "So help me, when the war is over, I'm going to take that little bastard home with me to play with my kids."

Eilers' right-hand man and the brains of the Administration Section was Eidmann, a well-educated, high-born German. Eilers, though superior in rank, was actually beneath him. A graduate of Heidelburg and other institutions, his face was decorated by the coveted saber scars of his caste. He would have been an officer of high rank had it not been for some kind of rheumatism that sometimes laid him up for days. He held the degree of Doctor of Forestry, had held a professorship before the war, and had spent some time in the Dutch East Indies. With his non-commissioned rank of *Oberfeldwebel*, he had a man-killing job.

He was caught between the fires of kriegies who would vent their wrath upon him, and the *Abwehr* people who would pester the living daylights out of him over countless petty things the kriegies did or didn't do. He once said he always had one foot in the *kühler* ("cooler," or solitary confinement), and often said he would much rather be at the front than here.

However, he was a died-in-the-wool Nazi, convinced that Nazi-ism was the only solution to Germany's troubles, and Europe's as well. He was so sincere in his beliefs he would almost cry. I was puzzled by his faith in a cause so obviously lost. He spoke English fluently, but being so well-educated in German he was never fully satisfied with his ability to express himself in another language. He kept a German-English dictionary handy. He would frequently attempt to wax eloquent in English, and get stuck. Then he would reach for his dictionary, saying, "I wish I could say it to you in German." My answer was, "In another six months I'll be able to understand you."

He told me this on 29 November 1944:

"I have just returned from my home. Seeing my old experimental station, my laboratory and my tools made me feel sad. I was amazed to find everyone here so optimistic about the war on returning (you Americans I mean). Morale is very high in Germany. The nearer you travel to the west front the higher it gets. The morale in Cologne is unbelievable. People here believe the war will be over this year. I will tell you frankly, I don't see how it can end before March or April. People here forget that all the fighting is taking place west of the Siegfried Line. I believe Eisenhower has enough supplies to last another fortnight. By that time he might have pushed us back of the Siegfried Line. "

"Then he will have to sit and wait for new supplies to be brought up. That will give us a chance to prepare new defenses and to further develop our new weapons. The We-2 (V-2) is a great weapon. It is not an improved We-1 (V-1); it is entirely new. It will go 100 kilometers high and hundreds of kilometers distance. You cannot shoot it down. True, it is inaccurate, but it will hit a city. Hundreds of them will destroy a city.

A commission of Americans gave a statement that no rocket

could go more than a certain distance because it's fuel-weight-range ratio reached a peak. But they didn't count on the stratosphere.

That is where our We-2 operates. We may soon bomb the USA by We-2. If we can gain a little time and raise your bomber losses and destroy your supply lines, perhaps you will think it too expensive to destroy Germany. Perhaps you will make terms, no?

I do not think we will use gas, but we are prepared to use it if the enemy does. The Nazi party will never lose power in Germany. The Nazi party is Germany. The war has brought hardships that have melted all Germany into a mass. We are completely united and strong. I am sorry the Gestapo was necessary, but we had to have it. I am sorry we made so many mistakes in the beginning. Our education system was all wrong. It taught our people to be over-confident and arrogant. We should never have lost respect for the rights and feelings of others. I am sorry the party infringed upon individual liberty. But I am convinced that these things had to happen and I know they were all for the best. These mistakes have all been rectified now. We have learned much in the few years of war. The German people will never submit to communism or democracy or to being bought by money. They have a will of their own and they demand to be allowed to govern themselves in their own way. The Russian Front will hold. The issues will be decided on the West Front."

Gambietz was a pleasant type, always smiling and courteous. He always saluted a Senior American Officer before addressing him. I never heard a derogatory remark made about Gambietz. Some Texan nicknamed him "Tex," and the name stuck. He even called himself "Tex."

Fischer was a good-natured former acrobat from Alsace-Lorraine. He was the most thoroughly Americanized one of them. After he got to trusting you he was always good for a juicy, anti-German crack.

It was the chief duty of those four Germans to count us twice a day. In order to count us, they used "*Appells*," something like roll-call parades. They were conducted as follows: First, a detachment of special guards with fixed bayonets would march in and be carefully briefed by Eidmann, who dispatched each one to a strategic spot where he could observe and prevent any foul play in which we might indulge to "screw up the count." We could accomplish screw-ups by having some men counted twice, by darting from one formation to another and covering up any shortage of men in the line-up.

Each block Commander, a captain or major appointed by Colonel Alkire, would assemble his men five-deep in a designated place on the parade ground. Colonel Alkire would stand in the middle with his staff two paces behind him. As Eilers and Eidmann approached, Colonel Alkire would call the parade to attention. Eilers and Eidmann would salute Colonel Alkire and Eilers would say, "Thank you. Stand them at ease, please." Colonel Alkire would then sing out, "At ease!" Eilers would walk over to the front of the nearest block and salute the block commander who had just called his men to attention. Eilers would then walk in front, counting by fives, while Eidmann would walk behind the group, checking each file to see that it contained five men. This took only a few seconds. Eilers would call out the total to Eidmann, who wrote it in a book. Then Eilers would salute the block commander again and pass on to the next block. The block commander would then stand his men at rest.

Eidmann and Eilers continued around the parade ground, repeating this procedure for each of the seventeen blocks.

Block commanders who had been counted would read aloud the latest orders from the American staff, or they would discuss any business with their men they deemed necessary.

While Eilers and Eidmann were counting, Gambietz and Fischer would scurry through all the barracks to count men too sick to attend Appell, or those who were left in the care of the block adjutant, who remained in the barracks for that purpose.

While Eidmann, Fischer and Gambietz were buzzing together trying to make their figures tally, Eilers discussed things with Colonel Alkire and his staff. Eilers would bring in the latest German orders, and Colonel Alkire would present Eilers with our innumerable complaints.

Those debates were endlessly amusing, though often exasperating. An outside observer would have had difficulty distinguishing captor from captive had it not been for Eilers' little pistol. At last Eidmann would announce, "*Alles im ordnung, Herr Hauptmann*," and Eilers would then hiss, "Please dismiss them."

There were two *Appells* daily, at 8 a.m. and 4 p.m. Sometimes there would be a surprise count in the middle of the night, or an extra *Appell* called during the day.

Obviously it was to our advantage to facilitate those parades as much as possible. If anything went wrong we could be kept standing in the cold for hours until the count tallied. If all went well we would often get them over with in twenty minutes.

The position of Senior Officer for a group of prisoners was a difficult and thankless job, at least. Although a senior officer was subject to the same treatment as any other POW, he was also responsible for everyone else's well-being. In addition, he was caught in the middle between his men's innumerable complaints and our captors' multitudinous threats. No one came with training or experience for such a job.

No higher authority assigned him his "command." His responsibilities were tremendous, and important decisions affecting hundreds of men's lives were his to make. But his most monumental decision could be, and often was, superseded by the lowliest German *Gefreidter*. Therefore, his biggest problem was his lack of power over his subordinates.

He could not give merit awards, had no way of motivating his men, nor of punishing miscreants. His duty was to enforce discipline upon his charges, but his only tool was his leadership ability. His men were mostly high-spirited youngsters, highly trained and efficient in their technical jobs, but mostly lacking in maturity and self-discipline. Many thought that when they became prisoners they were outside the jurisdiction of American authority. What's more, they could never be absolutely certain that the men professing to be their leaders were real Americans. In fact, they often suspected that the commanders were working against them, even when their leaders were working hardest on their behalf. Senior American Officers had only these universal axioms for guidance.

(1) Wherever two or more soldiers are together, one is in command.

(2) A combat commander in the field is permitted to make and enforce his own regulations as the situation demands.

(3) A soldier must always conduct himself in a soldierly manner, regardless of circumstances, unless relieved by competent authority.

(4) No act may be committed which might discredit the United States Government or the Army Air Forces, especially in the face of the enemy.

Our "Bible" was the Articles of the Geneva Convention of 1929. In view of all the obstacles, West Camp was extremely fortunate in having Colonel Darr H. Alkire and Lieutenant Colonel Wilbur Aring as our senior American officers.

While they had decidedly contrasting personalities, the two men each brought out the best in each other, and made day-to-day life in West Camp much more tolerable.

Colonel Alkire was senior to all the other Americans in *Stalag Luft III*, until Brigadier General Vanaman arrived later. Alkire had served twenty years as a flying officer with the Army Air Corps. He was Scotch-Irish, and was from Nevada. His mother was a Mormon. His father, nomadic by nature, had roamed the frontier territories of the west before becoming a miner. Colonel Alkire described his father as a man who spent much of his life chasing rainbows.

Before Darr's first birthday his family moved to a mining camp at Eureka, Utah, then later to Turlock, California, where Darr finished grammar school and two years of high school. He graduated from high school in Salt Lake City, then entered the University of Salt Lake as an engineering student. As a high school cadet during World War I he completed four years of infantry training. His military training continued in college, where he studied field artillery for two years in the ROTC.

In college he decided on a military career. He was appointed to Annapolis, but failed one of the examinations. He then decided on an army career, and applied for training at the Air Corps Primary Training Center at Brooks Field, near San Antonio, Texas. He was accepted and began his training there on March 10, 1924, in a class of 137 cadets. Their primary training was in Curtiss JN-6H's powered by 150-horsepower Hispania engines. Those who graduated this class moved on to Kelly Field for advanced training on DeHaviland DH-4's, and later Martin Bombers. From his original class of 137 cadets, only nineteen graduated. The best known of Darr's classmates was Charles A. Lindbergh.

Darr's class rejected the parachute as "an unnecessary and hated encumbrance" when it was first introduced to them at Kelly. Their attitude changed when one of their instructors broke his rudder and was saved by his chute. From then on, it was accepted by everyone.

Speaking about his class, Darr added, "One of the foolish things tried by new students was taking off in the rear cockpit and coming down in front. San Antonio, at the time, could either take its flying cadets or leave them."

"Aviation in general was still in the automobile race drivers stage, and the average civilian treated the average cadet as a cross between a moron and a damn fool."

Colonel Alkire's long and colorful career in the peacetime Air Corps sounded like the history of military aviation itself.

His first overseas assignment after the beginning of World War II was in England as an observer in operations and training; his particular concern was bombardment, and his job was to compare British installations with American bases for their possible use by our combat groups in the forthcoming air war with Germany.

When he returned to the States he was assigned command of the famous Second Group which operated an anti-submarine campaign from bases in Virginia, North Carolina, and Newfoundland over the next ten months. The planes used were B-18's, B-25's, DB-7's, and the now-famous war horses, the B-17's. The Second Group's task was to patrol vast areas of the Atlantic from Newfoundland to Yucatan.

After a period of temporary assignments, Colonel Alkire's next permanent assignment was command of the newly-activated 100th Group.

After the 100th was organized and trained, the group was broken up and its men reassigned to Second Air Force as instructors. Later, Colonel Alkire was ordered to activate, organize and train the 449th Group (B-24's). He reported to Forty Seventh Wing Headquarters at Manchuria, Italy, with his combat-ready group on December 17, 1943. They flew their first combat mission on January 8th, 1944. Leading his group on its nineteenth combat mission twenty-three days later, Colonel Alkire was shot down.

At the transient POW camp near Frankfort, he relieved RAF Squadron Leader Elliott as senior allied Officer. He was there until March 22, 1944, when the camp was destroyed by RAF bombs.

His next stop was *Stalag Luft III*. When West Camp opened

in April, he became its Senior American Officer.

The British had been at war for two years before us, and were entrenched at *Stalag Luft III* long before the first Americans arrived. Thus, most of our policies and operating procedures were already set up by them. Nearly all of our code words and slang were of British origin.

One British policy was "goon-baiting." The idea was to do everything possible to make life miserable for the Germans. Some goon-baiting methods were: Pour hot water on the backs of ferrets crawling under the floor to eavesdrop. Wait for hours with a stick poised over a knothole for a chance to poke it into the eye of a peeking ferret.

A small group would silently follow a ferret all day, right on his heels, never taking their eyes off him, until the ferret would be driven almost to distraction. They did everything imaginable to "screw up" the count at Appells. They would trick a gullible German into committing some act for which he would likely be punished severely, then they would blackmail the hapless dupe into smuggling contraband to them.

Although those sports were endlessly amusing to the bored kriegies, retaliation for them was often severe.

Colonel Alkire was against this and some of the other established British policies. Instead, he encouraged the following policies:

(1) Make every effort to get the maximum number of Americans home alive and in good physical and mental condition.

(2) Establish a well-organized and efficient organization to conduct housekeeping operations within the camp; this organization would take on crude combat functions in the event we should be faced with annihilation.

(3) Encourage prisoners toward useful pursuits, such as education, athletics, and competitive sports, to the fullest extent of our facilities.

(4) Conduct drills, calisthenics, parades and inspections to keep the men on their toes militarily as well as physically.

(5) Ascertain that absolute fairness prevailed in relation to distribution of food, clothing, reading material and other articles, without regard to rank, position, or prison seniority.

(6) Bring maximum pressure to bear on "the Detaining Power" (in this case, Germany) for strict compliance with the

Articles of the Geneva Convention.

(7) Attempt to furnish useful employment or responsibility to all who were able or willing to accept.

(8) Exercise maximum bargaining power while complying with German regulations. (In other words, weigh the merits of voluntary compliance with German regulations against the possibility of having them forced on us, always skirting the thin line between the cost to us in discomfort, and the cost to them in manpower. Walking this thin line was the biggest headache for SAO's, and kept us constantly in hot water with both Germans and kriegies.)

(9) Carry on whatever subversive activities that had a value commensurate with the risk involved.

I never envied Colonel Alkire his job. Many times, I wondered how he kept his sanity. His responsibilities kept him on the job an average of fourteen hours a day, seven days a week, fifty-two weeks a year. He had no place to go to relax, no "escape."

Colonel Alkire's staff was organized along military lines, and was similar to a military division. His staff officers headed the usual sections: A1, Personnel; A2, Intelligence; A3, Operations; and A4, Supply.

All activities were coordinated by Chief of Staff, Colonel Jack Jenkins. Each member of the staff organized his department down to the smallest detail by setting up sub-sections and departments for the operation of each of our many activities.

A1 Section, first under me, later under Lieutenant Colonel Darling, maintained personnel records and took care of housekeeping activities such as assigning quarters, issuing orders, maintaining discipline, setting up inspections, parades, etc. All liaison with the Germans and our three contacts with the outside world: the Protecting Power, the International Red Cross, and the Swedish YMCA, was coordinated under A1 as well.

A4 received and distributed supplies such as Red Cross food and clothing, German food, cigarette parcels, book parcels, personal parcels and mail. This job was very important and could have caused jealousy and hard feelings, perhaps rebellion, had it not been handled with extreme delicacy. In Lieutenant Colonel "Pop" Clark's able hands, A4 operated smoothly and efficiently.

A4 also ran a store called "Food Aco," short for food-tobacco exchange. Store economics was based on supply and demand and the barter system. If a kriegie received a parcel from home and it contained articles that were in greatest demand he could take them to Food Aco and practically buy out the place. For instance, a pocket knife, a dozen pipe cleaners, or a box of powdered eggs could buy him two loaves of black bread, a large amount of blood sausage, or all the English cigarettes he could carry.

Clothing articles, concentrated foods, American cigarettes and matches were in greatest demand. German food and non-American cigarettes were at the opposite end of the economic scale.

Matches were almost non-existent. Since cigarettes were rather plentiful and cigarette lighters *verboten*, cigarettes were lit from other cigarettes. In this way, a single chain of unimaginable millions of cigarettes might have been lit from a single match. The habit of getting lights from other butts was so widespread that words became unnecessary; we'd merely hold our un-lit cigarette toward someone with a burning one and he would automatically light it, exactly as his own cigarette had been lit a minute before. (This is just one example of thousands of little oddities about our strange and unique world. I expect there are ex-kriegies who still, even today, get a sense of luxury from owning a whole box of matches.)

Another of A4's departments was Purchasing. Under the Articles of the Geneva Convention, a captured soldier must be paid by "the Detaining Power" an amount equal to the base pay of a soldier of equivalent rank in the forces of the Detaining Power. Policy at Sagan was to pool this money and use it as a "slush fund" for the benefit of all prisoners equally. The money wouldn't have done us any good individually anyway, since we had no opportunity to spend it. Too, the Article failed to take into account the all-important ration points, without which the money was worthless. Therefore, a purchasing department was set up under the direction of Lieutenant Mike Wyse. His task was to spend our money. Many of the items Mike bought were useless to us, but we felt that we were helping the war effort in a small way by removing scarce consumer goods from the already-depleted German market.

I think Mike's most useful purchases were newspapers and periodicals. He distributed those daily. Though super-saturated with Nazi propaganda, they contained pictures, cartoons, maps, and sometimes news. Best of all, they were paper, which we could use to start fires, chink holes, and use for obvious sanitary purposes. We liked to save pictures of Hitler or Himmler for that last function.

Lieutenant Colonel Aring's Operations Section's job was to formulate plans for coordinated action for our self-protection in life-threatening situations that might arise in the camp. This called for an Intelligence section, which was under Lieutenant Colonel Hand. A2 and A3 sections maintained such close liaison as to almost be a single function commanded by Aring. Aring was particularly qualified for his job, having served in a similar capacity on the Air Staff in Washington. He'd been with Eisenhower during the initial invasion of North Africa. He had commanded a B-26 group until he was shot down over the Mediterranean. He had been a kriegie longer than most, and thus knew what tactics worked in the camps. One of A2's duties was security-checking new kriegies. When a new purge arrived, everyone in it was segregated for a time and not exposed to any information concerning our subversive activities until we felt sure they were genuine Americans. In this way, we maintained a fair degree of security from German stooges posing as prisoners.

A2 was also responsible for internal and external security. They would place kriegie sentries, called "duty pilots," at strategic positions all over the camp to watch the ferrets. Those duty pilots, or DP's, maintained a constant check on the number of known ferrets in the camp and their locations. When a ferret approached, the DP's would give a prearranged signal, whereupon the kriegies could quickly transform subversive meetings into innocent activities like play rehearsals, lectures or games. One DP, on seeing a ferret approaching his barracks, would sing out, "Goon in the block!" The ferret, not understanding English, learned to repeat the phrase, but not what it meant, and would stride into a barracks and shout, "Goon in de block!"

One important function of A2 and A3 was to obtain and operate a radio which they used to monitor the British Broadcasting Corporation (BBC). To accomplish this task without being detected by ferrets required great ingenuity. The fact that it was accomplished so well, and that we were seldom without BBC news, speaks very highly of Aring, Hand and their associates. Where those men hid the radios from ferrets' prying eyes was a mystery. But at times Aring walked with an unusually stiff-legged gait. If a ferret had opened Aring's overcoat, perhaps he would have seen an awkward lump in Aring's pants leg.

Dispensing BBC news each day to 3,000 news-hungry kriegies without slip-ups was sometimes impossible. It was hard to keep BBC battle lines from showing up on a situation map supposedly maintained entirely from *OKW* communiqués.

It was even more difficult to prevent kriegies from talking enthusiastically about things they could not possibly have known about from the *Rundfunk*.

، One time the ferrets were hot on the trail of our radio. During *Appell*, they searched Navy Lieutenant Johnny Dunn's barracks. When Dunn returned and saw that he and his boys were locked out for the search, he yelled in to his adjutant, who hadn't gone to *Appell*, to be sure and count the cigarettes and chocolate. The Germans, usually meticulous about not taking our personal possessions unless ordered to do so, were highly insulted by this remark. The ferrets found the radio, but instead of charging Dunn with possession of it, they charged him with insulting Germans. He was sentenced to two weeks hard cooler. Of course, they confiscated the radio too.

Colonel Alkire tried to go to bat for Johnny. He told Eilers to send him to the cooler instead, that Dunn was acting under his orders. After that incident, both Dunn and the Old Man were heroes of West Camp.

After a few weeks without a radio, old "Cloak and Dagger" somehow managed to get another one. This time, however, A2 decided that the risk of directly disseminating BBC news to all prisoners was too great, notwithstanding the tremendous morale factor that news provided. No one worried about punishment for being caught with a radio; it was just that radios were so difficult to obtain. Thus, the cloak of secrecy that enveloped our second radio was so impenetrable that only a few knew we even had it. In that way, A2 and A3 were able to keep it operating for the remainder of our stay at Sagan.

Roughly, here is what daily life is like here at West Camp.

The average day for the average kriegie is quite dull. He rolls out of his sack at first call just in time to dress for *Appell* at 0830 hours. He shivers through *Appell* and rushes back to his combine for toast and coffee. He then washes up and either goes back to bed or starts reading. This is interrupted by another brief session of toast and coffee at lunch time.

After lunch he either takes one turn around the compound or goes to the reference library or to the news room for a few hours. It is then time for afternoon *Appell* at 1630 hours. During winter, the sun sets just after we're dismissed from *Appell*. The perimeter lights come on, meaning that in order to travel out of the barracks he has to follow a designated blackout path. Rather than bother, he probably goes back to his room and starts a heated discussion with his fellow kriegies on religion, politics, the war, Roosevelt, the army, or anything else that may enter his bored mind. He loses interest fast because people start raising their voices and the discussion becomes an argument. Arguments lead to fights. He can't fight with his roommates, having to live under their noses, so he either picks up his book or gets into a game of bridge. After dinner he is "all tired out" and hits the sack early, thinking longingly of home and better days until he finally drops off into the restless sleep of the idle.

The above, from my diary notes, is not intended to be disparaging. It may not even be representative. But I believe more days were spent in that way than in any other. The camp was probably the easiest place in the world in which to just give up and follow the path of least resistance. You might think that would be the ideal place to study. But it was surprising how few people really studied there.

Of course, there were outstanding exceptions. One was Navy Lieutenant Johnny Dunn, the oldest kriegie (not in age, but longest time in prison) in West Camp; he learned Spanish and French, and thoroughly studied military tactics while a POW. There was Lieutenant Kious who became fluent in German. There was Carl Abele who studied agriculture and designed a complete farm, down to the tiniest detail. And there were many others who attended classes regularly, or spent all their spare time in the reference library, sweating over some subject they fancied.

But I believe those men were the exceptions rather than the rule. Most kriegies were young, around twenty-three years old.

Most were accustomed to having someone look after them and tell them what to do. Even as soldiers and airmen in combat, most were skilled technicians without any responsibilities except when on a mission. The average kriegie was at the age where most young men sow their wild oats or go to college. He was also at the age of indecision. He wasn't sure he even wanted to amount to anything. Often he believed it wasn't worth the effort. He knew little about self-discipline. He often had a vague belief that his government would see him through; that he would never have to worry; that after the war he would be wined and dined as a conquering hero. I feared he would be disappointed.

A young man would often refer to his country as "they," not realizing that maintaining a democratic government would be his responsibility in a few years, not "theirs."

Not that the atmosphere in a prison camp is conducive to study; far from it. The overwhelming veil of futility hanging over us was hard on everyone's ambition, and there was much day-to-day "grunt work" to be done. While chances were five-to-one against a man getting a camp job, there were numerous block and combine jobs. Each combine needed a cook, two KP's, and a water carrier each day. Then, too, there were the time-consuming chores of washing, cleaning, sewing, darning, and endless other insignificant little duties which would eat away a man's time, especially if he was inclined to be fastidious about his personal appearance. And there was simple boredom and lack of diversions that so often dull the mind and kill ambition.

An important physical detriment to our vigor was malnutrition. We had almost enough to eat, but the diet was far from balanced. At least one man in two seemed to have ringing in the ears, weak or dizzy spells, poor circulation, or some other symptom of an unbalanced diet. Skin ailments were common.

The barbed wire itself created in us an attitude of futility after a while.

Aside from all those considerations, educational facilities were extremely limited. The Germans were bound by the Geneva Convention to encourage and facilitate educational pursuits, but I never saw any evidence of it. If not for our own charitable organizations I doubt if there would have been a single book in the compound, except perhaps a few copies of Mein Kampf. We complained about this lack to the Protecting Power (the Swiss Legation in Berlin) but they quoted Germany's same old story: "How can we be expected to worry about the education of enemy prisoners when we're fighting for our lives?"

Our reference library was superb, thanks mainly to the YMCA. But it could accommodate only fifty people, and the books wouldn't have lasted a month if they had been allowed to be checked out. There was one small classroom for 2,300 prisoners.

Books from the fiction library were read until they literally fell apart. I have never seen books take such a beating. Often the fiction library had to close so the books could be overhauled and rebound. The most popular books were in such demand that you often had to wait four months for your turn.

I have been a kriegie just over six months. I'm just beginning to get adjusted to this life, physically, mentally and emotionally. I don't know whether that's good or bad. It's better from one point of view not to "sweat it out" so much. On the other hand, it isn't good to become resigned.

If we could only tell how long the Germans can hold out we'd be much better off. I doubt if anyone knows, not even the Germans themselves.

I had a very interesting talk with a goon yesterday about the whole setup. Seems as though the whole thing is stretched to the breaking point. Might break any day, any hour.

Diary, 1 November 44. Today has been cold and dreary with a low ceiling and a light drizzle. Morning and afternoon *Appells* were held in the road instead of on the athletic field because of deep puddles on the field from last night's heavy rain. Both *Appells* were held during light drizzling rain, but fortunately were of short duration.

Yesterday's new purge of twenty-four officers is comfortably bedded down. They're from the Italian theater via Budapest. One said the Russian line was thirty miles from that city. They were really sweating out Joe's (Stalin's) bombs and artillery while in the Budapest jail. However, we didn't hear the usual stories of atrocities by civilians.

The new purge brings the total camp strength to 2,245. One boy is badly shaken. Colonel Alkire says he can't remember his group

C.O.'s name even though he flew twenty-nine missions with him.

The weather has not been severe yet, and the coal supply is adequate so far. German coal is excellent fuel. It comes in neat, handy, compressed bricks, about two-inches by four-inches by eight-inches in size. Evidently it is compressed from pulverized coal from which the most valuable compounds have been extracted. It is very easy to start the bricks burning, it takes only a paper fire to start it. Once started, it will not go out until the brick is completely burned up.

You can throw three bricks into the stove at midnight and close the draft completely and your slow fire will keep the chill off the room all night. In the morning, throw in three more and you have a warm fire almost immediately. There is little smoke, and the ash is a feathery substance the color of sawdust.

The coal ration for end rooms, which are the coldest because they have two sides exposed and are outside the swinging doors and have fewer occupants, is eight bricks per day, with an increase for every ten degrees drop in temperature.

This fuel ration is supplemented by pine stumps which we dig up ourselves. The Germans furnish a few tools for this purpose. There are about six shovels, four axes, and two picks for the entire compound. These are very closely watched by the Germans. Since there are seventeen blocks in the compound, a block gets the use of the tools every seventeen days. On this one day, the block commander sets up a time schedule specifying the hour when the tools are available to be used by each room, depending on the room's number of occupants. This amounts to about one hour per room. The kriegies work furiously for the hour, happy to lay hands on a real tool, even though of poor quality, and wind up with one or two stumps to burn.

The Germans get their land cleared quickly, the kriegies get a lot of exercise and a little firewood.

The stumps burn furiously but not for long. They are "lightered" from having been left in the ground a few months, and so they ignite almost as easily as kerosene.

The roots present no problem for they are easily cut up into small pieces to fit into the stove. However, splitting the stump itself is a back-breaking procedure as anyone knows who has tried to split knotty wood. The stump is a solid knot.

At first the Germans gave us two antiquated, hand-operated stump pullers. All we had to do was dig the dirt from around the roots far enough to get a cable attached, then jack them out roots and all. These mechanical aids soon broke down, however, and we resorted to the elementary method of digging around the roots, chopping them off, and then twisting the tap root off by locking a twelve-foot pole between the big root and the stump, and pushing this around in a circle. This is the method most widely used because no tools are required. Digging is accomplished with nothing more than tin cans and bare hands. All prying and twisting is done with the pole. The athletic field (parade, or Appell ground) was cleared and leveled in this way in less than a week.

2 November 44. Lieutenant Colonel Darling came in this morning. Lieutenant Colonel Hendricks and Major Lawrence had been his classmates. They asked the Germans to send Darling to this camp after hearing that he was at *Dulag*. Strangely enough, the Germans complied.

Lieutenant Colonel Darling had been Air Executive of a P-38 group in the Ninth Air Force stationed in Belgium. He was *abgeschlossen* (shot down) between Cologne and Bonn. His wing man had cut off his tail booms, causing his ship to tumble end over end. Getting out was a problem, but he finally managed it at 5,000 feet. He was captured by the *SS*, who turned him over to a *Gestapo* agent (out of the frying pan and into the fire!). His *Gestapo* captor marched him up a road with a pistol at his head, apparently to *vernicht* (kill) him. An army soldier saved him from that fate and took him to a civilian jail.

Darling is fairly pessimistic about the war ending soon. He says we are short of supplies and the weather is too bad to permit air support for a big push. Further, the *SS* and *Gestapo* are in control of everything in Germany and they are fight-to-the-death fanatics.

The faint ray of sunshine that he brought was a rumor that the Germans are running out of ammunition. At the rate they were throwing up flak, I don't see how they've made it last as long as they have.

Lieutenant Colonel Darling moved in with the four colonels already in Block 170.

Major Houston sent in a walk parole for thirteen theater employees today; don't know whether it will be honored or not.

3 November 44. Finally stopped raining. Even had about an hour of sunshine. Today *Hauptmann* Eilers called Colonel Alkire into his office. Tonight the Colonel gave me a written order from Eilers that each block commander should appoint a man to supervise turning

the lights on and off.

He warned that if kriegies don't stop using lights indiscriminately, a guard will remove the fuse from the block and not replace it until lock-up time at ten o'clock. Further, lights should not be turned on before the perimeter lights come on, and must be turned off by midnight.

Oberfeldwebel discussed lights with me a few days ago; evidently there is an acute power shortage in *Deutschland*. I must discuss this with the Block Commanders tomorrow.

Another topic brought up by *Oberfeldwebel* Eidmann was empty food cans; they must not be left outside the block. Eidmann said if the *Kommandant* saw them he might start a big flap to enforce a German order that all cans must be returned to the *Vorlager*.

There seems to be a threat behind these apparently insignificant orders. Both of those threats, if carried out, would cause us no end of inconvenience. Since it gets dark at about six p.m., we would have to sit in a pitch dark barracks for four hours. And if the *Abwehr* takes away all our cans we will lose one of the most useful articles we have in the camp.

We wouldn't assign a corporal to handle trivialities like these in ordinary life, but here in camp such things as lights and tin cans are of utmost importance, and command the attention of the Colonel and most of his staff. Such is life in a kriegie camp!

Lieutenant Colonel Salzman came over from Center Camp today, escorted by *Oberfeldwebel* Schultz, to discuss YMCA supply problems with Lieutenant Colonel Hendricks. Colonel Salzman has many friends here among the old kriegies. He represents the YMCA for the whole *Stalag*; Hendricks has the same job for this camp.

The YMCA plays a very important part in making kriegie life bearable. They furnish all our musical instruments, theatrical supplies, sports equipment, some of our books, and numerous other items. The YMCA's Swedish representative for Germany is Mr. Soderberg. He paid us a visit recently and took some pictures. His assistant is Mr. Lundeen, who lives in Sagan. Both men seem very amicable, and Mr. Soderberg quite efficient. Their visit was clouded over by the ever-present German escort; we couldn't discuss the things we were fairly bursting to talk about with someone friendly from the outside.

Seems very pointless that contact between Colonel Salzman and his old friends is so rare, and that prisoners are not able to visit close friends, yet spend month after month within a stone's throw of each

Scenes as "Y" Workers visit different camps of Stalag Luft III

The staff at Stalag Luft III poses with the visiting Y.M.C.A. workers, Gosta Lundin and Henry Soederberg. The officers had the "Y" men as their guests for lunch. Mr. Lundin, director of Y.M.C.A. services in Germany, is seated in the left foreground.

Left: Lt. Col. Saltsman thanks Henry Soederberg as General Vanaman looks on. Center: Col. Goodrich, Lt. Col. Klocko and Lt. Col. McNichell get their picture snapped. Right: Henry Soederberg and Col. Delmar T. Spivey. Bottom, left: Mr. Soederberg and Col. Goodrich. Bottom, right: The boys try a few musical instruments that have just arrived from the Y.M.C.A.

Luft III scenes from the January 1945 issue of <u>War Prisoners Aid News</u> published by War Prisoners Aid of the Y.M.C.A., a participating service of the National War Fund.

other.

4 November 44. General Vanaman came over today from *Mittelager* (Center Camp). He is the Senior American Officer of all the *Stalag Luft III* camps, and a good man to have as SAO. He was *Air Attaché* in Berlin for several years. He speaks German fluently, and knows many people in and around the high command. He is a typical diplomat, very amiable and cheerful. The purpose of his visit was to discuss the Red Cross supplies for the entire *Stalag*.

Our last inventory showed nine weeks supply of parcels, at the present rate of consumption of a half-parcel per man per week. However, a mistake was discovered and we have 2,400 parcels fewer than we thought. Unless we get a shipment from Sweden or Switzerland soon, we'll run out before Christmas. That would mean going on goon rations.

The threat of going on goon rations has been just about the worst kind of disciplinary punishment that the American administration could come up with to keep kriegies in line. But it's not much of a threat to recent kriegies. Many of us still remember living on four slices of black bread and a bowl of soup a day while in solitary, not so long ago. The first three days are rough, but after that you don't much care. You just lie about in the sack in sort of a daze.

The SAO's will discuss soon whether or not to go on quarter parcels per week. Our Colonel does not favor this. We know there are thousands of parcels in both Sweden and Switzerland, but getting them here is the problem.

We get a sort of grim satisfaction out of knowing Germany's transport system has been knocked out to this extent.

The bad war news for Germany, and the gloomy prospect of spending the winter in *Deutschland*, naturally leads to thoughts of escape. But the more one thinks about escape, the more he realizes how small his chances are. Ever since the famous mass break from the North Camp last March 25th, escape has been a losing proposition. Before that both sides considered escape as an interesting game. Here is what I have heard of that tragedy:

The British in North Camp spent several months digging a tunnel from their camp beneath the *Revier* (sick quarters) compound, under the road and opening in the woods about 200 yards away. This was quite an engineering feat considering the lack of tools, the problem of disposing of dirt, and the necessity for perfect security. Eighty officers were involved in the actual break. As luck would have it, the air raid alarm sounded just as the escapees were emerging from the mouth of the tunnel in the woods. The Germans double the guards at night during air raids because of the necessity for turning off all lights.

One of these extra guards discovered the break and set up the alarm. Four escapees were captured on the spot. Seventy-six got away, but most were captured between here and Breslau. Out of the eighty escapees, only three made it back to England. Fifty men are dead, supposedly killed by the *Gestapo* for wearing civilian clothes, carrying forged German papers, resisting arrest, etc. Nineteen were returned to the North Camp and given cooler sentences. It is believed those nineteen men were fortunate enough to be caught by the *Luftwaffe* instead of the *Gestapo*. Four men are unaccounted for.

5 November 1944. Today is Sunday, so practically everyone went to church. Kriegies are ardent church goers, partly because there isn't anything else to do, but mostly because almost everyone here realizes he is alive today only by the grace of God.

We have two excellent Padres, both English. The Catholic chaplain, Captain J. V. McVeigh, is an Irishman who was serving with a British paratroop regiment. He was among the first of the invaders. He was dropped behind the German lines in France at midnight on June 5th. His outfit was surrounded and the survivors captured about a week later. Of the six chaplains in his division, one returned to England, three are dead, and two are kriegies.

Padre McVeigh delights in joining in the numerous diversified discussions that occur all over the compound, at all hours, and on all subjects. His pet project right now is a campaign to clean up the lecherous camp newspaper, "Kriegie Klarion."

McVeigh says, with an Irish twinkle, that he is starting a cult to develop yoga, a "mind over matter" activity. He says that'll be a valuable asset when we go on goon rations.

The other is Methodist Chaplain E. H. Metherall from Cornwall. Chaplain Metherall is the oldest English kriegie here; he's been a POW going on five years. He was captured in Belgium during the British army's retreat to Dunkirk.

Surprisingly carefree, cheerful, encouraging, he is everything we could want in a padre. His Sunday sermons are both useful and beautiful, with everyday philosophy as well as the lofty and spiritual side of Christianity.

I usually do nothing on Sundays except read and go to church, but today I'm busy working up the agenda for our meeting with the Protecting Power tomorrow and Tuesday. The Protecting Power representatives are from the Swiss Legation in Berlin. Their responsibility is to see that the belligerent signatories of the 1929 Geneva Convention adhere to agreements as to treatment of prisoners of war.

Up to now, Germany has made an effort to live up to the Convention, but now they are crowding camps and seem to have practically scrapped the Geneva Convention. So we have many complaints.

We probably won't get results. Germany is probably doing the best it can under the circumstances. I believe the country is in a bad way. They should have given up long ago but didn't. You can't blame a country for not worrying much over captured soldiers when they are fighting with their last reserves, but it's pretty rough on kriegies.

The goons seem very interested in the forthcoming American presidential election next Tuesday. Last night a ferret showed his first sign of intelligence by asking, "What kind of a man is this Dewey?" They seem to think Dewey will make peace, but they are so crammed full of propaganda and shackled by restrictions I'm surprised any of them can think at all.

Our little *Hauptmann* is really pathetic. He has been through a lot of grief, having lost his wife and two sons in the war. He tries so hard to keep the peace here in camp, but he is a broken, beaten man. Tonight he was a few minutes late for *Appell*. The kriegies got a little cold waiting to be counted, so when *Hauptmann* Eilers finally puffed into view, a chorus of hubba-hubba's went up.

The *Hauptmann* grinned, "Vas iss dis hubba-hubba?" The kriegies roared, and a good time was had by all. You can't hate Eilers; you can only feel sorry for him.

6 November 44. It's Monday. Another rainy day and quite cold. We're getting ready to receive another big purge of about 120 men. They're due to arrive any day. They will raise our strength to well over 2,300, so we're really having to hustle trying to find room for them. The best part of getting a new purge is meeting old friends, hearing late news, and discussing all the rumors which inevitably spring up.

Americans are spoiled by their high standard of living and by their super-abundance of news. Consequently, after spending a few months in a place like this, with only the bare *OKW communiqué* to listen to, a person becomes absolutely starved for news. We get all the German papers, but few of us can read them; those who can, quickly become disgusted with them because of the propaganda.

One wonders if the German masses are really so stupid they can't see through it.

The hunger for news is what causes many absurd rumors to get started. A little bit of accurate information, sometimes only a voiced opinion, is passed along by word-of-mouth to, say, sixty people. By the time it gets to the sixtieth man it is unbelievably distorted. The kriegies' natural yearning for good news causes many to flavor it a bit, too, as they pass it along. This week, for instance, we have heard that Goëring (1) has died, (2) has been assassinated, (3) has gone into exile, (4) is sick.

<u>7 November 1944</u>. Today two representatives of the Protecting Power arrived: Mr. Albert A. Kadler and Mr. Ashmon T. Rist of the Swiss Legation in Berlin. Colonel Alkire and I waited two hours for them before they finally got here. While we waited we had a pleasant talk.

The two diplomats were escorted by the *Lagerführer* and our General Vanaman when they arrived during heavy rain. We ushered them into our little Senior Officers' Mess and started the meeting. Typical suave, continental types, they listened patiently to our numerous complaints. After business we had lunch. The diplomats seemed to enjoy our simple fare. We had a very interesting talk, unhampered by the usual presence of a German.

When anyone comes in from the outside we are so eager to talk to them we all but climb into their laps.

I hope our complaints bring results, but I don't think that will happen. General Vanaman says 10,000 parcels are on their way from Geneva. That sounds like a lot, but it's really only one per man for all five camps of *Stalag Luft III*.

<u>8 November 44</u>, Wednesday. Yesterday was election day in the States. We still don't know who our new president will be. The *Reich Rundfunk* (German Broadcasting System) didn't see fit to broadcast it. Maybe we'll hear tomorrow.

The Germans brought in three of their *kultur* films today. One, in German, was the history of printing and bookbinding. The other two were travelogues of Germany, in English. The films here are fair, but they can't come up to American film standards. One of the travelogues showed winter sports in the Bavarian Alps. It reminded me of Mr. Kadler's statement yesterday that our fellow fliers interned in Switzerland are just now going up the mountains for winter sports. Rough!

Later Wednesday. The new purge just arrived. We'd expected them all day. They finally got in at eight tonight. There are thirty-five in all, one captain, the rest lieutenants, except for two flight officers. The men are from England, Italy and France. Some are recent graduates and will be hard to identify. None were seriously wounded. They were a little pessimistic about the end of the war. One was in Major Larry Jarnigan's B-24 anti-submarine squadron at the time Larry was killed. (Larry was my cousin - see photo on following page.) He said that Larry's plane was shot down over the Bay of Biscay by a German fighter. They were seen to crash into the sea with no survivors.

A thing I've noticed about these late purges is that heavy bomber crews do not predominate anymore. There are lots of fighter, fighter-bomber, and medium-bomber people now. An interesting trend.

I know we look and act funny to these fighting men fresh from the outside world. I remember how strange old kriegies looked to me when I came in. I didn't want or expect to ever become an old kriegie, but here I am, and there isn't much I can do about it.

This business of expecting the war to end any time certainly cuts down on escape plans and activities. One thing I'll never do is completely resign myself to being a prisoner.

The new boys say Colonel Zemke, reported ace fighter pilot, is at *Dulag*, that our armies are on the outskirts of Koln, and that the Russians have spilled over into Norway. The Norwegians won't like that.

9 November 44, Thursday. Finally found out about Roosevelt's re-election. Eidmann brought in the news this morning. Both my roommates received personal parcels today. I got two letters. We three feel like we hit the jackpot. I'm reading "Oliver Wiswell"; certainly a painless way to learn history.

10 November 44, Friday. Feeling miserable with a cold, I spent the day reading in front of the fire in our little Mess. Couldn't get far from the fire without freezing. Colonel Alkire came in shortly after noon from the *Revier* where he goes for heat treatments for arthritis; he said the *Revier* was radiating optimism. He had talked with our new American doctor who transferred here from the ground forces camp at Schubin; the doctor thinks the war will be over three weeks after the big push starts, and he believes it has already started. If that is true, we should be out of here around December 1st. The doctor also told the Colonel that Schubin had been on goon rations for three weeks.

Major Larry Jarnigan, a cousin to the author, was shot down over the bay of Biscay. Jarnigan flew a B-24 on anti-submarine patrols.

Captain Oliver, Red Cross parcels officer, came in during the day with news that another shipment of parcels was on the way, making a total of three shipments due here between now and Christmas. If we are still here then, at least we won't be hungry at Christmas.

11 November 44, Saturday. Rained all day. Indoor *Appell* didn't work this morning because some of the boys didn't get up. The Germans went into a flap and made us stand outdoor *Appell* in the rain as punishment. I believe indoor *Appell* will work better hereafter.

Eight enlisted men arrived today from Budapest. One of them was from my brother's group in Italy. He reported that Don is OK. (See dedication page) The men were very hungry; they had not had anything but bread and water since leaving Budapest three days ago.

12 November 44, Sunday. Stopped raining, and it seemed to be clearing up, but its cloudy again tonight. The weather fronts move through this part of the world, in this season, at the rate of three and four a day sometimes. I don't see how the weather forecasters keep track of all the storms.

Spent the whole day in Block 170 in the room occupied by Colonel Jenkins and Lieutenant Colonels Szaniawski, Hendrix, "Pop" Clark, and Darling. I picked up a radio fan magazine. I hadn't seen any kind of American periodical for so long I spent the whole day engrossed in it, although at home I would never glance at one. Also started reading Gypsy Rose Lee's book, "G-String Murders". All in all, a very uneventful and restful Sunday.

13 November 44, Monday. Light snow last night, the first of the year. At lunch we got to reminiscing about wartime England, and the wonderful job the Red Cross was doing there, its club-mobiles, aero clubs, and service clubs.

Nothing could give a person a more forlorn feeling than groping around blacked-out city streets after ten o'clock, with nowhere to go and nothing to do, plenty of money but no place to spend it. You couldn't get a cab, and you could never trust the directions given you. People might give you directions in good faith, but they were next to impossible to follow. The worn-out phrase, "You cawn't miss it!" was never true. Many a poor soldier has rushed to London for a hard-earned brief leave, only to wander helplessly around in the blackout.

The Red Cross remedied that situation with their service clubs. They built American havens in all the large English cities. Their "flak houses," or rest homes, provided a welcome, peaceful place for war-weary combat men to rest and play.

Another purge arrived from Wetzlauer and Oberursel; twenty-seven officers, including two captains and two flight officers. This brings our count to 2,330.

14 November 44, Tuesday. A German army general has taken over the *Stalag. Hauptmann* Eilers said that *Herr General* would be inspecting today, so we passed word around and had everyone ready to "greet" him all day, but he never arrived.

The *Luftwaffe* personnel joke that they will have to exchange their air force blue uniforms for army green. We are going to have to be very careful. This may be the first move toward running the *Luftwaffe* camps by the dreaded *SS*. We hope fervently that never happens.

15 November 44, Wednesday. This has been a big day for me, as days go in a kriegie camp. The German general came in at noon. While we were having lunch, Gambietz announced excitedly that *Herr General* was in the compound. The Germans really get excited over their generals.

Colonel Jenkins went down toward the gate to meet *Herr General*, while Gambietz and I ran up to get Colonel Alkire, who was in his room, since he never eats lunch. Jenkins and Eilers met the general and his party just inside the gate. Eilers was all-a-twitter. He was so excited he kept jabbering to Colonel Jenkins in German, a language Jenkins knows about three words of. The Old Man, Colonel Alkire, and I joined them a little further along the road and were introduced. There were salutes, Nazi and American, Heil Hitlers and "how-do-you-do's" back and forth for quite a spell.

The general was accompanied by the *Stalag Kommandant, Oberst Braun*; his adjutant, *Major* Simoleit (German); and his own army aides, a major and a captain. *Major* Simoleit, a former history professor, is ordinarily a suave, poised officer; but he completely lost his poise in scraping and kowtowing before *Herr General*. I got the impression that the once-mighty *Luftwaffe* is now depleted to such an extent that it is fighting for its existence. Otherwise I doubt if their officers would kowtow to the army to such an extent.

The general was like a Hollywood version of a Prussian officer, complete with gleaming uniform, bullet head, saber scars, monocle and all. We showed him the theater, the fiction library, and a fifteen-man room with triple-deck bunks. I was surprised to see him remove his cap upon entering a room. He talked constantly in German, and seldom listened. All about him, the others repeated, over and over, *"Jawohl, Herr General!"*

The kriegies really popped to for him. We learned our lesson from the time no one saluted the *Kommandant* and he ranted and raved all over the compound. This time, the men really out did themselves and went into twanging braces if the general came within twenty paces of them. Evidently his "royal sirness" was pleased; at least they haven't run in a squad with chatter guns yet.

I dropped into the Mess at a quarter to four, fifteen minutes early, to warm my feet, and there was General Vanaman talking to Colonel Alkire.

General Vanaman is one of my favorite people; his being there after our comic-opera ordeal earlier in the day was such a wholesome relief that I could only sit and enjoy his presence. His optimism about an early end of the war alone was enough to put me into a pleasant frame of mind. He brought the very welcome news that there are fifty army trucks in Switzerland. They are for the Swiss to use for the sole purpose of delivering our food parcels, personal parcels and mail. Good old Uncle Sam hasn't forgotten us yet, in spite of his more pressing problems.

Eidmann invited me to his office later to listen to his theories about the salvation of Europe.

It was getting dark by then. Someone had stolen the blackout shutters from his window, so he called in Lehman and asked him to tell the guards in the goon boxes not to shoot us for having light streaming through the window.

16 November 44, Thursday. Started snowing about lockup time last night. Continued all day today. With the temperature well above freezing, the flakes were melting when they hit, so the compound is a slushy mess.

Only the older kriegies who have received shoes from home have two pairs, so nearly everyone stayed indoors as much as possible. The shoes we have might have to last a long time. Many kriegies have worn the same pair every day for many months and they are nearly worn out despite the careful treatment everyone gives his footwear. We rub in German shoe grease frequently, keep hobnails in the soles, and big iron plates in the heels and toes. Can't ever tell when we might have to do a lot of walking. Everyone, too, is careful about his health. Getting sick here could be very unhealthy, especially now.

Colonel Alkire attended a meeting of all the allied camp commanders at the *Kommandantur* today.They agreed that all camps would remain on the present ration of one-half parcel per week. They expressed confidence that we would receive another shipment of parcels soon. Their present agreement is that we will stay on half-parcels until we are down to two parcels per man. Then we will taper off to one-quarter parcel per man for eight weeks. After that, we can only hope for the best.

The *Kommandant* wanted to move all the British from North Camp to Belaria and make *Stalag Luft III* entirely American. The Senior British Officer protested loudly on the grounds that they were here first and have made many improvements, which they naturally do not care to leave. We still do not know who is going to Belaria.

There was a showdown on the light situation. The Germans agreed to leave the master switch on in the daytime so we can have current in the kitchen, reference library and theater, providing each block commander sees that the main barracks switches are left off during the day. If lights are seen burning in the barracks at any time except while the perimeter lights are on, the Germans will cut the main switches.

I don't know whether there really is a power shortage in *Deutschland* or whether they just want to keep us constantly reminded of our complete dependence upon them. Last summer it was water, now it's lights; wonder what it'll be next.

The worst news Colonel Alkire brought was that the *Kommandant* had been ordered by the *OKW* to issue Red Cross food to us only one day's supply at a time, instead of a week's supply, as was formerly the case. I don't know how they expect to accomplish this. Each man now gets one-half parcel every Monday. A fifteen-man room, for instance, gets seven parcels on Monday, and eight the following Monday.

An average parcel contains one can each of corned beef, Spam, powdered milk; a quarter-pound each of sugar, crackers and chocolate; two ounces of powdered coffee; one pound each of margarine, prunes or raisins.

A room combine can take seven or eight of these parcels, add them to the meager German rations of mostly potatoes and bread, and plan one fairly satisfactory evening meal each day. Breakfast and lunch are never more than snacks of bread, margarine, jam or cheese, and coffee. With only one parcel a day for fifteen men, there will never be enough at one time for everybody. We are going to have lots of problems over this.

17 November 44, Friday. War news sounds good. The camp is alive with rumors, as it always is when our armies make advances.

One rumor is that Himmler is seriously wounded from an accident. Morale in a kriegie camp depends almost entirely on good war news; ours is high tonight. We have been expecting it to be over almost any day ever since the invasion. The present situation could easily be the beginning of the end.

But after expecting the war to end for so long and being disappointed time after time, we sometimes feel that it could go on forever. As one old kriegie said, "It's gone on so long now it would be a shame to stop it." A statement like that, even in fun, should be filed under "famous last words."

When it does end, though, this place is going to riot if we're not careful. There are an estimated 15,000 to 20,000 allied prisoners within a ten-kilometer radius. This includes Russian workers who are treated as slaves since Russia did not participate in the Geneva Convention. That many men will be hard to control.

News of the allied invasion of France had spread like wildfire when it was flashed over from another camp last June. In thirty seconds, every man in camp knew about it. The shouting and jubilation made the guards nervous. When peace news comes, I'll bet they'll hear us in Berlin. The problem for the American staff here will be to prevent young hotheads from impetuously getting themselves killed.

We want to get every man in the camp back to the States alive. We are helpless to make any concrete plans to achieve that goal, since no one knows how or when this war will end. There are so many possibilities to consider. We're nearest the Russian front, so we sort of expect to be taken by them. Some kriegies are going so far as to study the Russian language. Another possibility is that peace will be declared and our guards will surrender to us. Then we could only sit and wait. It would be folly to march out unarmed and unguarded, with no food, money, and insufficient clothing, into a chaos of conquerors, conquered and liberated. Such a chaotic scene was probably why so many prisoners failed to make it home after the last war.

Another possibility is that the German military organization will break down and the civilians will riot, as they did toward the end of World War I. In such an event we can only hope that our government will drop us enough weapons so that we can fight our way out. Otherwise we will certainly be torn to pieces by irate civilians and anarchists.

We hope and pray for a speedy cessation to this war, yet the uncertainties and dread of facing the confusion and violence which will accompany its end dampens the pleasure of contemplating freedom. As for making plans, we can only cross our bridges as we come to them.

Everyone is talking about the kriegie who received a letter from his mother telling him to "be sure to visit your Uncle Gerhardt while you are in Germany."

It must be difficult for our relatives to visualize our position here. They seem to envision the camps as everything from concentration camps to "gravy trains."

Actually, we could be infinitely worse off; yet, I don't know of a single prisoner who wouldn't rather be back putting his life on the line, fighting with his old outfit. The punishment here is mental. The sudden change from extreme excitement to extreme boredom is maddening. A common thought is: "Maybe I'm dead. There was violence that killed me, then suddenly I'm in a horribly strange world. I've just died and gone to hell!"

The worst thing is the feeling of complete helplessness, of being at the mercy of a desperate and ruthless enemy twenty-four hours a day, day after week after month. This mental depression is worse than war. We aren't contributing anything toward ending the war, but we're earning our pay!

I managed to get a pair of new shoes today in exchange for my old ones that were devoid of soles. In here a little thing like new shoes makes one feel rich and dressed up.

18 November 44, Saturday. Saturday is inspection day in the army, and our kriegie camp is no exception. Although most camps do not have inspections, Colonel Alkire has insisted that we have one here religiously, every Saturday. Though considered a chore by many kriegies, inspections have advantages. They break our time up into weeks, and furnish a periodical high point to the week. It's something to look forward to in a weird sort of way.

The officers and men are inspected in their rooms, standing by their own bunks; They are inspected for shaves, haircuts, cleanliness of clothes and cleanliness and orderliness of rooms.

In preparation for inspections floors are scrubbed, latrines and kitchens are thoroughly cleaned, and cooking utensils, food cabinets and containers are put in order. As one of the inspecting officers, I am surprised that inspections turn out as well as they do. It does seem that a small room serving as kitchen, bedroom, dining room, living room and workshop for fifteen men could easily become little better than a pigsty. I am told the rooms are filthy in other camps.

But here in *Westlager* they are kept neat and clean, and in some blocks, thanks to the diligence and pride of the block commander they are immaculate.

Each block has a set of barber tools so the men can cut each other's hair. Razor blades are scarce, but we have sharpeners, and by soaking the beard thoroughly, a blade can be made to last a long time.

For the majority who have only one pair of trousers, each block has a few pairs of "communal" pants which are loaned out to individuals while they are washing their own. Communal pants are really our own G.I. heat suits, but being U.S. Government property, they were confiscated as war booty, then reissued to us. Shoes are shined with polish furnished by the Red Cross. Tables, benches, stools and other woodwork are scrubbed white with German issue sand soap.

⌐ Today everyone is excited over the war news, which is increasingly good. Hope has been revived again of maybe getting out of here before Christmas. We can hardly wait to read tomorrow's communiqua.

19 November 44, Sunday. The news today was good, but slightly disappointing. The *OKW* never seems to put out bad news on weekends. Perhaps too many people are listening then. I expect better news tomorrow.

20 November 44, Monday. The news is about the same. The Swiss representatives of the International Red Cross will be here Wednesday or Thursday. *Major* Simoleit (German) sent word that he must have a copy of the agenda of topics we'll discuss with them. The letter I sent him gave our agenda simply as "delivery of Red Cross food and clothing to this camp." I don't know what else we could possibly discuss. I get the impression that the *OKW* is jittery about the possibility of an organized internal revolution with prisoners of war and foreign workers as a nucleus (in addition to the Russian laborers previously mentioned, Germany has many imported laborers from the other countries she occupies). I can understand their concern. There must be a million of us. We would be all for a revolution here if someone would only start it.

Just heard about Roosevelt's saying the war would not end this year. Our first reaction was acute disappointment, of course. But, after a while we were actually relieved; we finally had something definite to go on, and could stop "sweating it out" so much.

A statement in one of the papers cautioned Germans that they would have to eat only food grown in their immediate localities, due to the acute transportation shortage. That will be rough on us as well. I don't think anything grows here but pine trees.

21 November 44, Tuesday. Tonight we had a musical program in the theater. First there was a swing concert of recorded music, then a dramatic sketch from Edgar Allan Poe's "M. Bon Bon." This was followed by light classical records.

The last act of the evening was a concert of "memory melodies" by the "Melodiers," a six-piece string ensemble, with Lieutenant Bianco and Navy Lieutenant Palmer doing the vocals. The show was a one-night "quickie," but was well done and thoroughly enjoyed by all. Lieutenant Bianco, who also plays the guitar, was in the States recently enough to know the three leading Hit Parade songs of '44. Those were enthusiastically received, but the biggest hit of the evening was his delivery of "Soldier, May I Read Your Letter?"

The theater doors were to open at seven, but by 6 p.m., every entrance was mobbed. When the doors finally opened, there was a stampede that would have killed anyone unlucky enough to have fallen underfoot. In five minutes, all the seats were filled, and the aisles were packed with standees. The remaining hundreds left outside were dejected.

23 November 44, Thursday. Today, Dr. Rossel of the International Red Cross at Geneva arrived at the camp, accompanied by *Hauptmann* Eilers, General Vanaman, and the *Lagerführer* of Center Camp, a German major. Rossel's visit was disappointing. In the first place, he arrived just as we were sitting down to our meager lunch. C. H. Pearson, our Mess officer, hurriedly swept the dishes off the table and got our little Mess ready for the meeting. In the second place, Group Captain Willets, RAF Commander of East Camp, had gotten into a flap with the Germans over some small item; consequently, the *Kommandant* was "away" when Dr. Rossel arrived, but had vindictively limited the time of the doctor's visit. In the third place, Dr. Rossel spoke mostly in French, so most of his conversation was over the heads of everyone present except General Vanaman and Lieutenant Stanhope.

Stanhope, who had been called in as interpreter, was born in France of a French mother and an American father. Although he was an American citizen, he had spent only six months of his life in the U.S. He served with the French Air Force, then with the RAF after France capitulated, and later was shot down while flying fighters with the USAAF.

We did manage to get this much out of Dr. Rossel: (1) The army trucks donated to the Red Cross for hauling food parcels to POW camps from Switzerland will probably not be used until after the cessation of hostilities. (2) The Germans refuse to increase their rations to us on the grounds that the negligible amount of food they now give us is the same amount they give their own civilians who are not working. (3) A camp of NCO's was moved westward in front of the advancing Russians. They were treated atrociously. Some were shot, some were bayoneted, all were subjected to strenuous marching, exposure and starvation. (4) The only cheerful news that Dr. Rossel brought was that, in his opinion, we will never have to make do on less than our present ration of two parcels per month per person.

Rossel is returning tomorrow for brief interviews with those of us who haven't been receiving enough mail. "Enough mail" is about one letter every two months. One big headache will be finding individuals with justifiable complaints for these interviews without causing a stampede.

24 November 44, Friday. Dr. Rossel returned tonight with his friend, a Mr. Thudicum, and interviewed a few of the men who have not been receiving mail, personal parcels, etc. Rossel and Thudicum are two typically French "bons vivants" from Switzerland. It certainly is refreshing to be around them. They seem to have a good time traveling about the continent and enjoying their privileges as citizens of a neutral power. They and their colleagues are doing a wonderful job. A kriegie camp would be just another concentration camp without them and their employers, the International Red Cross.

They were escorted here by *Leutnant* Vickinghaus, a wounded combat man from one of the *Luftwaffe* ground regiments; he is serving as substitute *Lagerführer* while recuperating. There seems to be a universal understanding between combat men; I suppose that is why we all like Vickinghaus. Colonel Alkire asked General Vanaman to try to get the *Kommandant* to replace the blundering Eilers with him, but evidently the *OKW* has other plans for him. I guess they think he is too valuable to be wasted on us.

We had two flaps today. Colonel Alkire held a meeting of block commanders this morning, after which the block commanders held meetings with their room commanders to pass along the information. A ferret happened to observe one of those meetings, that of Major Salzarulo of Block 159, and called his *Feldwebel* (Glimowitz).

The two broke up the meeting. They thoroughly searched the room and all of its occupants. They found nothing more incriminating than a theater script, so, believing that the meeting was a play practice, they retired sheepishly.

The other flap started when Lieutenant Ashman was caught sitting on the roof of a barracks sketching a goon box. The guard leveled his rifle down on Ashman, and called for assistance on his phone, whereupon Ashman tore up his sketch. Fisher and Colonel Aring came to the kriegie's rescue, but Ashman will probably get a cooler sentence. The guard apparently thought Ashman was receiving a visual message from *Stalag VIII-C* which contains many allied paratroopers and ground soldiers. So now the Germans are putting up a camouflage screen between this camp and VIII-C; they are taking no chances on our communicating between camps for organizing a rebellion.

There are some movie films in camp this week, but our projector has a burned-out sound tube. We tried to replace it with one from another projector, but the *Abwehr* had sealed it in to keep us from using it to construct a radio. So we had silent movies. They were "The Spoilers," a cartoon, and an English travelogue.

Two days before Thanksgiving, I heard that General Vanaman would visit us for Thanksgiving dinner. I went to my room to "dress up" for his visit. I shined my G.I. shoes, shined my insignia with Dr. Vierling's *Zahnpulver* (German tooth powder), and put on a tie.

While at the office collecting the day's correspondence and *Appell* notices, we got word that a new purge was in. They were eight officers from a concentration camp. They looked pretty beat up. I arranged for coffee and sandwiches for them before I left for *Appell*, but I didn't get a chance to talk to them. I wanted to get a good description of a concentration camp from them, but never got a chance.

After *Appell* the General joined us for Thanksgiving dinner. Pearson really outdid himself. There was a snow-white table cloth with a brown and orange border of crepe paper. A papier-maché turkey made by one of our theater prop men sat at one end of the table.

Someone had managed to produce a bottle of sauterne. This was my first taste of any alcoholic beverage in seven months, and it was delicious. There was only enough for about two ounces per diner, but I think I actually felt mine. Dinner included soup, roast beef (probably horse, but good), gravy seasoned with smuggled onions, mashed potatoes, turnips, coleslaw, white bread and butter, strong coffee, pie a la mode, and cigars (the cigars were donated by Lieutenant Colonel Darling who had received them from his family.)

The ice cream was frozen in a home-made freezer with ice from the fire pool. It was the finest meal any of us have had since captivity. Everyone got into the holiday spirit. The General commented that we should be happy here, since we are completely free of man's three main sources of trouble: whiskey, women and money. General Vanaman regaled us, especially our Irish Padre, with his solemn stories of his *Scheisshaus* (latrine) Gremlin. This little informer of his has been telling him that the war would be over in November. Now, the General says, the Gremlin has gone to Berlin to be decorated with an Iron Cross, and from there to join the *Volkstrum*. Before the Gremlin left he was seen limping as though he had a club foot. (German Propaganda Minister Goebbels, who we heard frequently on German Radio, was known to have a club foot.)

I just heard a story that might be significant. Herb Mosebach came in from the *Revier* where he goes for physiotherapy treatments. An English kriegie from the East Camp (who has been down two-and-a-half years but calls himself a new kriegie because his friends have been down four or more years) told him our camp is located in the center of a rich food-growing area. It is true the Germans are giving us more fresh vegetables than they ever have before. He believes that the transport problem is so acute that they're giving us the vegetables because they would only sit there and rot otherwise.

30 November 44, Thursday. Thanksgiving Day, and the last day of November. The Catholics had their service at 6 a.m. After *Appell* there was a Protestant service. Chaplain Metherall gave an interesting historical account of our first Thanksgiving, even though he's an Englishman who has never been to the States.

That was followed by a historical "radio play" given by our theater group over the public address system in the theater. Singing the national anthem was next. That was the first time I had heard the "Star Spangled Banner" in seven months. We really made it ring out. We left the theater singing "God Bless America" and feeling very patriotic.

Today the ferrets found some broken knives in this Block, 159. They always confiscate such items, but now they also threaten the people who have them with cooler sentences. They couldn't pin ownership of the knives on anyone, so they wanted to lock up the block commander, Major Salzarulo. Eidmann apparently talked Griese (who is head ferret of the compound) out of this. I suppose Griese is afraid the kriegies might use those broken knives as weapons; he'll probably charge the block with destruction of *Reich* property. The knives are ordinary table knives issued for eating purposes. They get broken because they are the nearest thing to a tool kriegies have. We use them for all sorts of things: opening cans, repairing stoves, digging stumps, cutting roots for kindling, and making articles out of tin cans.

1 December 44, Friday. This has been a busy day. The announcement was made that we are to submit a cadre list for Belaria. Only about seventy officers and men are needed, but the idea is so popular nearly everyone wants to go. I've been swamped with requests. I have to get the list ready by next Wednesday.

Compound Scene 1: Herb Mosebach regaling "Old Snaggle Tooth," a ferret, with a corny Southern joke, in German. Old Snag shows his appreciation with a broad, toothless grin. Old Snag is a good reason for the term goon. He is a quiet, too-dumb-to-be-dangerous type, whose self-consciousness can be mistaken for shrewdness and hostility. Herb has worked on him patiently so that now he seems to trust Herb completely.

Scene 2: Lieutenant Colonel Aring absent-mindedly calls the *Appell* to attention, salutes the Colonel, forgets to dismiss the *Appell*, and walks away. He then almost spins in turning around and getting back, after he remembers to dismiss us.

Scene 3: Captain Runyan and *Unteroffizier* Gambietz, happily pulling together on the tongue of a wagon cart. An example of how hard it is to force ordinary people of good will to get mad at each other, even when their respective nations are at war.

I got a description of Belaria from Eidmann. It is the best residential section in the Sagan area. Unlike West Camp, the ground is fertile and rolling. The camp is situated on top of a hill and has a nice view of Sagan and the surrounding countryside. You can even see the airport from the camp. The main highway passes only 100 meters from the fence. There are two types of barracks: some are like the small barracks in the north end of North Camp, the others are like the ones here.

2 December 44, Saturday. War news sounds good. We're making advances east of Aachen. The Russians have a big spearhead across the Danube, now west of *Fünfkirchen*. Looks like they might be headed for the Trieste area in Northern Italy. That would cut off the Germans in the Balkans and anchor their southern front so they could drive through in the middle toward here. I hope.

I have again been swamped by applicants who want to move to the new compound at Belaria. Some of them are attracted by the glowing description of the place. Others would do anything for any slight change. Major Houston wants to go; he says he has opened every other camp in the *Stalag*, so he may as well be in on the last one.

A goon just gave us the disconcerting information that the *SS* might take over this camp at any time. He said that the *SS* searches them and their barracks periodically. To quote him: "They made us strip. They searched us thoroughly, even our rectums. One man was asleep. They clubbed him brutally with a blackjack, of which they carry two. Our *Kommandant* made a protest to this area's *Luftwaffe* headquarters in Breslau. He has made many protests before."

In reply to the question, "Isn't Goering strong enough to defend the members of his organization against those of another?" he replied, "Everyone thinks Goering has skipped the country."

The goon went on to describe the *SS*. The best I can remember his words, he said,

"Every man, woman and child in Germany hates and fears the *SS*. They are all hoping and praying that the Americans will kill every member when they take Germany. The *SS* troops who are picked for special details such as guarding prison camps are chosen for their natural brutality and sadistic qualities. They will come in with machine pistols and shoot first and ask questions later. I know there will be trouble. They will come in dressed as infantry soldiers, but don't let that fool you; they're still *SS*. We will all go to the front then. That is why some of us are trying so hard and perhaps causing a lot of trouble for you.

No one wants to go to the front. If they come in here and you take all you can stand, break out and ask a civilian to help you, they all hate the *SS*."

I have repeated his story as best I can remember. I don't necessarily believe him. I don't think the man has sufficient mentality to know exactly what is going on, but perhaps his story gives a clue as to the state of affairs in *Deutschland* today.

The boys are having a big food "feast" lately. Many are sick because of over-stretching their shrunken stomachs. They are eating up all the reserve food that they have taken months to store up. The goons have put out an order that only one day's supply of food can be on hand at any one time, so the men are frantically eating up their stores before the food is confiscated. Formerly, the goons punched holes through our tins before allowing them to be brought in, to keep us from storing food. That worked only too well in the summer, many men got food poisoning then. Now that the weather is cold, food keeps for a long time.

I think it is slowly dawning on the average goon that Germany is losing the war. Some of them even seem to think that the best friends they have in the world are right here in this camp. One said today that nobody in Germany believes the war can possibly go on past January. If it does any good to wish, there's plenty of frantic wishing on both sides for the war to end tomorrow.

3 December 44, Sunday. Today didn't seem much like Sunday after having a holiday with church services on Thanksgiving Day. And, too, I was busy drawing up the new cadre list for Belaria.

The goons are flapping all over the place. We hope it's the usual spurt that dies down after a little while.

At *Appell* this morning, Eilers called me aside. He told me he had a tough problem. He said that he must have the number of Jews in the camp immediately.

I said I didn't know and wouldn't make any attempt to find out. Then he asked if maybe the block commanders would tell him. I said I didn't think so, that if they wanted that kind of information they would have to get it the best way they could. I told him that in our country we didn't pay much attention to that sort of thing. (I was wrong about that, but we don't take it to the extremes the way they do here.) He then walked over to Major Carpenter, block commander of Block 157. Major Carpenter was taken by surprise by the question and gave Eilers the approximate number of Jews in his block. In the meantime, I had gone to Colonel Alkire and the rest of the staff and expressed my indignation over the matter. The Colonel called out, "Block commanders, front and center!" He then informed them of what was going on. He reminded them not to give such information to the Germans, and if approached on the subject, to refer the question to him. *Appell* was dismissed. Word got around quickly about the flap. I have heard from many sources that the Jewish men in the camp are pretty worried. And rightfully so.

Sunday, p.m. Nothing further has been heard on the Jew subject today. Eilers took his usual Sunday afternoon half-holiday and was not here this afternoon. However, we are having a picture parade tomorrow morning. That may or may not have any connection with the flap.

Eidmann came in tonight to give me the details of tomorrow's picture parade. He said it will be to our advantage to get it over as quickly as possible so we can get in out of the cold. A picture parade is a way of checking on each man's identity. This is the second one they've had since the camp opened last April. In daily *Appells* we are not counted by name; they are only interested in the total number. The reason for picture parades is to make sure the right people are still here. The procedure is as follows:

Five tables are placed at intervals around the parade ground (athletic field) with English-speaking goons at each table.

The goons have large files containing each man's picture and his name, rank and serial number. Each block commander lines up his men in alphabetical order. He orders, "Column of files from the left" and they march pass the table in their turn. The whole procedure takes about an hour.

It is disconcerting to see the picture of yourself that was taken on the day you became a kriegie. Identification photos make one look odd anyway, but those photos show drawn faces, tired and suffering eyes, wounds, and other physical signs that bring back vivid memories of the ordeal of being shot down in combat, then captured and manhandled. Now our faces have filled out a little, and the look on them is that of men who are idle and bored, and in some cases, resigned; and in still others, there is a repulsive look of smugness, but not many, fortunately.

4 December 44, Monday. I was trying to get together the new cadre this morning when I was interrupted by the announcement that Mr. Soderberg of the Swedish YMCA would arrive at once.

I asked C. H. Pearson to prepare late lunch for four, and rushed to my room to shave and clean up. Mr. Soderberg arrived, escorted by *Hauptmann* Eilers and *Major* Reinhard of the *Abwehr*. Both German officers planted themselves firmly in the dining room. We felt obligated to offer them a cup of coffee at least.

The YMCA representatives are the only ones of our outside contacts the Germans don't seem to trust. They leave us alone with the Protecting Power and with Red Cross representatives, but they won't let YMCA men out of their sight. It probably isn't so much that they don't trust Soderberg, but that the YMCA has less prestige than the other two groups, and therefore cannot bring pressure on the Germans to rid themselves of their watchdogs. So, we had two Germans over for lunch.

After our brief business with Soderberg, he called in a number of kriegies for whom he'd brought personal messages from the States via Sweden. While he and Lieutenant Colonel Hendrix were busy with that, Colonel Alkire and I talked with Eilers and Reinhard. We don't know Reinhard well. He is new here and doesn't come in much. I don't blame him, I wouldn't either. We offered them a cup of tea, which they accepted. We discussed the usual things: religion, politics, the war.

What a crazy situation! Our country is fighting a war to the death with the Germans. We have friends dying by the thousands because of the Germans. And here we are, 500 miles behind the German lines, having tea with the enemy! Is this treasonable fraternization with the enemy? No, it's perfectly normal; there is an irrepressible yearning for peace and friendship that surmounts any amount of indoctrination for hatred.

17 December 44, Sunday. A pretty dull day, although the weather continues to be beautiful. For the past three days the skies have been clear and the temperature has hovered around freezing. There was a slight thaw today, but it's below freezing again tonight.

We saw a lot of air activity today. There were about a dozen fighters

Military Funeral

above us high enough to make vapor trails. We heard intermittent flak all afternoon in the east and southeast. *Rundfunk* reported no *fliegers* in this area.

The mail has slowed almost to a standstill. We only get a few hundred letters per day lately. The mail is a big morale factor, naturally, even though six weeks is considered fast service. Most letters are about a month old. I imagine the average mail reception here is around three letters per man per month. There is a letdown feeling after reading a letter, because they are too short, and the writers are so cautious because of the censorship. This is true at both ends. Some even go so far as not to write at all, which, of course, is a big mistake. We are allowed to send out three letters and four cards per month. This is increased slightly commensurate with rank. A Lieutenant Colonel, for instance, is allowed six letters and four cards.

I recently got shocking and frustrating news about my brother, Don. A purge from some groups stationed in Italy passed within shouting distance of us in West Camp while being processed into the Stalag. I hollered, "Anybody from 464th Group?" (My brother Don's group).

Someone answered, "Yeah."

"Know Major Burton?" I asked.

"Yeah, he spun into the Adriatic."

There was a maddening silence as his comrades shut him up. The purge then moved into another camp. I couldn't find out anything more about Don as long as we were at Sagan. (Since there were many examples of miraculous survivals, military policy was, "Don't report anyone dead unless you actually see his dead body.")

25 January 45, Thursday. This long gap in the diary represents a period in the lives of kriegies, all over Germany perhaps, we'll not soon forget. Morale reached rock bottom during Christmas; we were inside these fences, and probably would remain here for another year. The low mood was accentuated by the war news. Germany's winter offensive drove a deep wedge into allied lines in the Belgium-Luxemborg border area ("Battle of the Bulge"). The German propaganda machine played this offensive up strongly. German morale soared, and kriegie morale slumped.

Two other depressing incidents occurred. First Lieutenant R. N. Burks, 0-810106, died 28 December 1944 after a mastoid operation in the French Hospital. A small party of Germans and Americans led by Colonel Alkire went out to bury him in the allied cemetery on 2 January 1945. He was buried with full military honors and wrapped in the Stars and Stripes.

The other incident concerned two officers and two enlisted men, all from the same crew, who were taken out under heavy guard and locked up in the cooler. The men, all of whom arrived in Europe 30 April 1944 and were arrested on 23 December 1944, are Second Lieutenant J. R. Clary, 0-685000; Second Lieutenant J. J. Walsh, 0-809778; Staff Sergeant E. J. Martin, 35491958; and Sergeant E. J. Walsh, 32461350. Their offense was a mystery until recently, when we learned they were charged with inciting Italian civilians against the Germans behind the lines in Italy while wearing civilian clothes. Previous to their arrival here, they had sent word to us that they had been tried and sentenced to death. That is, three of them got death and one got life imprisonment. So far, the Germans have denied that those men have even been tried. All this came on top of our very un-merry Christmas.

Lieutenant John Dunn (USN) outdid himself putting on a series of first-rate Christmas programs. Everyone went around wishing everyone else a Merry Christmas, but the acting was poor and the words fell flat on unappreciative ears. We tried hard, but a pall of gloom hung over the camp. We resigned ourselves to another year of imprisonment and tried to occupy ourselves with various time-consuming tasks. Colonel Alkire started a comprehensive review of mathematics. Lieutenant Colonel Darling took over the A1 section and started setting up a detailed staff system. I resumed my study of the German language.

About ten days ago, the Russians started their great offensive along their entire western front. At first the news was received coolly. No one wanted a repetition of our gloomy and disappointing Christmas week. Darling wrote an editorial called "Appeal to Reason" imploring kriegies to "follow the middle of the road."

But the Russians advanced 400 kilometers, from the Vistula to the Oder, in four days. They outflanked the little Ruhr and cut off East Prussia. They took thousands of localities and drove spearheads to the Oder.

Aring, acting in his capacity as A3, ordered everyone to walk ten kilometers a day around the compound to toughen our feet. We're to walk in squads. A pack was designed employing the G.I. overcoat as a carryall for personal possessions and food. The camp is slowly awakening from its lethargy.

Tonight the Russians are on the Oder River, just forty-five kilometers east-southeast of here. Breslau and the little Ruhr are almost surrounded. East Prussia is cut off. One gets the impression that there is no east front left. We could hear artillery in the east today. There has been more air activity than we've seen before.

All is quiet tonight, but the camp is tense. I think few of us will sleep. We've been waiting to be moved westward, but now it looks like the Germans have waited too long. The Russians are practically here.

It is still very hard to believe. If we aren't moved tomorrow, we expect to be liberated by the Russians very soon. The Germans seem stunned. They can't believe what's happening. This is the most excitement we've had since getting shot down. The suspense is terrific!

26 January 45, Friday. Last night was quiet. Today there was no evidence of external activity except for a lot of planes flying, in spite of the bad weather.

- A long column of old men in civilian clothes have moved into the *Truppenlager* next door (west). I was told they are 60-year-old recruits for the *Volkstrum*, and that they are taking the place of the army garrison which was moved to the front.

There was another arrest the day before yesterday. S/Sgt K. O. Henson, 6955909, tried to escape by slipping across the parade ground between the two guard towers at night; he only got about halfway across the parade ground.

The camp is a beehive of activity. We are doing ten kilometers a day trying to get our feet in shape for a march. We want to be ready in case of short notice to move. The Russians are still only forty-five miles east of here at Steinau, on our side of the Oder. The Germans say we are not likely to move westward. I think they are seriously worried about a mass escape if they try to move us. With an estimated 20,000 allied prisoners in the area (15,000 Americans and Englishmen, 5,000 Russians), a mass riot might be the straw that breaks the camel's back. However, we are busy designing packs and sleds just in case a move is called.

Tonight Colonel Jenkins (Chief of Staff) held a block commanders meeting and laid down the law: iron-clad discipline from here on out.

At *Appell* we could plainly hear sounds of the battle going on in the east. Aring asked Eilers what they were going to do with us now that the Russians are almost here. Eilers placed his fingers together and answered calmly, "We will stop them."

Herb Mosebach has gone to the news room to get the 2100 news. I am anxiously awaiting his return.

Part IV
Chaos

Following are my diary notes dating from 28 January to 3 April, 1945, recalling the evacuation of Sagan and our relocation at Nurnberg-Langwasser.

Diary

28 January 45, Sunday. Freiwaldau, Germany. *Stalag Luft III* is being evacuated! We were given notice last night at 7:30 p.m. to pack our food, clothing and blankets and be ready in one hour for a forced march westward. We packed and lined up on the road, then were kept standing in the snow until midnight before finally departing. We then double-timed out of the camp through the *Vorlager* where one full Red Cross parcel was thrown to each of us. We marched all night and all morning arriving here at noon today. We've heard that the Russians are close on our heels. We can hear their guns in the east.

Freiwaldau is about twenty-five kilometers southwest of Sagan. We're stopped here for a five-hour rest. We are at a prison that can accommodate only about half of us at a time; the others have to stand out in the frigid weather waiting their turn to come in.

We are in dreadful condition. Our hastily built packs are falling apart. Many are having to discard valuable equipment and food so as to keep up. We hear that many have either fallen by the wayside or have intentionally escaped. Escape would be easy because of the confusion and the fact that our guards are old men who stagger under the weight of their packs and rifles. They, and others we pass along the road, eagerly glean the food, clothing and blankets that are discarded by our weakest and most exhausted kriegies.

At West Camp last night we organized into six sections, each consisting of about three Blocks. The Blocks are divided into Squads. Some Squads are pulling quickly improvised sleds.

North, South, Center, East and West compounds are traveling

together. We number about 10,000. Walking three abreast, we stretch out in a line fifteen miles long. We're quite a traffic problem for the *Wehrmacht*, who are keeping the roads hot with their transports.

We rest frequently, but the stops are too long and we have to be careful not to freeze our feet while resting. There seems to be confusion to the point of chaos, and there are many wild rumors.

Our problem right now is simply self preservation. Fortunately we have sufficient food since we each have a Red Cross parcel. But the packs are very heavy and the weather is bitterly cold.

As I write this we are preparing to set out on our second all-night walk.

30 January 45, Tuesday. Muscau, Germany. We have been through the most agonizing experiences. We arrived here Monday morning at 6 a.m. after an all-night walk of thirty-six kilometers from Freiwaldau. During the thirty-six hours we covered sixty-six kilometers with only two hours sleep or less, and one meal. The temperature was well below freezing, the road was covered with ice and snow, and it snowed frequently during the night. We out-marched three sets of guards, and the horses that were pulling the wagon load of German supplies gave out. Many kriegies are missing, we fear some are dead, and a few seem to be insane.

Soon after leaving Freiwaldau, Colonel Alkire's old wound caused him to drop out and Colonel Jenkins took command. Colonel Aring went to the rear of the column with a crippled foot. The misery he saw there caused him to return to the head of the column and implore Eilers to discontinue the march for the night, but Eilers was unable to find a shelter for us. Shortly after that, Aring dropped out, along with 400 men who could go no further.

Then some German soldiers opened fire on the rear of our column thinking we were Russians. At the same time, some kriegies saw two airplanes overhead and thought we were being strafed. The alarm spread and several blocks either dived into ditches or made for the woods. Then our own guards, thinking we were starting a riot, opened up on the column. Fortunately, few were seriously hurt.

When our guards started firing, the soldiers who had fired on us saw our long column and, thinking they were outnumbered and surrounded, came forward to surrender. They walked up to Eilers with hands raised, and were very embarrassed to find they were trying to surrender to their own forces.

All this was unknown to us at the head of the column until Eilers came forward and told us what had happened. Meanwhile, at the head of the column, we were having our own flap. Eilers left another *Hauptmann*, named Deutsch, in charge while he was at the rear. When the flap started there, we halted and almost froze waiting for them to catch up. Many guards came forward, threw down their rifles, and told their *Kommandant* that they were through. Their discipline just went completely to hell. Mosebach translated all he heard.

Deutsch told them that he could guard 2,000 prisoners alone if necessary, and he was fifteen years older than they. But the guards are old and starved; I saw one fall into a snow bank and lie still, his face against the snow.

Block commanders continually came forward with stories of freezing, fatigue, and other suffering. We might have rioted but for everyone's weakened state.

Colonel Jenkins remained calm. At last Eilers came forward and we continued the march. Eidmann and Gambietz rode ahead on bicycles to try to find accommodations for the sick. At our third halt, Lieutenant Colonel Tiller and Lieutenant Colonel Hand fell out with another 200 exhausted men.

The horses were becoming tired and stopping more frequently, and they finally gave out. We walked around them while a guard stayed to unload the guards' packs. Two guards who were preceding us by almost 200 yards left their rifles in the wagon; they didn't know the wagon had stopped, so the whole front half of the column was then guarded by only two unarmed guards leading a dog.

From about 2 a.m. on, many passed out on their feet. Some wanted to lie down and sleep in the snow. Others were talking to themselves. Almost everyone was seeing visions or hearing strange noises. We were afraid to halt and rest, afraid too many would fall completely asleep and freeze to death. Our feet were wet from snow melting through shoes, so that if kept still for thirty minutes they would have frozen solid. We had no choice but to keep moving.

The last six kilometers were pure hell. Eilers knew nothing of what shelter was ahead for us or where we would stop for the night. He had depended entirely upon Eidmann for that, and Eidmann was nowhere to be found.

We arrived in Muscau during predawn blackness, a sad-looking string of suffering humanity. Many were half-crazy by then. Eilers located the *Bürgermeister's* house and went in to make arrangements for us to rest one day and night. After we'd waited twenty minutes Colonel Jenkins sent me to follow Eilers, hoping for some word of encouragement to pass along to our miserable troops.

The sight that confronted me at the *Bürgermeister's* house was devastating. Men had forced their way inside the house and packed the corridors. More were pushing at the door. I angrily ordered the door closed and everyone outside. When the door was finally closed, someone pounded on it. I opened it. A kriegie, apparently frozen, was shoved in. "What are you going to do about him?" someone asked. I dragged him in.

His skin felt cold and inflexible. He descended to the pile of freezing bodies. A weak voice said, "Please, please move him." I moved him a little and rushed upstairs.

I pounded furiously on the door at the top of the stairs. A woman came to the door and I asked for Eilers. She said he was telephoning. I said I had to see him immediately. In my very poor German I explained that men were dying each minute.

Then Eilers came back. Two women brought hot tea, took it down the stairs and began giving it to the worst cases. I told Eilers we must have shelter immediately or the men would riot. Eilers was unimpressed; he pointed out that he had walked the whole way too, and he was past fifty. I was ready to choke him when he went on to explain that North Camp had arrived ahead of us and were housed in the glass factory where we were to have stayed. He said we could go to the churches. Thinking that news might be somewhat encouraging to the others I rushed out and made the announcement, imploring them to keep their heads. When I got back to Eilers we learned we could go to a pottery factory nearby which had heat for the curing process. Eilers told me, an enemy prisoner, to take along a few German soldiers, our guards! One of the women volunteered to show us the way.

With a few guards we hurried to the rear of the column, which was in the direction of the pottery factory. I left Major Lawrence and Captain Butcher in charge of the people remaining at the *Bürgermeisters*; they had already been there when I came in.

At first the *Feldwebel* of the guards would not allow us to move, despite the German woman's and my assurances that it was *Hauptmann* Eilers' orders. He had to go see Eilers himself before he would believe us. He returned surprisingly fast and ordered his guards to let us go.

The heroic German woman who saw us through all that deserved three cheers at least, but no one was able to cheer. She walked with me at the head of the column of miserable, staggering kriegies. Our column snaked right through the town with the population staring unbelievably.

At the pottery factory we found that it could only hold 1,000. I am now with this group. Colonel Jenkins has taken the others to the churches.

I couldn't get any casualty figures when we'd settled down at the factory, but I feel they must be high. There are lots of frostbite cases. I am afraid there will be some amputations when medical attention is available.

There are many foreign workers at the factory; they are friendly and helpful.

Colonel Aring came to the factory in the afternoon with about 100 men. We sent 200 on to the next stop with South Camp.

German rations of bread and margarine were delivered to us at the factory. We will walk eighteen kilometers tomorrow, then eight more the day after that, before we entrain for an as-yet unknown destination.

1 February 45, Thursday. Glaustein, Germany. We left Muscau yesterday noon for the eighteen kilometer march here. We regrouped just out of Muscau. We're in better shape now; the much-needed rest revived us in body and in spirit. Losses are not nearly as high as I had guessed. The senior officers who dropped out are slowly coming in, along with their men. We arrived here last night after about eight hours on the road. We're split up again, however, and billeted in eighteen barns.

I brought my section here, but most of the men were sent to other places. I have only part of Block 163, my lead block. Major Wheeler is here with his Block 162. Also here are Lieutenant Colonel Aring and Padre McVeigh. Padre McVeigh seems stunned. Herb Mosebach is with me as interpreter and friend.

There are about 150 of us packed in this barn. Nevertheless, the straw was the softest bed I have slept on in over nine months and I slept well.

The civilians here are not hostile. Some are even friendly. The kriegies are busy trading cigarettes, chocolates and coffee for bread, apples, potatoes, beer and wine. The family that owns this barn gave us hot water.

So far we have enough food, clothes and blankets. We are waiting to move on to Spremberg where we'll entrain for some permanent camp in Central Germany.

We're surprised so many of our bad cases pulled through. The kriegies are adapting to the hardships and learning road discipline.

Only about fifteen out of the 1,000 men at the pottery factory couldn't walk after they'd rested the night. Colonel Alkire and Lieutenant Colonel Aring are doing much better now.

Our walk this morning is only eight kilometers. We will then entrain, probably in boxcars. Most of our escapees have been rounded up. In addition to us, we have another fifty men from South Camp and about 500 from North Camp under Lieutenant Colonel Bland, totaling about 2,500.

A thaw last night left the road extremely slippery; the sleds can't function where the snow has melted, and are being abandoned.

"Chief" Masterson lightened everyone's mood with his Texas wit; he says he is still on his first mission, that he was a prisoner of war four days after he left his home in Texas.

There have been many cases of heroism on this march. Captain (Doctor) Pickard, Lieutenant Wilcox, Captain Travis, and others work tirelessly providing first aid.

The wild rumors are becoming more plausible. We hear the Russians are just forty-five miles from Berlin.

3 February 45, Saturday. We're on board the prison train now. We were given forty-five minutes notice on Thursday and marched out of our farm billets at Graustein. It was a rainy day. A warm storm had caused a thaw, and the muddy roads were crowded with military transports and refugees from the east. Although we kept mostly to second and third class roads, we still got cluttered up from time to time with swarms of retreating masses. Many of the refugees are peasant families driving crude wagons pulled by two, three or four scrawny horses. They carry what household belongings they were able to pack in their haste. One group carried a large frozen hog in the back of their wagon. The guards ran along behind it, sliced off hunks of pork and ate it raw, with the hair still on the skin. I got a piece also; it was surprisingly good.

We heard sounds of the battle raging all day in the east. Mosebach had heard the *OKW* communiqué in the farmhouse at Graustein and told us that the Russians had taken a town on the Oder forty-five miles east of Berlin; they are just over sixty miles from us.

In Graustein troops were everywhere. As we marched out the usual groups of civilians offered various products for trade for our cigarettes, chocolate and coffee. Now and then men would leave the column, dicker and trade for awhile, then rejoin their column with their new prizes. It was all very crazy.

The march from Graustein to Spremberg was an easy one of only eight kilometers, but the thaw had made our sleds useless and they were soon discarded.

When night fell, pitch black and with a blustery wind, we were herded into an armored force base. The base's former occupants had apparently moved out hurriedly; only a few tanks and troops remained.

Our billets were gigantic concrete and steel hangars, with about 1,000 men per hangar. We were given a few bags of excelsior to spread on the concrete floor. It was so crowded it was almost impossible to walk about in the hangar.

An army *Feldwebel* who had lived eighteen years in the States greeted us and gave us the latest news. What he said, roughly, was:

"The Russians are forty-five miles from Berlin and only sixty miles from here. They have thrown in 180 fresh new divisions. We cannot stop them. The Bolsheviks are overrunning Europe. They will overrun America too. You cannot stop them on the west front with your puny eighty divisions. Germany and America must join together to stop the Bolsheviks."

His propaganda explained the relatively good treatment we've had so far. The army gave us all the soup we could drink that night-good soup. The green-uniformed *Heer* personnel were a new sight to us; Except for brief experiences with them after being captured, we'd been guarded totally by the blue-uniformed *Luftwaffe*. *Heer* personnel were surprisingly friendly. Even the officers seemed solicitous of our well-being. What a change in attitude compared with when we were captured!

There were two air raid alerts during the night. We heard the flak. Fortunately, no bombs dropped in our vicinity.

Next morning (Friday, February 2nd), we marched about two kilometers to the train station. Since my section had become scattered beyond hope of regrouping, Mosebach and I went to the head of the column and joined Colonel Alkire's staff. After a short wait we were broken into groups of fifty and assigned to our cars.

The train is an ordinary German freight train with small "forty and eight" type cars. No drinking water was provided. There are over 2,500 of us being transported, so some cars carry as many as sixty-three men. Mosebach and I are in a car "equipped" for the Colonel's staff, the German medical group, and our own medical group, under Captain Pickard. Major Carpenter and a few of his men were added, for a total of twenty-three Americans and four Germans in our car. Our "special equipment" is a stove, some coal, and one bale of excelsior. We constructed a stove pipe from a discarded metal drum. This car serves as prison train headquarters as well as storeroom for extra rations.

On the Colonel's staff here are Colonel Jenkins, Lieutenant Colonels Darling, Hendrix, Clark and Burton (author); Lieutenant Mosebach, interpreter; Lieutenant Pearson, rations officer; Lieutenant Murphy, bugler; and Padre McVeigh. With twenty-seven men in this small car we are too crowded for all to lie down at once. In cars that are more crowded they have to take turns to even sit down.

Captain Pickard, head of our medical group, was a paratrooper doctor from Oklahoma. He is assisted by Second Lieutenant (Pilot) Kennedy, who was the Camp Dental Officer at *Stalag Luft III*. Pickard is probably the busiest man in the group. He also supervises our one qualified medical orderly, Private McNeeley. The medical men, with their meager supplies, are scattered all up and down the train. Most patients are foot cases. Other medical personnel are three German *Sanitäter* with the rank of *Obergefreidter*. These men are apparently well-equipped, but only treat Germans.

Our guard is an *Unteroffizier*. German-American relations in the car are friendly, almost cordial. Our guards often leave their guns sitting around, and seem to trust us completely. I suppose they realize we are helpless on the train without them.

Before leaving Spremberg we learned from Major Simoleit that each man would get eight-tenths of a Red Cross parcel and one-half loaf of bread. Eilers told us we are fifteen hours behind schedule.

We stopped for a few hours at Russen that first evening. Many children, including Hitler *Jugend*, offered to fetch water in exchange for cigarettes. One of the German medics, Giesel, brought beer to exchange for cigarettes.

One of the German medics speaks English and plays the harmonica. Another sings. Together with Murphy playing hot licks on his trumpet, we had a concert as the train chugged along toward an unknown destination.

At Riessa there were 1,000 bowls of hot soup ready, but it ran out just before it got to this car.

4 February 45, Sunday. Another day spent on board the prison train. We made good progress last night and slept well, at least in our car. As we passed through the province of Franconia (which looks like upper New York State), Eidmann told us we are 140 kilometers from Nurnberg, our destination.

As we travel we pass many hospital trains crammed with Germans wounded at the front.

Several of our men came down with severe belly aches and thought they had appendicitis. Fortunately they were only puffed up with gas from too much goon bread.

Colonel Alkire said we've lost only twenty-eight men, a surprisingly low figure. We've picked up many stragglers from other camps, and all of the Americans from North Camp. The British from North and East were sent to Bremen. We 2,500 are going to the Nurnberg area. South and Center will go to Moosberg.

There are no sanitary facilities on the train, so we hurriedly do whatever we have to do, usually in plain view of the public, wherever we stop. We try to get everyone to at least get away from the tracks when defecating so that feces will not be tracked back into the cars.

We are due to arrive in Nurnberg tonight, Sunday, February 4th, but we're running late, so the train is making no stops for water or evacuation this last morning of our journey. We have been on the train forty-eight hours and on the road for eight days. We are becoming accustomed to tramp life.

5 February 45, Monday. Nurnberg, Germany. We pulled into the Nurnberg railroad yards on Sunday, February 4th at 1:30 p.m. At about 4:30 p.m., we finally disembarked for the short march to our new quarters at Langwasser, a suburb of Nurnberg. After the usual confusion and milling about in a cold rain, we were herded into a pigsty of a camp about one kilometer away. It had been occupied recently by Italians. The camp has about fourteen small wooden barracks, each with 144 closely packed, triple-decker bunks. The barracks I am in has 250 men, as does many others, which leaves over 100 men sleeping on tables, benches, or on the floor.

We arrived after dark and there were no lights. No latrines or *Aborts* could be found, and some of the more careless defecated on barracks floors. The meager fresh water supply is overtaxed by kriegies trying to fill tin cans for drinking or washing.

We have many North Camp people with us; they seem almost to have reverted to animals. Some have not shaved or had haircuts for months.

Eventually we got some lights on and enough fires going to prepare food. An air raid alarm sounded, but fortunately no bombs fell.

This place is called *M-Stammlager XIII-D*. It is in an area called Langwasser that had been used by Nazi party members as a meeting place. There is a mammoth stadium, still under construction, across the railroad tracks from us.

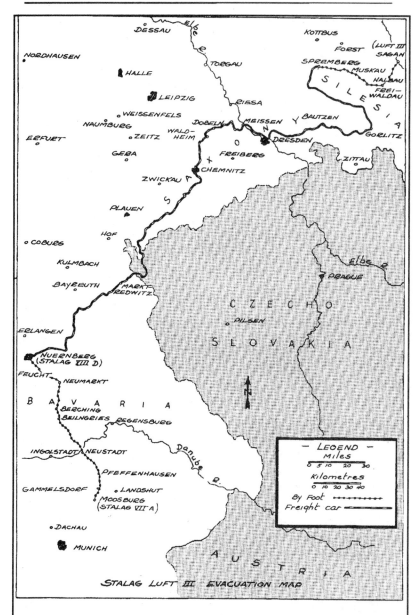

Based on a sketch by war artist Bob Neary, this map shows the prosoner route from (Stalag Luft III) Sagan to Nuernberg (Stalag XIII D) and Mooseburg (Stalag VIII A).

I believe that area was once used for the Olympics. There are signs in Russian, English, French and German. At one intersection the streets bear the names Adolf Hitler and Hermann Goering.

We were assured that the crowded conditions of the first awful night would be temporary. This morning Eidmann and Gambietz came in to look over the situation and make a report to the *Kommandant.* We have cleared the men out of the kitchen and expect to be able to issue hot water soon, but Pearson says the three boilers will only accommodate 1,000 men.

There is mud everywhere. Many squads have built fires, despite the crowded conditions. The whole place is unbelievably filthy, but we are too crowded to do much about it.

American enlisted men from various branches are located across the road. We heard most of them were taken during Germany's winter offensives on the West Front. They are hungry and very short of cigarettes since they've received very few Red Cross parcels and only short German rations.

7 February 45, Wednesday. We are beginning to get settled in our depressing surroundings. We were given an additional area to expand into, and now have twenty-two barracks. In addition, we have an infirmary set up by Captain Pickard and staff, a recreation building under our two English Padres, and three kitchens under Lieutenant Colonel Bland. The Block Commanders are Majors Eagan, Carpenter, Ingenhut, Salzarulo, Hill, Orriss, Brown, Kramer, Lawrence, Ott, Hogan, Cox, Hammet, Taylor, Quillan, Haltom, Cortner, Low, Exon, Murray, and Captain Wheeler. The last four majors and Lieutenant Colonel Bland came with the group from North Camp. Major Hill has two blocks to house all the enlisted men. Each block now has about 120 men. There was a great deal of confusion when the moves were ordered. Efforts were made to keep established combines together.

The weather is cold and damp, and there is a sloppy mess of mud everywhere. All the buildings have an inch of mud on the floors, and that situation is aggravated by the paddling of thousands of feet. Everything smells sour. There are fleas in the straw sacks. We have no bedding except the blankets we brought along.

We received some German rations on Tuesday: meat, bread, margarine and jam. Pearson managed to turn out a tasty little soup, served with bread, for each man. After *Appell*, we moved into the new area.

Two exciting things happened Tuesday: One was that one of our officers located his brother two fences away in the ground forces camp; they hadn't seen each other in two years. The other was, five of our "oldest" kriegies were repatriated "as a token of German appreciation for our good conduct during the move from Sagan to Nurnberg." Colonel Alkire chose the lucky men strictly on a basis of time in prison. They are: Lieutenant Newton, Texas, August 1942; Captain Croteau, Washington State, September 1942; Major Houston, Maryland, September 1942; Major Wheeler, California, November 1942; and Captain Frost, Illinois, December 1942.

The men departed Wednesday night: five bewildered kriegies headed for Berlin, and from there to Sweden.

Our organization was set up and humming by Wednesday, February 7th. We've retained our original staff, except Major Rosener replaced Captain Owens as Adjutant, and Lieutenant Colonel Sears replaced Lieutenant Colonel Hand as A2 (Captain Owens went with South Camp and Lieutenant Colonel Hand remained in the hospital at Muscau). Lieutenant Colonels Tiller and Tuttle were appointed CO's of the two areas.

All majors and lieutenant colonels, except those on the camp staff, will live and eat in two field grade officers' messes that were set up in two of the kitchens. The camp staff of colonels and lieutenant colonels will live and eat in the kitchen of Building 103.

These messes will also accommodate the two Padres, Captain Pickard and Lieutenant Pearson, Mess Officer.

We had our first meal in the Colonel's Mess Wednesday night; the fare was soup, one potato, bread, jam and coffee.

Corporal Murray, representing the Man of Confidence of the ground forces camp, came over with many tales of woe from his camp. There are 312 British and American Air Force personnel in that camp who, having heard of our good fortune at being in the hands of the *Luftwaffe*, are very anxious to join us. We also hear there are 1,500 new men from *Dulag* coming in on Thursday; that probably means we will open a third area soon.

8 February 45, Thursday. We opened the new area, Area Five, today. Immediately after *Appell*, 1,500 air combat enlisted men arrived from their camp near Stettin, from which they'd been evacuated in front of the Russian drive. They had been packed in boxcars for nine days, and one man died en route. Major Haltom was taken out of his block and given charge of the entire area.

Major Carpenter moved his men from their temporary quarters in Building 118 into Major Haltom's block. Building 118 will be used as a recreation building.

There are twelve barracks in the new area. Each has approximately 150 NCO's and is commanded by a senior NCO, usually a technical sergeant, elected by his constituents. In addition to those 1,500 men, 312 allied Air Force personnel arrived from Area Four where they had been imprisoned with ground personnel under the supervision of the *Heer*. With them are Major Dow of the USAAF and S/L Smith of the RNZAF. There are also four officers of the Free French Air Force and fifty-five NCO's from all over the British empire. That group of 312 had no food, no blankets, no cigarettes, and few overcoats. The kriegies came through in grand style, though, and shared their meager supplies. The NCO's from Stettin were especially generous; they had somehow managed to save most of their belongings. They had been given twenty-four hours notice before their move, something that would have saved our own group much grief.

All is well tonight, and 4,335 kriegies with at least partially-filled bellies are under a dry shelter. Last night the men in my building poured soup ladles full of hot water over each other in the kitchen, and thus we had our first baths in two weeks. Tonight all is peaceful. Some are playing bridge, some are washing or sewing; others just sit around the coal stove chewing the everlasting fat.

10 February 45, Saturday. Friday was a normal day. Today, we received eighty-six new kriegies. That number includes officers and enlisted men of both the USAAF and RAF. There are four Staff Sergeants from Italy who were shot down only four days ago. We also are getting in some stragglers who had dropped out during the moves. Among them are Major Linfest and a lieutenant; they were free for four days before they became exhausted and were picked up by civilian police.

Our Red Cross food is practically exhausted. There is no assurance of any immediate resupply. We are on German rations of potatoes, bread, kraut, margarine and soup. We are hungrier than we've ever been before in a *Stalag*. We have no reading material or recreational facilities. There is a complicated maze of barbed wire fences all around us. We know that as soon as our people get a little more rest and finish their cleaning and settling-in processes, those fences will become very oppressive.

11 February 45, Sunday. Today, 480 British and American officers and enlisted men arrived from Sagan. They are the group who'd stayed in the hospital because they couldn't walk; They were transported all the way by train so were able to bring most of their belongings and lots of Red Cross food that we had to leave behind.

In this group, too, are many recaptured escapees, including Johnny Dunn, USN, Lieutenant Colonel (Jonsey) Szaniawski and Mike Wyse. They were done in by exposure, exhaustion and hunger.

The train they were on was supposed to have brought our camp supplies, especially our extra Red Cross food. When they entered our camp they came in with all the food they could carry. Some had stretchers made on which they carried six or eight parcels. Lieutenant Colonels Clark, Edna and I and Captain Oliver stood at the gate and tried to get them to leave their extra food in the camp pool to be distributed evenly later. But only a few of them complied. We called the block commanders together. Colonel Alkire told each one to confiscate all food from their personnel in excess of a fourth of a parcel per man and place it in our storeroom to be issued out on an even basis. This proved quite successful and netted enough food to at least flavor the soup for everyone for several days.

. Among the new arrivals are Colonels Martin, Arnold and Stevenson, and Major Fitzgerald, all of the USAAF; Lieutenant Colonel Loocke, RSAAF; and W/C Hope, a Scotsman of the RAF. There are several S/L's and Majors. (See Glossary for British Commonwealth symbols and the American equivalents.)

There is a rumor that the British will all be moved out to Bremen tomorrow. If that is true we will have to return all their food. Our total strength is now 4,892.

12 February 45, Monday. A purge of eighty Anglo-American officers and enlisted men arrived from *Dulag* today.

A few days ago I heard the story of the sad march made by several thousand British and American Air Force NCO's from *Stalag Luft VI* at Hydekruge, East Prussia, to *Stalag Luft IV* at Kiefheid near Stettin. We'd heard scattered reports about that march before at Sagan.

Hyderkruge is located about twenty kilometers northwest of Tilsit. When the Russians pushed dangerously near the prison, the *OKW* issued an order for the prisoners to prepare to leave within twenty-four hours.

There were 6,600 men in that particular contingent, 2,400 of whom were Americans. They departed on 15 July and were thirty-six hours en route to Memel. They were herded aboard a prison ship bound for Stettin. The British were manacled together while on board the ship.

The sixty-hour trip to Stettin was a nightmare. They were so closely crowded that they had difficulty turning their heads. Nearly everyone was seasick. There were no sanitary facilities. The men described that trip as one of the worst experiences of their tempestuous young lives.

On disembarking at Stettin the Americans were also manacled, so they had to abandon many of their precious belongings.

The last leg of the journey was even worse than the first. Before starting out for Kiefheid from Stettin, the guards, *Luftwaffe*, *Heer* and *Kriegsmarine* personnel, were given a fiery speech by their *Kommandant, Hauptmann* Pickard. The Hauptmann told his guards that those were Anglo-American *Terrorfliegers* and that this was their chance to get revenge for their bombed-out homes. He told them they could be as rough as they pleased as long as they did not kill anyone. The guards made full use of their authority. They beat the men with clubs, pounded them with rifle butts, and prodded them all over with bayonets. One man had over fifty bayonet wounds when he arrived. The guards also amused themselves and filled their pockets by cutting packs off the prisoners and allowing their Red Cross parcels of food, clothing and blankets to spill. What the guards didn't want or couldn't carry, they left for civilians to grab.

The men arrived on July 18th and were left standing all day without food or water. Those were the same men who the week before had made the nine-day boxcar journey here from Kiefheid.

This Monday, February 12th, is dreary, cold and damp. The morning rain turned into heavy snow in the afternoon. We had indoor *Appell*, which was a blessing. The men are in poor physical condition from having no decent food recently. Almost everyone has a cold. We are running out of coal. Even before, our coal issue was so inadequate as to be almost funny.

Food confiscated from new arrivals will be added to the 1,000 parcels on the train. After setting aside two parcels per man for the British in case they are moved out, an issue of roughly a fifth of a parcel per man will be made. Both Eilers and Eidmann feel the British will not be moved.

We connected up our loudspeaker to try to hear the *OKW* communique, but were not successful. We are anxious to get the news so as to dispel the many wild rumors that spring up in the absence of hard news.

I am running out of writing paper and there is no more available. That, however, is the least of our many shortages. We don't see how the mess we are in can last much longer.

13 February 45, Tuesday. The weather has turned much warmer. At least one does not shiver all day. It is really a Godsend in view of

our coal shortage. There is no coal left in the barracks and today the kitchens ran out of coal too. However, a load came in today just in time to keep the kitchen fires from going out completely. We've been assured of enough coal for the kitchens only for the next ten days. After that, we don't know. Already the barracks are without washing facilities. That probably accounts for the many cases of dysentery in the camp. Dirty bodies also encourage proliferation of the fleas and lice left here by our Italian friends before us.

German orders prohibit leaving the barracks for any reason after eleven p.m. The men with dysentery are going to have to use cans after that time and during air raid alerts when we are also confined to barracks. The alerts occur daily, although we haven't had an actual raid so far.

The Germans have ordered us to segregate the British into their own barracks. They have turned down our request to expand into Areas Three and Four and said that the immediate area will have to accommodate 7,000 prisoners. We already have close to 5,000 in an area no larger than West Camp at Sagan, which was considered overcrowded with 2,300. Hundreds are already sleeping on floors and tables. They have at least one consolation: they're less subject to attacks from bedbugs, fleas and lice.

We knew our plight would probably get worse before getting better, but we certainly hope it doesn't get much worse than it is now.

There is one bright spot in this dark day: a Red Cross parcel issue of one-fourth parcel per man raised kriegie morale considerably. But that completely exhausted our supply. We don't know when to expect more.

14 February 45, Wednesday. We have been on air raid alert almost continuously over the past twenty-four hours. Flak artillery thundered for hours last night and few of us could sleep through it. We heard that only five bombs were dropped on Nurnberg, but they must have been big ones! They jarred our buildings and rattled the windows. Although we have a few small shelters we are not permitted to use them. We are ordered to stay in the barracks during all alerts. The shelters wouldn't hold a tenth of us anyway. Padre McVeigh was caught here at our headquarters last night and was obliged to sleep on the floor with only one blanket.

This afternoon two groups of B-24's passed to the north of us, headed from east to west. They lumbered along slowly, well within our view, gleaming brilliantly in the sun. Tonight we are still on alert.

15 February 45, Thursday. We had quite a raid last night. There

was flak, searchlights, flares and quite a few bombs dropped.

We are completely out of coal now. Tomorrow, if none comes in we'll have no hot water. Eidmann says Germany must reach a decision in the next fourteen days.

Our rations are very sparse: barley for breakfast, potatoes for lunch, potato stew for dinner. We have asked two neighboring camps for cigarettes and books. We have few cigarettes and no books. Our clothes are almost worn out; we darn and patch. We have learned to turn socks upside down so that the worn-out heel is over the arch. We ravel thread from our blankets for darning. There is an acute shortage of soap, and the water is quite hard, so clothes are just as dirty-looking after washing as before. But at least they smell better.

So far this evening we are not alerted, but we expect to be any time now.

17 February 45, Saturday. We had our first inspection here today. Couldn't expect much, but it was surprising how the guys had gone out of their way to tidy the place up as much as possible with nothing to work with. They scrubbed the tables with plain sand, and everyone had a fresh shave. Many need haircuts, but there are only three or four sets of clippers and shears in the whole camp.

Yesterday and today we had only about two hours on alert, a welcome change. No bombs were dropped here, but we heard bombing and flak in the southwest. We were on blackout last night.

Today 270 officers and enlisted men came in and were put into Areas Three and Four with the ground personnel there. We have no contact with them and don't know yet whether they will be assigned to us or not.

Our two ex-German-American "friends" of the *Heer* who took care of us at Spremberg came in today. They brought enough letter forms for three-fifths of one per man. They are working directly for *OKW* in Berlin and seem to be contacting all American camps in Germany. They act in a sort of "special services" capacity and appear to have the job of propagandizing us against the Russians. They say they are trying to get recreational facilities for us, but we don't expect much from them.

We heard today that Sagan was taken by the Russians. We left there three weeks ago tonight.

22 February 45, Thursday. The past two days have been exciting, to say the least. There were two heavy daylight raids on the city of Nurnberg. They were both conducted through cloud cover; on Tuesday, through about seven-tenths, and on Wednesday, through

ten-tenths. Each raid seemed to employ two air divisions of about 300 planes per division.

On Tuesday we could almost see the whole show. We watched group after group of forts drone almost overhead on their bomb runs. They would drop marker flares, then a row of smoke geysers would appear in the city. In about twelve seconds the thundering would reach us here.

We saw a beautiful silver fort spinning vertically into the inferno. Another exploded and its pieces floated down through the clouds and smoke. Six planes were seen to fall. Several chutes drifted overhead, their occupants swinging like pendulums. One chutist pulled his ripcord too soon and was buoyed up by the explosions and fires; we watched him fully ten minutes during which he didn't seem to descend a foot.

Here in camp everyone was scared stiff. Windows rattled constantly and the ground trembled. Flak fragments screamed overhead and banged into roofs. Occasionally the terrifying swish of bombs falling much too close caused us to fall flat and wait breathlessly for the deafening crash that would follow.

A tremendous explosion, then what sounded like sporadic artillery fire, told us that an ammunition dump had been hit. The blast from that explosion, far greater than that from a bomb, fanned us here and broke some windows.

There was at least one case of hysteria. Not surprising, since we have no bomb shelters and the guards are waiting to shoot anyone who steps out of the barracks. Those facts, plus our poor physical condition, and the tendency toward claustrophobia from our crowded conditions, all contribute to make our plight when the bombs fall, hard to endure. To top it all off is the realization that we're in the target area and might be killed by our own people.

On the night of the first raid (Tuesday, 20 February), the fires and explosions were still going and a smoke pall hung over the ancient city of Nurnberg. Suddenly a gigantic geyser of flame rose hundreds of feet in the air. Our lights were off, of course, but the flame clearly illuminated the room we sat in. Some of us rushed to the windows but were thrown back by the concussion that blew the windows open and seemed to almost cave the wooden walls in. Thousands of smaller explosions followed. The ammunition was apparently still burning. About a half-hour later there was a repetition of all that. The fires and explosions continued throughout the night.

Yesterday (21 February) the sky was completely overcast. The visibility was so poor we couldn't tell where the bombs were falling except that the terrific swishing sounds told us they were much too close. Most of us spent the whole time as near to the floor as we could get.

Pamphlets and ration cards were dropped too. We haven't been able to find out yet what the pamphlets say. When the all-clear sounded, everyone was relieved to find himself still alive. It seemed incredible that no bombs had hit the camp. Kriegies spent the afternoon collecting flak fragments as souvenirs.

Last evening the fires and explosions were still raging. A smoke cloud covered forty-five degrees of the horizon and a black smoke cloud rose thousands of feet. The explosions continued all night. This morning Nurnberg continues to burn. We were on alert for three-and-a-half hours, but our bombers spared us this time and bombed some other place near here instead. We could plainly hear the bombs and flak, but none were near enough to worry about.

Last night we had no lights, as usual, but we are becoming accustomed to sitting about in the dark. We were alerted on and off all night long by "nuisance raiders" who dropped a few scattered bombs. The mission of those bombers seems to be to keep people in their bomb shelters all night.

Mr. Eric R. Berg of the Swedish YMCA visited on the 21st of February. He had visited the president of the International Red Cross four days earlier. He reported they know we are here, and promised to drop his YMCA duties and concentrate on the more important Red Cross duties of supplying us with food, medical supplies and clothing. He gave us a few items which had been destined for camps of other nationalities but which could not be delivered because of transportation difficulties. The most important of those was 600 kilograms of medicinal foods.

Colonel Alkire approached *Major* Simoleit with an offer to sign a parole if they would give us a two-weeks supply of food and march us to the Swiss border. There, we would be near our food supplies and away from the bombing. Simoleit didn't think much of the idea. Instead, he offered a counter-proposal: he offered to "lift the restrictions here" if the Colonel would sign a similar parole. That proposition was vetoed.

Colonel Alkire then asked Mr. Berg to find out if our government would approve a parole for us to be moved into Switzerland for the duration of the war. Mr. Berg promised to do all he could.

Senior Medical Officer here is Captain Rochet, a South African doctor who was captured while serving with the British Medical Corps. He says there have been three cases of pneumonia, twenty-five cases of flu, and about 3,000 of gastroenteritis since we arrived eighteen days ago. The diet here is insufficient to sustain life, he said, and unless it is supplemented soon we are liable to suffer permanent health effects. According to Rochet, the outlook is gloomy, and our only hope is for the war to end. As a doctor, he expects a disease epidemic to break out at any time because conditions here are ideal for the outbreak of disease.

26 February 45, Monday. The air offensive in this area has continued day and night. Although we hear the battles almost continuously, they have remained at a safe distance from us since the last two big daylight raids of the twentieth and twenty-first.

Our food situation has become steadily worse. The caloric count of our rations is well below that required to sustain life. In other words, we're starving. We think and talk of nothing but food. We go to bed and dream about food. All of us are losing weight. Every face has the gaunt look of hunger. Our buttocks have dwindled away to such an extent that it is painful to sit down. It is nearly impossible to keep our bodies warm, particularly our hands and feet. We haven't the strength to exercise to keep our circulation going. Previous feelings of apathy and lethargy are now interspersed with bitterness and hatred. We will be lucky indeed to live through this ordeal.

Our indefatigable "cloak-and-dagger" people have somehow managed to acquire another radio, so being able to listen to BBC cheers us somewhat.

Yesterday our guards brought in some cheese that had been bombed; a great deal of it had either been soaked in ammonia or was rotten. The German doctor, Hildebrandt, admitted it was not fit to eat. Nevertheless, we ate it. The dehydrated vegetables we get are full of bugs and worms. We figure the insects and worms will at least bring up our protein deficiency! There have been no issues of ersatz jam or honey (those delicacies made from coal tar) for two weeks.

They say it is always darkest before the dawn. We struck an all-time low this morning just before Bland came in with the glad tidings that two carloads of Red Cross parcels had arrived! In spite of our weakened condition a loud cheer went up. The food, said Bland, is in the town of Furth, about five kilometers northwest of here. It is being transported from there to our *Vorlager*. We estimated there should be 4,000 parcels if the cars are full. This would be about four-fifths parcel for each man. The news spread quickly, almost magically, as it always does in a kriegie camp. Morale has jumped 100 percent. Kriegie needs are simple and kriegie morale is easily elevated by good news.

On top of the good news about rations, the war news, too, is good. The long-awaited offensive has started on the west front, and the Russians are on the move in the east. Things are looking up!

27 February 45, Tuesday. Last night we went through one of the most harrowing experiences of our kriegie careers. An alert sounded shortly after dark. No one paid particular attention to it; we thought it was the usual RAF "spoof raid" like we get every night. But when the glow of a red chandelier flare showed through the clouds over Nurnberg, we knew we were in for a rough time.

It got scary after the first bomb went off. It was a 4,000 pound blockbuster. A red glow first illuminated everything clearly, then came the explosion and a shock wave that knocked us down. Bowls and windows broke, and walls were pushed in. We could hear the roar of the big Lancaster and Halifax bombers' engines directly over our heads. The first bombs fell in the city. Then they became wild. A few fell off to our right, then two fell behind us. We were bracketed! One bomb fell behind us in a pine forest. It exploded within a thousand feet from where we pressed our bodies to the ground. Had it not fallen in the trees, thereby losing some of its force, it would surely have flattened our barracks. When the concussion reached us the wall of our building bent inward like an archer's bow. Realizing the danger, we ignored the guards and dashed for the slit trenches.

Fortunately, the raid was of short duration, but I'm sure there was not a man in the camp, German or American, who was not shaken to his very foundation.

Today, Colonel Alkire gave orders to dig slit trenches enough to accommodate everyone. The Germans objected violently, in fact ordered us to stop digging. They were afraid we were going to use the trenches for an uprising against them in case our airmen should start dropping weapons for us to use. We flatly ignored their objections and continued digging furiously with tin cans and bare hands.

Tonight the *Kommandant* sent in a written order forbidding digging any more trenches, or using the ones we already have; but we have our trenches now, and if there's another raid like the one last night, it will take a lot of Germans to stop us from using them.

About 1,000 parcels came in today. Captain Oliver is issuing them out as fast as they come in. His crew must open each can in the presence of the *Abwehr*. They want to make sure the cans contain no contraband. They also want to ascertain that the cans are opened so that the food cannot be stored for escape purposes.

4 March 45, Sunday. This morning a guard was found dead. A *Gestapo* man came in to investigate. Although it was very hush-hush, we heard from a reliable source that it was a case of suicide.

Another example of Germany's cracking nerves is the story we heard about a guard becoming hysterical during one of the recent big daylight raids. Seeing that the bombers were going to drop their bombs through a solid overcast, he started screaming, "They can't see us, they can't see us!" The kriegies told him for crissake to shut up. He quieted down, but whimpered like a child for the duration of the raid.

During the past five days things have been rather quiet. We won the battle of the slit trenches. We can now use them day or night, but the Old Man had to sign a parole that they would not be used for escape, or plans for escape.

Although we have been on alert almost constantly and have seen a few American fighters, we have been spared the horrors of another raid. Yesterday no aircraft were reported over the area all afternoon; that was so unusual we wondered if the war was over.

An example of our air supremacy over Germany may be interpreted from one of *Unteroffizier* Fischer's cracks: "The reason we don't raise our arms high above our heads anymore in giving the Nazi salute is that, now, up there is allied territory."

The usual 8:15 p.m. "immediate danger" alarm sounded tonight; but it is now 9:30 p.m., and we are again relaxing after the "all clear."

The weather has turned cold. Heavy snow has fallen for forty-eight hours. Cold weather is a bitter enemy here.

Our rations have been cut again. The worst shortage is in sweets like jam, honey and sugar. We feel this lack intensely since our bodies seem to crave those heat-giving foods. Without sweets we don't have enough energy to generate body heat by exercising.

The coal supply is very meager and sporadic. The Germans brought in a few scrub trees for us to cut up and burn in the kitchen, but there is still no fuel for the barracks. However, the barracks are so crowded that accumulative body heat is almost sufficient, although ventilation must be ignored to maintain it. Here in the main kitchen, we spend most of our time crowded around the kitchen stove. There aren't enough of us to warm our room with body heat alone.

Our meals at present are as follows. Breakfast: one cup of very thin barley soup, ersatz coffee, and one slice of black bread. Lunch: one cup of thin vegetable soup made from the cheapest dehydrated vegetables, one slice of black bread with a flat square of margarine, and ersatz tea. A couple of times a week we have about one ounce of rotten cheese. Dinner: one cup of stew flavored with meat from our parcels, two baked potatoes, two slices of bread with margarine, ersatz tea, or coffee flavored with real tea, or coffee from our parcels. Sometimes there is a dessert made from barley with Red Cross chocolate, raisins or prunes added. Not a crumb is left over. The bowls are scraped so clean they scarcely need washing. The only meat and cheese we get is that which has been bombed and has absorbed ammonia from the destroyed cooling system. By soaking it in water for many hours it is rendered edible. There is such a small amount that it barely flavors the soup anyway.

I have had a severe cold for a month. The doctor said I had pleurisy but he couldn't do anything for me since one has to have pneumonia to be administered a sulfa drug. When the parcels came in I traded cigarettes for chocolate, then ate the chocolate, which gave me enough calories to have a fever all night; the next day I felt much better.

Our best hope is an early cessation of hostilities. *Major* Simoleit said that they can't help us; He said our government ought to swallow its bureaucracy and allow the trucks in Switzerland to bring us food.

He also said the telephone central office in Nurnberg was bombed, so he can't call anybody.

His attitude has certainly changed lately, after his recent flap with Colonel Alkire, when the Old Man cursed Simoleit to the fullest extent of his remarkable vocabulary. Along that line, the Old Man is more adept than any trooper, sailor or mule skinner. Simoleit became so intimidated he turned white and trembled all over. Since then, the swaggering Simoleit has been as meek as a lamb in the presence of Colonel Alkire.

5 March 45, Monday. There was a long alert this morning. We heard a formation of our fighters flying over, and heavy flak rattled our windows. The fighters were above the clouds so we could not see them.

Seventy-seven *Luftwaffe* personnel are leaving here today, apparently for the front. Among them are many whom we have known well for the past ten months. We hate to see Gambietz and Lehmann go. Grieser is also going. We understand that they will be replaced by very old *Volksturm* troops.

According to our best calculations there are sixty-nine former West Camp personnel missing since our move from Sagan. Three sergeants escaped and supposedly are still at large. Three were hospitalized at Priebus and sixty-three were hospitalized at Muscau. We can't find out how many have succumbed or what has become of those who have recovered and been released from the hospitals.

6 March 45, Tuesday. The war news continues to be good. From all appearances the war is practically over. We often speak of it in the past tense. As Colonel Kenneth "Sleeper" Martin puts it: "It's been over a long time, we just can't get it stopped." (Colonel Kenneth R. Martin (Sleeper) was the author's escape companion. See "Part V, Escape.")

The Germans are fast coming down off their high horses. Some of their officers are shabby and a little dirty. I imagine they are almost as hungry as we are. We are miserable, but whenever two or more Americans get together we manage to find something to laugh about. So we talk and laugh and try to hide our true feelings.

The little wash sheds between the buildings have all but disappeared. Kriegies take the wood and splinter it for fuel in their small home-made stoves. But today the Germans issued an ultimatum that if the practice did not stop, they would lock us in the barracks after dark, air raid or no air raid. So Colonel Alkire ordered us to support the German order so that we will not be denied use of our trenches.

7 March 45, Wednesday. There is a tense atmosphere in the camp. The allied armies are all along the central and lower Rhine. The food shortages are more acute than ever. We hear the German food issue is not likely to get better because the Germans themselves are starving. Foreign workers are carrying on trading activities with kriegies on the quiet. We manage this during shower parades or delousing parades. We trade our cigarettes for bread or salt (we are now completely out of salt except what we can obtain in this way).

I swapped one package of cigarettes to a Russian for about a one-fourth loaf of bread he was carrying unwrapped in his pocket. He handed it to me with his dirty hand. It was delicious.

The German guards are now quite open with their defeatism and criticism of their government. Today a *Heer* soldier, emaciated and pot-bellied from hunger, tried to take a GI blanket away from a kriegie at a delousing parade. The kriegie won.

Tension was heightened today by the visit of an *SS Colonel-General, Kommandant* of the Nurnberg defense area. Six-feet-five, saber-scarred, immaculate, fierce, he struck terror into the hearts of Germans and kriegies alike. He was *Obergrupenführer* Dr. Martin. He pulled a surprise inspection to investigate our slit trenches. He cursed and berated us, calling us "cowardly swine" for being "afraid of your own bombs." Surprisingly he did not deny us the use of our trenches.

Tonight the loudspeaker was moved into our sleeping quarters (Camp Headquarters). At 10 p.m. we could plainly hear the air raid announcements. A large force of RAF heavy bombers hit Leipsig and flew right over us on the way home. Three searchlights marked a triangle on the overcast clouds. Not a shot was fired. We were mystified by the whole procedure.

8 March 45, Thursday. At 6:30 a.m., we had the pleasure of listening to the *Rundfunk* in English.

The weather continues to be cold and snow falls constantly. The temperature is just above freezing so the snow melts and creates a sloppy condition that makes it impossible to keep our feet dry. We all have persistent coughs. Many have serious colds.

Our bread ration has been substituted by *Knickebrot.*

9 March 45, Friday. The Protecting Power is going to visit us next Tuesday. We hope they will be able to do something for us. Our German rations have been cut again. There is no sugar or salt, only enough potatoes for about a week, and the dehydrated vegetables have been cut. We are getting weaker and can't shake off our coughs and colds.

Eidmann looks pale and thin. He told me he has lost ten pounds. He said he and his men are on exactly the same rations as we prisoners.

He also said there is no hope for the German rations to get better, that they will get worse instead. He hopes we will be able to get Red Cross parcels. Perhaps the representative of the Protecting Power will be able to facilitate the delivery of the parcels.

The irony of the situation is that there are thousands of parcels in Switzerland. There are plenty of trucks there to haul them to us, but our government will not allow them to be used on the grounds that it is Germany's responsibility to transport food to us. In the meantime, we are starving.

12 March 45, Monday. The Germans have finally admitted that the allies have a bridgehead across the Rhine between Bonn and Koblenz. The Russians are fighting near Muscau and are attacking on both sides of Kustrin, also at Stettin Bay.

We are still hungry and continue to lose weight. Faces are more drawn than ever. No one has any energy. Starvation is unpleasant, but seems to be accompanied by a contentedly weary feeling.

We are still without sugar and salt. Eilers said yesterday two carloads of parcels are on the way. Typically vague, he says that he has no idea when they will arrive. We have had one parcel per man over the past six-week period. Today *Major* Kirscher (German *Abwehr*) told Captain Oliver that he has received a telegram from Switzerland indicating that many carloads of parcels are en route here. Those statements by Eilers and Kirscher are probably part of the build-up they give us just before the arrival of Protecting Power representative so as to prevent our complaining too much to them. The latter is due tomorrow. We have a voluminous list of violations to present. It would really be much easier to mention what we do have-nothing.

This is the first time most of us have ever had to do without soap. Clothes have long been getting slick, but now they are getting black too.

Our cook here in the senior officers mess, Sergeant Norman Krauser, a recently shot down ball turret gunner, does wonders with our measly rations. He made a delicious potato peel soup for lunch. He makes desserts by grating the crusts from loaves of bread and adding odds and ends. The breakfast barley is now so thin it's harder than ever to find a grain of barley in it. But somehow Krauser manages to make it retain its taste. Krauser was once a professional cook. We knock ourselves out thinking what he could do with some real food.

Food racketeering has become a real problem. We have three officers up for investigation into a deal that involved selling two pieces of cake for a $500 IOU (to be paid on returning home) Some hospital people are under investigation, too, for swapping "D bars" for watches, rings and other valuable items. These are the people who manage to stay fat while people around them starve.

How they manage to do this I don't know, but it must have to do with taking the food from patients too sick to eat. The thing that most disgusts and infuriates us is that Germans have lately been seen eating Spam and other American food, and smoking American cigarettes.

The main allied prisoner hospital near here received 3,000 parcels. They are mad at us because they say they asked us for ten parcels to save the lives of some amputation cases, and that we refused.

We never got their request, and besides, we didn't have the parcels anyway. Now they don't want to share with us any of theirs. That is OK with us because at the rate we're starving here we'll all be over there soon.

Twelve senior officers have returned from a parole walk. Some of us didn't go because we are too weak. They only walked about two miles. They went to a suburban tavern and had a liter of beer and a little potato salad. They were guarded by Eidmann and another *Feldwebel* who speaks American from having spent many years in New York. Eilers joined them later. The whole thing seems to have been for the purpose of pounding out a little propaganda. No sooner had our officers settled down than the three Germans launched forth on their studied discourse. The general theme of the lecture apparently was to make us feel admiration for the German people. The twelve were outside the fence about six hours. They reported a very pleasant trip on the whole, despite the propaganda.

13 March 45, Tuesday. The two representatives of the Protecting Power arrived this morning and stayed in conference with our staff all day. They were the same two who came to Sagan last year. This is roughly what they had to say in answer to our many complaints:

Your rations are the same as those of the German civilians and all other Germans except those who do heavy work. German officers have the same rations as you have. The German ration situation will not improve but will probably worsen. The chance of getting Red Cross supplies to you is almost negligible. The U.S. Army trucks in Switzerland have been released by our government to haul in supplies. The hold-up is finding drivers. German or American drivers are not permitted to do this work, and Swiss drivers are hard to recruit because your fighters are strafing everything that moves. Your people who are awaiting repatriation are still in Germany. They have not yet been accepted by your government. Meanwhile, they are in some Stalag where they are receiving the same treatment as German officers. Compared to other POW's in Germany, you are well off. There are 100,000 allied prisoners on the march all over Germany with no more supplies than you have here.

At least you do not have to march. One group has been strafed five times. One of your colleagues was killed by the strafers. No, we haven't the slightest idea when the war will be over. Yes, we will do everything in our power to get food in to you as soon as possible.

Two telegrams came in today. The gist of their contents was that five carloads of Red Cross supplies left Geneva on February 23, bound for Nurnberg. That shipment includes 5,000 food parcels, plus clothing, blankets and medical supplies. All that is in addition to the 4,800 parcels which we have already received the bill of lading for. This gives us four separate batches of food bound this way: the two mentioned above, the supply which is supposed to be bound this way from Lubeck, and the American trucks from Switzerland. At least we should have food from one of those sources soon, thanks to the good old USA, and the International Red Cross.

Our fighters seem to have a free run over Germany now. This afternoon we were sitting outside taking advantage of the first sunshine in weeks when two P-51's flew toward us. They were at about 200 feet, and from the direction of the nearby airport. We were startled at first, and some dived into the trenches, but the fighters wagged their wings and turned away sharply. They seemed to be shooting up the airport. Later, several fighters flew directly over the city. Not a shot was fired at them. The air raid sirens didn't even blow.

We have started a very interesting and entertaining series of lectures here in our Mess. Lieutenant Colonel Loock of the South African Air Forces has talked about South Africa. Colonel Stevenson (shot through both legs by a guard at Sagan) talked about the West Indies tonight. Tomorrow, Lieutenant Colonel Clark will give a talk on Central America. These lectures are excellent substitutes for reading, and much appreciated since we have no books. All of us find it difficult to amuse ourselves without books to read, since reading was the principle pastime for most us before our Sagan evacuation.

14 March 45, Wednesday. Things are looking up again! Today has been warm and sunny, but the high point of the day, if not the whole month, was the arrival of three big, beautiful GI trucks from Switzerland loaded with Red Cross food parcels! They were eight-wheel drive, five-ton trucks, painted solid white with enormous red crosses painted on top of the white tarpaulins. Each truck carried 1,200 parcels. Their time from Switzerland was three days. The drivers said they are going from here to Moosberg just out of Munich to get another load for us. Moosberg is a *Stalag* reputed to be well-stocked with parcels. The round-trip shouldn't take over three days. If all this is true we should certainly get a full parcel apiece this week. Morale is zooming!

Today, Second Lieutenants J. R. Wood and J. J. Dzikoski arrived after being released from a hospital in Breslau. They had been on the road forty-three days, during which they traveled 720 kilometers. For thirty-seven days they walked, but the two officers were allowed to ride the last six days on horse-drawn wagons. Wood had had an operation to rejoin his right jawbone, which had been separated by a piece of flak. On his last day in Breslau, when the Red Army was very close, Wood's German doctor got drunk and Wood had to unwire his jaw himself. That, he said, took half a day.

While en route, and still near the front lines, the two were thoroughly strafed by American fighters. The column they were traveling with was composed of many nationalities. The Russians in the group, wearing their long, green coats, apparently were mistaken for Germans. Everyone took cover in the woods and ditches except the Russians, who remained standing upright in the road and were soon mowed down by repeated passes from the fighters. An estimated sixty of them were killed. The following night the roof was blown off the house where they were sleeping by a near-miss from a bomb. Their German rations were so sparse that they were forced to trade everything in their possession to civilians for food.

Earlier this evening the usual air raid alert sounded. Our loudspeaker announced that two heavy formations were directly on course for Nurnberg. We listened breathlessly to the announcements as they progressed, hoping fervently that they would turn off in another direction. A major night raid on Nurnberg was the thing we had been dreading most, but also expecting as inevitable. The bombers continued on into the inner circle. We had the bugler blow the prearranged signal telling the men that bombing was imminent and for all to go to the trenches. In our barracks we gathered coats, pillows and blankets, and trudged out to our cold trenches. Loock stayed inside until the last minute to translate the announcements as they came. The night was clear and beautiful, and we knew we were in for a severe pasting.

Loock announced bombers over the city, then joined us in the trenches. The chandelier flares dropped down and the flak went up. We steadied ourselves and prayed. The first formation flew over. Nothing happened! We couldn't believe it! But the radio announced their departure.

We waited for the second group, thinking the first had dropped delayed action bombs, and that soon all hell would break loose. But the second group skirted around the western edge of the city, and after a while the all-clear sounded. Our spirits rose.

About an hour later we were alerted again. The bombers were returning! They had pulled a clever trick to get people out of their shelters, we thought. But again they skirted around the western edge. We got a reprieve for another night from one of our most frightening dangers - a maximum effort night raid.

15 March 45, Thursday. Today two American Ford trucks bearing Swedish flags arrived, loaded with musical instruments, toilet paper, writing paper and notebooks. The instruments were those salvaged from Sagan. Our wonderful technical library had been destroyed. Technical books would have been a godsend here, but none were included in the shipment.

16 March 45, Friday. When a situation gets so bad it seems it can't get any worse, then it can only get better. After today we hope we're on the upgrade. The three wonderful trucks arrived from Moosberg loaded with parcels. The Swiss drivers said we can expect a regular flow of parcels from now on; apparently Moosberg is being used as a depot for this area. Fifty Canadian and English kriegies were paroled as drivers for those trucks.

In addition to the trucks, two railroad cars of parcels arrived.

Although one of the cars had been seriously damaged by bombs, the other was intact. That gives us something over 7,000 parcels, or just over one full parcel for each man for this week. Many of us had enough to eat this evening for the first time since leaving Sagan.

The food didn't arrive a moment too soon. Everyone had lost weight markedly, except the sick quarters personnel.

This evening we had three-quarters of a bowl of dehydrated vegetables, topped off by a wonderful dessert made from cereal and "D bars" The icing was made by mixing powdered milk, margarine and sugar, and flavored with a lemonade powder. I imagined I could feel the weight flowing back onto my bones. I left the table feeling not stuffed, but moderately satisfied that I'd had almost enough to eat. Breakfast and lunch are still sad affairs though; here, we live for dinner.

This evening, as Colonel Martin was in the middle of a very interesting lecture about economics, the siren wailed a warning and the radio announced RAF heavies approaching from the southwest on an easterly course. We figured they were bound for Munich, until suddenly they changed their course to the northeast. Soon after that we stood terrified in our trenches and watched and heard the greatest, but a most terrifying show - a four-engine night raid.

Lovely pyrotechnics of red, green, amber, blue and white lit the sky and the ground. It was almost as bright as day. The deafening roar of bombs, guns, shells, and engines beat steadily on our eardrums, while explosions fanned our bodies. Three burning airplanes, distinguishable because their flames were larger than those of the flak explosions, brought back sickening memories of our own experiences on bombing raids. One plane had a runaway engine and we could hear it whine as it revved up beyond its mechanical endurance. The flame grew larger as the plane increased its speed in its death dive. Another bomber spurted flame from each wing before it went into a spin. We could follow its lazy rotations as it spun into the inferno that used to be Nurnberg. Rows of ugly, reddish, pinpoints of light among the bombers indicated the tracking of flak artillery. Large fragments from those shells screamed over our heads and showered down around us. Our only protection from them was pillows and chairs which we held over our heads, weak substitutes for steel helmets. A huge fire with accompanying smoke cloud appeared as the first bombs dropped, and the fire grew as the raid progressed.

In just under twenty minutes the raid was all over. We staggered hesitantly back to the barracks, our legs stiff from crouching in the cold trenches, and our spirits shaken by our predicament. But tonight, now that the raid is over and we're still alive, our spirits have soared again to heights accessible only with the impetus of full bellies.

Our newly organized provost marshal's department has acted on its first case. A lieutenant was convicted of stealing food and placed under guard for a week. He will be deprived of Red Cross food during that time and will face further, more serious punishment on returning home.

18 March, 45, Sunday. Last night we were subjected to our fifth bombing raid. A relatively small number of Mosquitoes (English fighter-bombers) dropped about 100 large bombs, a few of which fell uncomfortably close. There was the usual spectacular display of pyrotechnics. The raid was over in about fifteen minutes. The worst part of it was that our loudspeaker wasn't working. We were almost caught with our pants down. But when the three-burst flak signal went up we knew it was time to take cover.

Today we had a big food bash. For breakfast we had a large portion of mixed cereal which, in spite of a few weevils, was a pleasant filler after the watery barley we have been having every morning for a month. We called this treat cereal-with-cereal-in-it. For lunch there was meat loaf made from bread and liver paté, and some "green death" (dehydrated vegetables). Our dinner consisted of three real courses: soup, Spam, and vegetables, and a delicious dessert made of bread crumbs, prune seed kernels, and "D bars".

Later this evening we had fish spread on toast and tea as a bedtime snack. This evening snack is now a nightly institution, but the forthcoming Sunday bash is something we will have another week to look forward to.

This afternoon we heard another heavy raid in the west. Our loudspeaker is still not working, so we are at a loss for news except for sketchy reports from the Germans. If their reports are to be believed, our armies, and those of our allies, are making appreciable gains on both fronts.

Two truckloads of parcels arrived today, but they turned out to be for the French.

As previously mentioned, another of the constant threats here is the breakout of a disease epidemic such as typhus. Conditions and surroundings are ideal for such an epidemic since we are starved, unclean and vermin-ridden. Heretofore we have been consoled by the thought that the Germans, too, are concerned and would take preventive measures, knowing that an epidemic would quickly spread to the area surrounding the camp. Now, however, with their own medical supplies and facilities exhausted, we can only hope for the best.

19 March 45, Monday. Last night we thought we would get a letup from the steady bombing. But at 2:30 a.m., flak signals went up (without most of us hearing any other warning) and we hurried out of our warm beds into cold trenches. Though we dressed as quickly as possible, the marker flares were down and bombs were falling before we got out of the barracks. Apparently the bombs were 2,000 pound blockbusters dropped from Mosquitoes. The raid lasted fifteen minutes.

We went back to our beds, only to be rousted out again at 4 a.m. by another flak signal. No bombs dropped this time, but at 9:30 a.m. we heard bombing in the northwest, near enough to rattle our windows. The explosions were as steady as falling rain. They continued for half an hour. We sincerely hope no similar raid occurs here.

Today we have been on alert all day long. There have been two flak warnings. The only bombs that fell were four 500 pounders dropped from fighters. Many fighters have been cruising about, apparently at random, throughout the day.

Explosions continued intermittently all last night, apparently from delayed action bombs. A few explosions were much stronger than the others, indicating that explosive material had been hit.

The question in everyone's mind was, how have German civilians withstood these attacks so long? How can they bear them any longer? The answer is probably best summed up by these words from *Unteroffizier* Fischer:

"Germans who want to quit outnumber the others ten to one. You ask why we don't do something about it. You prisoners outnumber your guards ten to one. You don't like it here. Why don't you do something about it?"

Maybe Fischer has something there. Germany is a solid prison camp!

20 March 45, Tuesday. Last night we had the usual numerous alerts we're becoming uncomfortably accustomed to. The Germans evidently got their wires severely crossed on their alarm systems and security measures. We had no radio, and therefore could not tell exactly what was going on, but what we saw and heard was actually funny. Everyone seemed to be in a humorous mood at the same time, perhaps because of the combined effects of sufficient food, better weather, and good news. This example of the breaking up of traditional German efficiency hit us all just right and we derived a most cheerful evening from it. Here is more or less what happened, although it will be impossible to recapture the jovial mood:

The evening was beautiful, with bright stars, a young moon, and soft, balmy air. Some of us were sitting around the kitchen stove reading and talking. Others had retired, for it was after nine o'clock. The sirens announced aircraft en route to Nurnberg. Those who were still up made hurried preparations for either retiring or going to the trenches before the lights went out. But the lights went out almost immediately, and quiet cursing could be heard as men stumbled over chairs and tables.

A few went to the trenches. The others decided to wait for the flak signal. In a few minutes a single siren blew a long, steady note - the all-clear. We knew there was something wrong because we could hear the sound of engines overhead. Besides, they always blew a pre all-clear first. So we waited, not trusting the signal.

Then someone in the trenches remarked, "Funny, I've never seen the Milky Way in Germany before."

"All milk comes in powdered form in *Deutschland,*" replied Pearson.

Then the all-clear blew on many sirens and the lights came on immediately. We hurriedly closed the blackout shutters.

Those who had gone to the trenches returned and started preparing for bed, grateful that there was light to undress by. We had no sooner settled into our sacks than there was another *Voralarm*, soon followed by the *Flieger*, or general alarm. This time, there were more customers for the trenches, all cursing bitterly.

After a very short stay there, the pre-all-clear sounded again, followed by the all-clear. We disgustedly trooped back into the barracks. Pearson was in bed before he realized that he had forgotten to take off his shoes.

Once more we settled down. By now the wisecracks were beginning to fly over the stupidity of our situation. The perimeter lights and floodlights were on so we figured we could relax.

Suddenly there was a terrific explosion. Although it sounded like a blockbuster we were at a loss to explain why we had not been alerted and why all the lights were on with bombs falling.

Colonel Alkire was up immediately. "That one blew me right into my shoes," he said. And then a single, lonely siren again screamed out the general alarm. Still there was no sound of aircraft, flak or other warning, and the lights continued shining brightly. Ed Bland said, "Wolfgang probably figured those controllers are asleep - *Himmel*! There's a raid on, I must blow my siren!"

Colonel Stevenson added, "Yeah, Wolfgang says, to hell with this radar, I got ears!"

After awhile, another all-clear blew. Jack Jenkins said, "There's the all-clear; everyone take cover!" Whereupon we all decided to give up and go to sleep.

Today has been sunny, but cool and quiet. Our loudspeaker is back in operation and we are thankful that we can hear aircraft position reports and German news again.

Three-course dinners have been resumed as a daily function on the strength of a good food supply, thanks to the American trucks which are now operating regularly between here and Switzerland.

25 March 45, Sunday. With kriegies, there always seems to exist a state of feast or famine. At present, we're in the feast stage. After the famine of November, December, January and February, which became progressively worse until it could not have continued without some very serious consequences, the present series of good events seems too good to be true. All last week the weather was beautiful.

We peeled down many layers of clothing (I was wearing seven) and allowed the sun to bathe our emaciated bodies. We were dismayed to see how not only fat, but muscle too, had dwindled away from our frames. Many had lost forty pounds or more. The only ones who had escaped this forced dieting were the ones in on the sick quarters racket.

Several trucks arrived today from Moosberg and Switzerland. One shipment contained French parcels. Since they were addressed to us, we naturally started unloading them. A French officer came from a French POW camp nearby and demanded the parcels. He said he had 1,400 starving men. Colonel Alkire gave him all but 600 of the parcels, that many having been distributed already to our various barracks. Yesterday, when another shipment arrived, we paid him back, thereby avoiding another "serious international situation."

Today *Major* Kirscher (German *Abwehr*), who doesn't come in unless he has good news, gave us the glad tidings that there are twelve carloads of food in the railroad yards. This news is so welcome and so unexpected as to almost throw us into a panic. We knew some food supplies were on the way by railroad, but in view of transport conditions here as a result of constant allied bombing and strafing, we hardly expected to see them. And, too, when things are really bad, it's hard to realize they will ever be otherwise. Since good news here is accepted with skepticism, we figured the food would be bombed, strafed or stolen before we ever got it.

But Captain Oliver, with his very hard-working and efficient crew, has managed to get down to the yards and to unload some 35,000 British, American and Canadian food parcels. They are now safely (more or less) stored in a coal warehouse in our *Vorlager* here at Langwasser. If they are bombed now, we will be too, so it won't make any difference. Our present strength is something over 6,000, so we can now issue a full parcel a week to each man for the next five weeks. That amount of food will not be an ounce too much, since the already meager German rations have dropped off to practically nothing. At least we won't starve before the end of April. That is, if nothing happens to our parcels and if not too many new kriegies arrive.

On top of all this good news the war news is prima. Today the *OKW* announced that we have three more bridgeheads across the Rhine, making a total of six. Patton has driven across in lower Alsace and the English have started a major drive between Wesel and Rece with airborne troops dropping behind enemy lines in front of their advance.

All week the air raid sirens have been going crazy. Day and night fighters and fighter-bombers have swarmed over the entire country.

We see American aircraft frequently in the daytime and hear British ones every night. They are taking full advantage of the beautiful weather to keep Germany in a constant state of tension. The heavies haven't been near us lately, but we know they're still operating because we can hear their position reports broadcast by the *Rundfunk.*

The front is just over 100 miles from us now in the Manheim area. We can hear and feel the constant rumble of artillery. We pay very little attention to air raid alerts now. Only when heavy formations are reported headed this way do we observe the rules. Otherwise, the Germans would have to keep *Appell* guards in the camp twenty-four hours a day and we would be in the trenches almost that long.

Morale is probably higher now than its ever been before, even at Sagan. At least here we don't have the maddening monotony we had there.

27 March 45, Tuesday. The war news is out of this world! Patton has broken through south of Frankfort and is now well east of Ashaffenburg, less than eighty miles from here. The Fifteenth Army has broken out of the Remagen Bridgehead and is headed southeast, obviously to contact with Patton. There is terrific fighting on the lower Rhine with considerable progress being made there.

We are trying hard to believe we're witnessing the final phases of the war. How the war's end will affect us is causing considerable concern, but for the average kriegie with a belly full of food and the war's end in sight, all is well.

The compound staff is again feverishly making plans for evacuation, either to the east or to the west. Of course we hope to go west, but must be prepared for the worst. We hope never to have another experience like our last move. The problem is a little different now. We're about 7,000 in the seven camps, but the camps, especially Five, Six and Seven, are much more closely related than was the case at Sagan. The commanders of these three camps are Colonel Jenkins, Camp Five; Colonel Martin, Camp Six; and Colonel Arnold, Camp Seven.

Since we can now communicate between camps I have found a man from my brother Don's group in Italy. This officer actually saw Don's plane disappear over the Adriatic. Don was leading his group on his thirtieth mission. The officer told me that pilots flying in Don's formation that day figured Don was having autopilot trouble because his wing dipped several times at a faster rate than was normal with manual control. Finally, the wing dipped so far down that the aircraft suddenly dropped sharply into the clouds.

The pilots who witnessed the sudden disappearance assumed that Don's plane had gone out of control and had spun all the way down and crashed into the Adriatic. One aircraft from the formation was sent down to search. That pilot reported that the clouds were solid all the way down, almost to the sea, and that he could see no sign of wreckage on the surface. The witnesses theorized the plane probably disintegrated on impact with the water and disappeared without leaving a trace. (Don and his crew, eleven men in all, were officially declared dead one year later.)

This week we were issued half a British parcel and one American parcel, and an extra issue of bulk Argentine food. This is by far the biggest food issue we have had. This issue has a three-fold purpose: to make up for the deficiency of German rations, to give personnel an excess of food for the purpose of making iron rations for an emergency, and to build up personnel physically for the eventuality of another forced march.

The iron ration for our mess was made last night. We used oatmeal, margarine, chocolate, sugar and cracker crumbs. It is much too rich to be used as anything except an emergency ration, but as such, will urge a man further when he is nearing complete exhaustion. We have about one pound each, wrapped in wax paper and sealed on a hot stove. We hope to make another batch of it soon so we will have two portions each.

Everyone is eating well now. The effect is amazing. The men are snapping out of their lethargy and showing spirit. Faces are filling out, and the gaunt expressions disappearing. Some are overdoing it, with the resulting nausea and vomiting. The policy in many combines is to starve all day and bash at night. This practice is obviously detrimental and is being discouraged.

One of the most noticeable changes after the starvation period is the different topics of conversation. While starving, we talked only of food—not only of eating food, but of cooking, canning, preserving, growing, buying, selling and manufacturing it. High-ranking officers made serious plans along those lines. Almost everyone compiled long lists of good eating places all over the USA. Those who had never been hungry before didn't realize, of course, that this was only a passing fancy and would, in nearly all cases, soon be forgotten after a few weeks with a full stomach.

Last night we had a snack of two cups of cocoa and a jelly cracker sandwich. This morning we had the most delicious breakfast of our kriegie careers, and perhaps the most appreciated and enjoyed of our lives. We had oatmeal, bacon and powdered eggs, two slices of bread with plenty of margarine and jam, and two cups of cocoa. Some had difficulty negotiating that amount with a shrunken stomach. Morale is soaring!

Later Tuesday: It looks as though things are going to start happening here at any minute. Eidmann, representing the *Kommandant*, has just conferred with Colonel Alkire. He says they have been alerted to move us southward. The *Kommandant* wants to know if we will cooperate in a move out of this area. The Colonel's answer was that he will do anything and everything necessary to get all kriegies home safely.

What the final outcome will be, no one knows, but it will be to our advantage to get out of the city area at least, in case the Germans decide to make a fortress of Nurnberg.

Good rumors have it that Patton is in Wurzburg, about fifty miles west of here. The *Kommandant* expects tank spearheads here this afternoon or tomorrow. The atmosphere is tense and expectant. Everyone has been ordered to be ready to leave at any time. We are making packs and bashing food. Today for lunch we had Spam, vegetables, two brews, margarine, bread, peanut butter, and a very rich dessert. One major got sick.

29 March 45, Thursday. We were ready to move all day yesterday and today, but nothing happened. In tonight's communique the Germans announced having cut off Patton's spearhead which was threatening Wurzburg. Eidmann says we won't move until our armies get east of there. That probably accounts for the delay in moving, which suits us fine. We figure the longer we stay, the better our chances of being liberated here. Meanwhile the weather has become lousy, with low ceilings and drizzling rain.

The five repatriated fellows have returned. There was some tie-up which prevented their going home. I think our own government refused to accept them. They had a very pleasant stay in *Stalag IIIA*, however. The place is at Luckenwalde, fifty miles out of Berlin. They were permitted to go out on parole all day and were given full Red Cross parcels weekly. It was quite a letdown for them to be returned here. With them are Colonel Kennedy, G/C MacDonald, and a Lieutenant Brown, who were on the same deal from other camps. They reported that General Vanaman and two other Senior Allied Officers had been living in the *Truppenlager* at Luckenwalde, but were now in Berlin. We expect them here any day.

The weather continues to be bad, but the news is good, particularly that from the lower Rhine. Our armies are approaching Munster and are fifty-five kilometers east of Dortmund. The situation appears to be temporarily static.

This evening the weather cleared and is now CAVU (ceiling and visibility unlimited) with a full moon. The atmosphere is tense again. Everyone expects to move tonight.

3 April 45, Wednesday. We are finally leaving Nurnberg! Tomorrow we'll start walking the 100 miles to *Stalag VIIA* at Moosberg.

Part V

Escape

During those final, unbelievably confusing days at Nurnberg the decision to escape or not was truly maddening: On the "Not" side was official notification from our government that escape attempts were no longer our obligation. This resulted from the well publicized failure of the mass attempt at Sagan in early 1944. The other strong deterrent was that German indications, both visual and verbal, were that any kind of organized war couldn't possibly continue.

To the contrary, however, two rumors, later verified, were extremely demoralizing. (1) Hitler had sentenced all Air Force prisoners to death for bombing Germany (2) Germany was to move us to a redoubt area in the Bavarian Alps, there to bargain us as hostages.

Martin and I resolved to risk dying from results of our own positive initiatives rather than to continue trying to survive as senior officers under such unpredictable odds.

I had planned to escape with Herb Mosebach, but those carefully made plans came to an abrupt end when Herb informed me one day that he had decided to escape instead with Ulich, an English-speaking German whom we had Americanized. Mosebach and Ulich were caught by the *Gestapo* shortly after their escape; Mosebach was brutally beaten and Ulich was shot.

I had not known Martin except by hearsay prior to our arrival at Nurnberg. He had been in Center Camp while I was in West. Briefly, here is his story:

Colonel K. R. Martin of Kansas City had commanded the first P-51(Mustang fighter) group to enter combat. While on a fighter sweep one day, he engaged in a head-on attack with a

German ME-109. Each pilot was determined not to "break," but to force his opponent to give way. With incredible momentum they collided. Miraculously both pilots survived. Martin regained consciousness on the ground with no knowledge of how he had survived the crash or of parachuting. His only awareness was intense pain and blindness. A German doctor arrived on the scene and inspected Martin's injuries. A deep wound in his scalp was bleeding profusely. This was the cause of Ken's temporary blindness. In addition, Martin's left arm, hand, leg, and right foot were broken, and his back was painfully sprained.

The doctor gave him a shot of morphine and drove him to a local hospital. While at the hospital Ken was introduced to the German pilot who had also miraculously survived their head-on collision. Martin was kept at the local hospital for a few days, where he received minimum medical attention and very little food.

His next six weeks were spent at *Dulag Luft*, in solitary confinement, on a bread and water diet. He received almost no medical attention during that time, and was interrogated ruthlessly and constantly during his six weeks in solitary. When he was considered sufficiently well, he was taken to *Stalag Luft III*.

When I met him at Nurnberg he wore a brace on one leg, but appeared to be in good condition otherwise.

Because of his injuries he had not been forced to walk from Sagan. He therefore had managed to bring along considerable food and contraband that he had been hoarding for a year.

During our daily walks around the compound Martin and I made our plans. We adopted the attitude that we had rather be dead than to remain in prison any longer. Since no American had successfully escaped from a German *Stalag* up till then, that fatalistic attitude enabled us to proceed with our plans without worrying over the tremendous odds against us.

We made innumerable laps around the perimeter, both to toughen our feet and to talk over our plans. Also, those laps provided the only way to ensure the privacy of our conversations.

We agreed on the following basic plan:

(1) We would leave the marching column under cover of darkness during the forthcoming evacuation of Nurnberg, at

the first reasonable opportunity. We decided on an early escape so as to have maximum energy for our first dash.

(2) We would walk westward until we felt safe from recapture, and then find a safe hiding place to hole up in while we waited for the American lines to pass by.

(3) We would travel only during darkness, and hide and rest in the woods during daylight.

(4) We would contact no other living person until we were behind American lines.

(5) If we were challenged in German, I would answer in German that we were Spanish civilian workers returning from work in the woods. If we were challenged in English, Martin would make whatever answer the occasion demanded.

With those points as our outline we tried to foresee and forestall every conceivable obstacle that might prove to be a stumbling block when our big moment finally came.

Colonel Kenneth Martin, the author's escape companion.

Fifty years later, Martin would write: "Paul, I still remember you staying with me at the river crossing and on the autobon crossing where I went down. I probably wouldn't have made them without your help."

In the ensuing weeks various clandestine activities kept us busy. Unfortunately, the tiny compass I had brought into Sagan hidden in my ear was useless because I had accidentally washed it in my pants pocket, and the strong GI soap had melted the

A portion of the Hand Drawn Escape Map used by Burton and Martin shown near actual size.

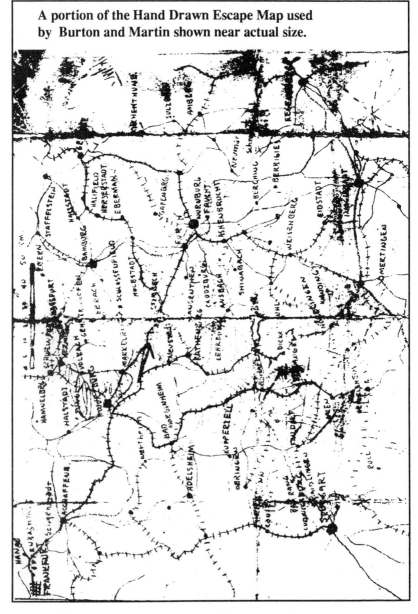

bowl. But I made an exciting discovery. The steel knife sharpener in the kitchen was magnetized from having been stroked by knives. So by rubbing Red Cross needles against it I could make dozens of compasses! I made three of them by simply stroking the needles on the steel knife sharpener until they became magnetized, and then mounting them on pivots made from bent safety pins and tiny pieces of leather from my shoes. After testing my kitchen-made compasses I dismounted them, concealed the mounts in match boxes, and pushed the needles into the cloth of my trousers.

We soaked our GI clothing in coffee to give them an inconspiciously dirty color, and we partially concealed our rank insignias by pinning them as far inside our coats as we could without hiding them completely.

We made packs by tearing German bed sheets into strips and using them as straps to lace through our GI barracks bags and thence over our shoulders.

The escape kits many of us had when we were shot down had contained escape maps. Fortunately one such escape map was available. We had a copy made of it, and using the latest German communiques, we drew in the battle lines. Martin also managed to secure a copy from a detailed map of the Nurnberg area.

Our most important item of equipment by far proved to be Martin's escape kit compass. It was smaller than a dime and had luminous dots on the needle, two dots for north and one for south. How he'd managed to hold on to this high-priority contraband, I still don't know. He mounted the compass on a small piece of wood that fit snugly in his watch pocket, then tied the wooden mount to his belt loop with a leather thong.

Our maps and compasses, though crude and inadequate in many ways, gave us confidence that we could go where we wanted to go once we'd broken free of our captors.

When all our arrangements were complete and our plans clear, I reported to Colonel Alkire. "Sir," I said, "I request to not be given a command for the march for I plan to escape."

The Colonel seemed un-surprised; during those days no one was much surprised by anything.

"You know what I think?" he finally barked. "I think you're a God-damned fool!" He stomped away.

Later that day, he put his hand on my shoulder and addressed me by my first name for the first time.

"Good luck, Paul," he said. "I hope you make it. When you make contact tell them the kind of signal we're carrying so the dam fools won't strafe us."

I was delighted to hear him say <u>when</u> you make contact, not <u>if</u>.

Martin and I were fairly well stocked with food, clothing and equipment. Our clothing was good and warm. We carried three blankets each, two German and one American. We considered discarding some items, but decided to take them along, realizing that we could always discard things but we could never go back for them. The most impractical items we took along were books; we carried two, "Good Night, Sweet Prince" and a Spanish grammar. That may seem odd, but I think it typified our tremendous thirst for reading material at Nurnberg.

On Wednesday, April 3, 1945, we formed up for the long march to Moosberg. Martin and I left the group we had been ordered to march with. Carrying our heavy packs, we made our way into the column of another group we knew was to billet in a different place from our own group that night.

Before slipping in with the other group we hid our rank insignia, pulled our knit caps way down and turned our coat collars up. We had two goals: we wanted to make ourselves supernumerary to the group we were marching with. That way we would not be missed when a count was taken after we left. When we were missed from our original group, we hoped to be too far away for it to matter. Our second aim was to be as inconspicuous as possible; we both were well-known to the German staff due to our ranks and duties on the American staff.

At 10 a.m. we departed. As we marched through the gates at Nurnberg my heart pounded with exhilaration at finally being outside the barbed wire compound. Now, only armed guards stood between us and open country. At last we had a chance to put our plans into execution.

Luckily the weather was cool. We were able to carry our heavy packs without having to discard any of our clothing, most of which we were wearing. However, before we'd gone very far I realized that I wasn't nearly as strong as I had been on our march from Sagan. The stressful Sagan march, followed by starvation and illness at Nurnberg, plus the fact that I had been too weak there to keep my muscles and feet tough, all had taken their toll on my stamina. I knew immediately that I would have to lighten my pack. I discarded a blanket before we had gone a mile.

Our destination that first night was the town of Neumarkt, twenty-three kilometers south, and at right angles to the direction Ken and I had to go to reach American lines. We knew we had to leave the column as soon as possible or increasingly lengthen the distance between us and our destination.

Our decision was strengthened by the fact that I had developed a blister that covered the entire ball of my right foot. Fluid from the blister was seeping around my toes. I feared that if it became swollen or infected I would not be able to make the crucial first long dash away from the column.

We stopped in a village for lunch at noon. During our stops, the guards spaced themselves at intervals well out from our flanks. That allowed us a little room to mill around and fetch water for our brews, and carry on the inevitable trading with civilians. I was busily engaged in trying to negotiate a trade for some bread or potatoes to supplement our food supplies of mostly concentrates when an air raid alarm sounded. I looked up and saw a flight of P-47's at about 3,000 feet. That brought an abrupt end to our trading efforts. The Germans became very excited. Screaming *"Tiefflieger! Tiefflieger!"* they disappeared as if by magic.

As I watched the fighters, I pictured eager young pilots, their necks craned searching for targets. By this time strafing targets were no longer easy to find, due to our overwhelming air superiority over the Germans. I imagined seeing their eyes bugging out eagerly as they spotted our column, not knowing, of course, that they were strafing Americans. They peeled off and came down on the rear of our column with each of their six fifty-caliber guns spouting death. They attacked the NCO section of our column; we heard later that six American sergeants were killed.

That evening, as we approached Neumarkt, the guards were tired and had become a little lax. Martin and I noticed there was considerable confusion at the rear of the column, as many stragglers gave the tired guards plenty of trouble. We decided to straggle back toward the rear too to take advantage of the situation.

The sun was setting as our snake-like column wound itself around a long, sloping curve. At the crest of the rise a dense-looking forest lined each side of the road. We were just ahead of the blue-uniformed RAF group which was bringing up our compound rear. A hundred yards ahead of us was the preceding American group. Martin and I looked all around for guards. Apparently none was in sight.

Was this our chance? My heart seemed to practically jump from my chest, and my palms dripped perspiration.

Suddenly, as if by mental telepathy, we sprinted off the road and into the woods together. Martin and I became separated as soon as we entered the woods. I darted past a shallow ditch which I momentarily considered as a hiding place, then discarded the idea and put on more speed.

My insides dropped as I suddenly sprang into an opening, and parked there was a German vehicle surrounded by guards. I heard a shot behind me. At the same instant I saw that I was confronted by a steep incline that would make me a perfect target. Those observations, coupled with sickening feelings of being trapped and defeated, all took place instantaneously.

I instinctively fell flat on the ground when the shot was fired, causing the guard to believe he had shot me. That he missed must have been due to the fact that he was running when he fired the shot.

I lay still as he came toward me. I could understand now what had happened. In all our careful planning, Martin and I had overlooked one very important point: the blue uniforms of the RAF were the same color as those of the *Luftwaffe* guards. We had made our break in plain view of guards who had become mixed, probably intentionally, with the RAF group, so that they were indistinguishable in the dusk. My running out into the clearing was just plain bad luck. However, the presence of guards in that clearing was not coincidence. It simply meant that we had underestimated our enemy, a serious mistake in any undertaking.

Those thoughts ran quickly through my mind. I had narrowly escaped death and was still in imminent danger, but that didn't occur to me just then. I was just very disgusted that our escape had failed.

I wondered how Martin had fared. I was almost certain that

he, too, had been recaptured, since he could not run as fast as I.

I got to my feet, panting loudly. When the guard saw I wasn't hurt he became furious, cursing me to the full extent of the German language. For some crazy reason I told him I had tried to escape because my feet were too sore to walk anymore.

That remark made him even more angry.

He replied, adding the appropriate curses, that If I couldn't walk, I could certainly run. Then he started beating me with the butt of his rifle. Oddly, I hardly felt the blows, perhaps because I was so glad he hadn't killed me.

In a little while we came on Martin, lying where he had been caught, only a few yards off the road. I was glad to see he hadn't been hurt. We both were hustled back into the column, still panting and sweating.

We dreaded punishment less, I think, than the close surveillance we knew would hamper our future escape attempts. Thus, we were delighted to notice that the guard who had recaptured us was not keeping a close watch on us individually. However, my confidence was badly shaken, and I had expended most of my energy. I reflected that the failed escape was probably all for the best; when we made another attempt we would know better than to go off half cocked.

As though to add insult to injury, word passed up and down the column about our abortive escape attempt. We half-saw, half-imagined derogatory looks on the faces of all who knew us. I reached a new low in mental depression as we trudged along. I wasn't sure I would ever try to make another break. Good old Ken brought me slowly back to my senses with his confidence and his reasonable encouragement. That was only one of many occasions to come when I would realize what superior character, intellect and determination resided in my friend's broken body.

When darkness came we were still on the road. The guards hustled us along, hoping to get us locked up somewhere before the situation got out of their hands.

Soon after dark we came to a small village. We were divided into groups. My group was herded up a narrow, ascending street with a farmyard at the top. It became apparent that we were to be locked in the barn for the night. The canyon-like street, with the enclosed farmyard at its end, formed an ideal funnel through which we could be poured into our prison without undue risk of having some of us leak out into the darkness.

This farmyard seemed to follow the familiar pattern of others we had observed on our previous march. Perhaps in a holdover from medieval times, German farmers grouped themselves together in tiny villages instead of living on their farms. Their livestock and tools, as well as they themselves, stayed inside a compact, carefully guarded area immediately adjoining their houses. This square area, formed by outbuildings jammed compactly together created a fortress- like enclosure.

When we were all inside the farmyard we stopped. At the front of our column the guards squeezed our men into the small barn. That caused the rear of the column, where Ken and I were, to stop moving. The blind street through which we had entered the farmyard was the only opening into the enclosed area. Ken and I stood near the opening, which was adjacent to the back door of the farm dwelling.

We waited for the column to move into the barn. We imagined the Germans were making a careful check of their charges. We at the rear were forced to remain stationary for a considerable length of time. During that time Ken and I surveyed the situation as best we could in the darkness, and continuously consulted with each other as to our chances of making another break. After a while we sat down. Though we hadn't left the column, a guard ordered us to get up. We remained sitting. We were relieved when he moved on into the black night, probably too tired himself to be very conscientious. The guards, too, had been subsisting on starvation rations at Nurnberg, and they, too, had walked all day with us, with the added responsibility of having to guard us. I imagined most of them were thinking of the glass of schnapps they would have at the local tavern as soon as they had us safely locked up in the barn.

After a few minutes, when no one else made an attempt to get us to our feet, we started inching away from the column, still in a sitting position. In about an hour we managed to squirm six feet away and into the dark shadow of a chicken house. There we tried to blend in with piles of rubbish heaped into the corner formed by the chicken house and a high fence.

We remained absolutely still then, for a very long time. Confident that we were not detected, we proceeded to camouflage ourselves thoroughly. First we covered ourselves with a dark blue German blanket. With this perfect night-camouflage we felt confident that we could not be distinguished from the pile of rubbish on which we were lying. Next we smeared handfuls of earth into our hands, then rubbed the dark earth into our white bed-sheet straps, and into any light-colored places we could find on each other.

Our position was six-feet away from a line extending from the back door of the farmhouse to the barn entrance. After the column moved away from us this line became a path along which guards continually scurried back and forth between the house and barn. They were escorting prisoners carrying hot water into the barn for the other prisoners, who were preparing their evening meals. They constantly passed almost within reach of us as we hugged ourselves to our pile of rubbish, hearts pounding wildly. Once a guard, accompanied by a female member of the household, stopped within three feet of us. The guard was trying to force his affections upon the woman. Although they were talking in whispers we could hear every word of the brief but amorous conversation. We thanked God for the triumph of virtue as the woman repulsed the guard's advances and they moved away.

After what seemed like many hours had passed, activity around us quieted so we felt it was safe to start planning our next move. Martin was in favor of rising and walking boldly down the street from whence we had entered. I strongly opposed that. My once boundless confidence was gone.

I simply couldn't face the prospect of walking down the street and risking another experience like that of a few hours before. I wanted to try to get through, or over, the fence behind us and go away from, instead of toward our captors.

We argued these two possibilities for a long time, in whispers, of course. Each of us was convinced his own plan was better, and neither of us was willing to yield.

Finally, we realized we would have to act soon if we ever expected to put any distance between us and our captors before dawn, so we each made a proposal. Mine was that I would investigate the chances of getting through the fence, and unless I found a stronger selling point I agreed to accept Martin's alternative.

I squirmed cautiously along the fence, feeling each picket and trying its strength. The fence was constructed of large, round stakes driven deeply into the ground at about three-inch intervals. I found one loose stake. I pulled on it as hard as I dared, but found it unyielding. Clearly we couldn't get through the fence, so I stood up to see if we might get over it. The fence was much higher than I had imagined. Try as I might, I couldn't find a foothold on it. Finally I conceded to Martin that my fence plan was out. By that time it was about two a.m. and all was quiet. We summoned our courage, then rose, and without hesitation or a sideward glance, we strode down the quiet street. It seemed as if our footsteps thundered throughout the village, and our hearts pounded as though trying to drown the noise of our footsteps. I never had a stronger urge to run in my life. It took every ounce of my willpower to maintain a slow, casual gait. It seemed we would never arrive at the end of that little canyon.

Finally we came out onto the main highway where we had entered the town. When we started southward on it we found our troubles were far from over.There was a lot of traffic on the highway, so we would fall flat into the muddy ditch each time a vehicle passed by. We hurried to the outer edge of town and got off the highway as soon as we could without running into someone's grounds or buildings.

When we took a side road we thought would bring us back around to the northwest edge of town we ran into more trouble. We saw we were headed back into a thickly settled part of the town. Occasionally in the darkness we would walk into a fence. The infernal dogs would hear us and start barking. We wondered if we would ever work our way out of that entanglement of civilization.

Eventually we reached a large, open pasture with a few comforting trees. We fell exhausted beneath one. We lay there quietly for awhile, feeling relaxed for the first time since leaving Nurnberg.

But in a few minutes it started raining and we were soon soaked to the skin. Nevertheless we were glad to see dark clouds covering the stars and tightening our cloak of darkness. The rain also decreased visibility and thus lessened the possibility of our silhouettes being observed by strollers. We didn't particularly mind getting wet.

Ken took out his tiny compass and we set out on a westerly course, steering slightly south of west in order to give the heavily-defended area of Nurnberg a wide berth. We felt thankful for the little compass with its shining luminous dots. My homemade compass was useless in the night's blackness, and we didn't dare light a match, knowing the rigidly enforced blackout regulations would bring immediate investigation of any light. As dark as it was, we had to steer by compass constantly because no tree or star was visible enough for us to get a line on and aim for.

Ken walked in front, intensely concentrating on the compass. I tagged along behind, holding onto a strap on his pack so we wouldn't become separated. I tried to see through the inky darkness to locate obstacles before we stumbled into them. Then we would swap places, Ken on the lookout while I navigated.

It was essential to stay tied together, else we would drift apart and lose sight of each other. That would have necessitated talking dangerously loud to find each other again. It would have been easy to totally lose each other. Neither of us relished the thought of separation, since we were discovering traits and abilities in each other we both needed to succeed in our escape.

During that first night out we stumbled onto some sort of industrial plant shortly after leaving the farm. We spent some anxious moments trying to get ourselves away from there without setting off an alarm or arousing anyone. We knew it would be certain death if we were found near a military or industrial establishment.

At the first sign of dawn we looked for a place to hide. We found a thicket that we considered satisfactory and tumbled into it. We were dead tired, and soon asleep. I slept fairly well despite my wet clothing, but Ken stayed awake watching most of the day.

The rain awakened me in the afternoon. Walking in the rain hadn't been bad, but sleeping in it was another matter. Ken told me two people had walked through the woods dangerously close to us while I slept. One was a kriegie, the other was a German NCO, apparently in hot pursuit. Martin was shaken by the close call, and swore we would never again spend the day in such a carelessly chosen or poorly prepared hiding place.

I was increasingly grateful for Martin's determination and thoroughness. Although I was often exasperated by those very things and by his attention to tiny details, I was beginning to appreciate those qualities in my companion.

That afternoon we lightened our packs. I discarded the Spanish grammar and a suit of khakis I had laboriously scrubbed and pressed back at Sagan. I rearranged my pack straps so that I could get them around my shoulders without Ken's help.

We tore off the backs and fly leaves from "Good Night, Sweet Prince." While waiting for darkness, Ken would read a page, tear it out and hand it to me. I would read it, then bury it.

We ate a fairly good meal, then prepared brews from dried coffee, cocoa and sugar. This we carried in small cans in our pockets to drink en route. At the first stream or puddle we would fill those with water, shake them up, and there would be our drink for the night.

At dusk we moved cautiously to the edge of the woods and stayed put there until darkness blurred our silhouettes. Then we set out eagerly, wondering what new perils the night would bring.

We started out in good spirits on the second night. The rain had stopped. There was an occasional star or silhouetted tree to help us find our way. We could stay together without tying ourselves to each other, and there was less stumbling and falling in the dark. We had lightened our packs, and both of us felt good about the distance between us and our guards.

Our cheerfulness soon ended when we found ourselves in a dense swampy thicket. There was no choice but to blunder through as best we could. Limbs and briars tore at us. In the thicket the inky blackness enveloped us again, and we would often run smack into a tree. But at least we didn't have to tie ourselves together; We were making so much noise crashing and thrashing about that we had no trouble keeping track of each other.

When we reached open fields again we quickly learned how densely populated Germany really was. We would stumble into villages suddenly, often when we least expected to encounter one. We soon learned to detect these villages in advance by using all our senses. Except on very dark night we could usually tell the angular silhouette of a row of houses from the more curving outlines of nature. We also developed our sense of smell to such an extent that we could distinguish the smell of a village in the distance from the pure, fragrant odor of the forests and fields. Other things warned us of civilization and danger: sounds of dogs barking, babies crying, roosters crowing and motors running.

Despite our alertness we occasionally would run into a village and have to walk right through the center of town. We would find ourselves suddenly at someone's front door, or tangled up in some farmhouse fence; we'd then beat a hasty retreat to the woods.

About fences, it was very fortunate for us that German farmers kept their livestock at home with them in their villages rather than fencing them in the fields; otherwise we would have had no end of trouble running into and climbing over fences.

Our goal the second night was to get across the Regnitz River. But when the gray dawn arrived we knew we would not make it.

We began a frantic search for a dense patch of woods to hide in until darkness came again. We found a place that looked good, but found after we settled in that we could see light on all sides. Eventually we found a small thicket in the center of a plowed field where we could conceal ourselves. We camouflaged our nest as best we could, covering everything that was not of a brown or green shade. We then made our bed, using boughs to hold us above the wet ground. We had a snack, then took off our wet shoes and overcoats and covered up with our wet blankets.

Most of the time we slept with one eye open. Either of us who saw or heard anything unusual would squeeze the arm of the other, the signal to freeze and remain motionless until the danger passed, remembering that a well-camouflaged object was conspicuous only when it moved.

On that day a farmer plowed the field around us all day. We could hear him talking to his horses as he worked. Several times we were almost certain he saw us.

That evening we set out as soon as it was dark, determined to get across the Regnitz. It rained again, and in the darkness we fell every few steps. Our packs made us top-heavy, and when we started falling the packs would seem to push us on down. We would often lie where we fell for several minutes, too tired to get up.

I smoked a lot during the day, but at night I allowed myself only three cigarettes because the risk of lighting a match was so great. I would cover myself completely with a blanket during our rest periods; Ken would check all around while I lit up. He didn't smoke so he often was impatient with me for exposing us to such risk for a cigarette.

That night we came upon an industrial plant surrounded by a high cyclone fence, We heard engines running inside. We thought it must be an important plant to have a fence around it as there were few fences in Germany. Therefore we proceeded with extreme caution.

We were walking along the fence line in one direction, trying to find a way around it, when we ran smack into a town. We quickly decided to retrace our steps. After we went quite far in the opposite direction and still had not found a way around the fence Ken decided we had to climb over it. I was very opposed to the idea; I'd had too much of being inside fences. I thought, too, that we might set off an alarm or get electrocuted. He persisted, though, and we started the climb. We didn't have too much difficulty scaling the seven-foot height. First we took off our packs and Ken boosted me to the top. As I hung there he handed me the packs and I threw them over. Then I pulled him up, and we jumped to the other side together, feeling surprised and lucky that no one had come to investigate.

We then resumed our westerly heading and soon came to the opposite fence without running into anything at all in between.

We repeated our fence-climbing procedure, crossed a highway, and at last, there before us stretched the Regnitz River.

We worked our way to the river, eager to cross it. When we arrived at the river's bank, however, we could readily see we would have to cross by bridge. There were no boats along the shore, and the river appeared too wide and too deep for us to swim.

We walked southward along the shore until we came to a road we thought would take us toward the bridge we'd seen. But after a few steps we reached a locked toll gate. It was a toll bridge! The Regnitz River itself was an obstacle we'd anticipated, but discovering that the only bridge across it within miles was a toll bridge was quite a blow. Toll bridges, of course, always had attendants, and attendants were people. People were our enemies who at the very least would demand money, if not our freedom, or our miserable lives!

As dawn seemed about to break we retreated to a thicket on top of a hill overlooking the highway and the river. Another night was gone and we still had not crossed the river.

We estimated from our map that we were on the outskirts of the city of Roth.

Our bivouac that day was highly unsatisfactory. We had spent too much time investigating the river crossing and had to hurry into the first thicket we found. It proved to be a sparse growth of scrubby pines. Although we camouflaged our nest as well as we could in the swiftly brightening dawn we were sleepless and apprehensive all day lest someone stumble upon us; the sounds and smells of civilization were far too close to suit our fast-developing animal instincts.

That night, the fourth of our escape, we crept cautiously down the hill, across the highway, and through the narrow valley to the river bank. We washed, drank and filled our water cans, then proceeded upstream to the bridge and hill where we had been nearly caught by the dawn that morning. This time, instead of following the road which ran through the gate we stayed by the water's edge until we had sneaked our way to a position directly under the bridge. From that position we were able to determine whether the bridge was guarded, how much traffic was going across it, and study our chances of climbing up over the bridge's railing in order to bypass the toll gate.

I guess we remained under the bridge for hours, whispering and listening, before we decided to risk the climb. We shouldered our packs and climbed up the embankment to a point not twenty feet from the toll gate. We climbed quickly over the railing, strode nonchalantly across the bridge whistling "Lily Marlene," the only German tune we knew.

At the opposite side of the bridge we found ourselves in a residential area. However, it was getting late so not much was stirring. We quickly made our way into open country.

The road we followed then was very satisfactory. There was no traffic and the road followed our heading nicely. It ascended steadily and we soon came into a hilly, forested area. The night was clear and cool, the air was pure and fragrant from the forests, and we were making good time. Our spirits soared.

We must have gone a long distance before we realized the road had made a decided turn away from our course. We were trying to steer westerly to avoid heading back into the Nurnberg area, then to veer northward. We estimated that course would intersect with the Heilbron-Nurnberg *Autobahn*, which our armored forces spearhead seemed to be driving toward. Our plan was to approach to within a mile or so of that four-lane highway; we figured that from that distance we would know when the spearhead passed us. Then we could continue westward, paralleling the fighting until the main spearhead had passed.

Unfortunately our information concerning the war situation was almost nil, so our plan was based almost entirely on conjecture. But we believed that any plan was better than no plan at all. We could alter our plans when conditions demanded. We knew that the most difficult part of our escape lay ahead, and that we had no experience or training that might assist us. We had no way to formulate an iron-clad plan for getting through to our own lines; we simply had to solve those problems as we came to them.

Germany was famous for its well-kept forests. That worked both for and against us. The scarcity of underbrush made it difficult for us to hide in the woods. There were numerous fire towers that increased our chances of being seen by fire watchers. But the network of fire trails through the forests gave us rather secluded paths that we could walk along with relative ease and safety. So we turned down one of these, again following our westerly heading.

We followed many such trails. At times the forests would close in, shutting out the starlight. We would lose sight of each other and would have to tie ourselves together and stumble through the woods, falling often, and occasionally crashing headlong into a tree.

By now my foot blisters had healed and my soles had toughened nicely. I developed a sensitivity that enabled me to feel my way along a trail with surprising accuracy. This new animal instinct became so reliable that Ken and I could walk at normal speed even when we could hardly see a foot ahead.

Toward morning our course brought us down a long decline. We were pleased for two reasons: First, we could double our normal speed going downhill. Second, streams would be found eventually so we could satisfy our thirst and refill our containers.

In walking all night we consumed large amounts of water. The small containers we carried contained coffee or cocoa. This would be consumed long before our daybreak stop, so we were without fluid except what we could find in a stream, ditch, or hole. On high ground such places were scarce.

At the bottom of the decline we came upon a stream that we thought must be the Rezat River. We drank and rested on the bank a long time before trying to cross. Recalling the time we had wasted at the Regnitz we decided to try to proceed directly across.

We probed the depth with sticks to assure ourselves that it was shallow enough. Then we removed our lower garments, pulled upper clothing as far up as possible while holding our packs on top of our heads. The water was frigid. It was difficult to keep from yelling as it closed into our armpits. Once across and dressed, however, the cozy feeling was luxurious.

We hurried toward the woods since dawn was fast approaching. I wanted to flop down and rest my weary body at the first likely looking hiding place, but Ken was never satisfied until he found the very best place in the area. To him the ideal hiding place was a thicket of saplings so low and thick that we would be warned of anyone coming near us by the noise of small twigs breaking. After he would find such a place he would laboriously camouflage it perfectly. When we'd eaten and put away our things he would crawl all around our nest to see if he could see a spot of blue or white, or the glint of a can shining through, in glaring contrast to the natural coloring of the forest.

We really appreciated the olive-drab color of our clothing and blankets; those colors were almost indistinguishable from the browns and greens of the forest. When Ken was completely satisfied with his job, he'd have me check it, too, to see if I could find any flaw he might have missed. Then, at last, we would snuggle into our damp blankets to sleep.

On that afternoon it rained again and we were soaked. Sleeping was impossible. We tried to shelter ourselves with our blankets. The rain only formed puddles on them, then poured through. We were chilled to the bone. Rest was out of the question. All we could do was take off our clothing, wring out some of the water, and put them on again. We also wrung out our blankets, then packed up our diminishing supplies and waited miserably for darkness to come so we could generate some body heat by walking.

We were very tired. Our bodies craved a warm meal and some roughage to fill the empty space in our stomachs. Our only remaining food was concentrates, mostly sugar.

I was reaching the point of fatigue that could trap an escapee;

the point where carelessness replaces caution. I desperately wanted to build a fire to dry out our clothing and have a warm drink. I had plenty of matches that I had kept dry in small bottles. I became obsessed with the thought of lighting a fire, and nagged Ken about it frequently. But he would remind me of the high risk. He pointed out that even the tiniest light would be visible for miles in the countryside's blackout. He was right of course.

That night we discovered the folly of following roads. We had had numerous close brushes with pedestrians, cyclists and motorists while following roads and trails, and always felt uneasy on them. We would normally follow a road just long enough to find a sign to check our position or until it veered away from our course, then we'd take to the open country or the forests.

On that particular night we were following a narrow country road when we suddenly came to a barricade. We backtracked hurriedly and turned at the first side road we came to. We proceeded up that road a little way, then found that it, too, was barricaded. There were heavy logs piled high across the road. We felt certain it was a gun emplacement. From then on we stayed on roads only for as long as it took to cross them at right angles and then only after we had stopped, looked and listened.

Ken was having a lot of trouble with his right leg and ankle. The ankle had swollen to twice its size the first night. He said his leg occasionally felt as though someone had hit him on the shin with a hammer. He seldom complained, but he had to slow down often. In ticklish situations my feet automatically sped up. I tried conscientiously to control that tendency, but nevertheless, Ken had to repeat over and over, "Slow down! Slow down!" I would then realize yet again how he must be suffering as he clack-clacked along on his brace, and would try hard to keep my mind and speed under control.

It was especially difficult for Ken to walk through plowed fields. But there was no way to avoid them. Once, as we stumbled through one, we paused to rest by what appeared to be a straw stack.

There seemed to be something vaguely familiar about that heap. My mind went way back to my childhood days on the farm. "Could this be?" I asked myself as I plunged my arm up to the shoulder through warm manure and straw. When I felt what I expected to find I was too excited to talk. I pulled out two huge potatoes and shoved them at Ken. When he felt them and slowly realized what they were he was more excited than I had ever seen him. We joyously loaded up with as many potatoes as we could carry.

We resumed our journey westward, eagerly anticipating the dawn when we could stop and camp for the day and try out our new food. We wondered how they would taste raw. What luck that German farmers plant whole potatoes, and not just a small piece, as is the American custom.

As we rested in another plowed field we found many rows that had been planted with the whole potatoes. Our first impulse was to load up again. But after passing through numerous fields similarly planted we realized that it would be silly to carry them around. They were everywhere for the taking. We found other fields with tasty green plants we couldn't identify, but we greedily ate them anyway.

We peeled and ate the raw potatoes and they were delicious. They had a crisp, sweetish flavor that reminded us of apples. We discovered that we could mix a bouillon cube with a spoonful of margarine, then by spreading the mixture on a slice of raw potato we would enjoy a food combination that almost satisfied our craving for meat.

We must have sounded like two parrots champing crackers as we noisily chewed our raw potatoes. We felt we no longer needed to worry about a food supply, and that the problem of hunger was eliminated.

My sensitive feet learned to recognize a potato field almost as soon as we stepped into one. Whenever that happened we would drop to the ground and run our hands along the furrow, just under the surface, until we found enough potatoes to last a day or two.

One night we inadvertently stumbled into a town. After the usual confusion we found the open road again. We hurried toward the nearest woods to relax and rest a bit. But just as we entered the woods our sensitive nostrils picked up a strong smell of motor vehicles. We halted, intent and cautious, and peered into the black night. We made out a truck just before we ran into it. It was probably part of a motor convoy that was parked in the woods to hide from allied aircraft. We turned and fled just as someone came into sight, searching with a flashlight.

We were just barely able to slip back into the night before his torch could spot us.

We hurried to another forest, more cautiously this time. We walked for a considerable distance and came to a steep downward bluff. Below us we heard the loud but muffled roar of engines. The sounds seemed to come out of the very ground we stood on. We searched fearfully for the source of the noise with our highly developed night vision. When we saw nothing alarming we figured the roars were coming from far away and the sounds were nothing to fear. Had we reasoned this better we could have saved ourselves from the grief that followed.

We skirted the bluff, searching for a way to descend, and came out on a railroad. We followed its tracks until they brought us to a level where we could clamber down the embankment. There appeared to be a large, flat meadow directly ahead and on our course. "Smooth sailing at last," we thought, elated. Finally we could make better progress.

When we entered the meadow we tripped over a tightly stretched wire, about a foot above the ground. Once again our logic failed to warn us, and we continued on with our suspicions unaroused.

A few hundred feet further we came upon what appeared to be the highway. Since we had made many deviations from our course since starting out I wanted to follow the road until we found a sign by which we could check our position. Ken was not in agreement with that, due to our earlier bad experience with roads. I persisted and eventually he gave in.

We walked down the road for perhaps a hundred yards when I reflected that it was the widest and straightest road I had ever seen. Also it was surfaced with a curiously familiar substance. For the third time our tired brains failed to assemble the alarming facts. The roar of engines continued emanating from the cliff from which we had descended. We now walked parallel to and about half a mile from the cliff's base. A suspicion slowly seeped into my brain. I stopped to touch the soft substance we were walking on. It was coarsely ground wood.

My mind jumped back to England where we had seen that same substance on runways. The English painted it green so that from above the runway would not be distinguishable from the surrounding grass. I then could feel the unmistakable prints of fighter planes' tires in the adjoining earth.

Everything was suddenly clear. The underground hangers, the roar of airplane engines being tested in underground shops, the alarm wire, and now the runway. We were in the middle of a German air base! We fought panic and trotted as fast as we could away from those hangers. Suddenly we saw a row of barracks before us. We wheeled away, imagining German soldiers inside.

Back in the temporary safety of the airfield we held a panicky conference. We didn't dare go back in the direction from which we had tripped over the wire because of the probability of our having triggered an alert.

We agreed to try another route, but found our way blocked by more buildings. We tried other directions, but met with failure each time.

After spending two hours on the base we began losing hope since dawn would soon catch us there. We decided to make one more desperate attempt. Somehow a hole opened for us through the maze of buildings. We darted through it and raced for the woods. Putting aside exhaustion we rushed for the nearest clump of trees only to skid to a stop when the long barrel of an anti-aircraft gun appeared directly over our heads. We were so close we could see the mesh of its camouflage net. We were afraid the gun crew would be sleeping nearby.

Again we wheeled and ran, with an awful feeling of being trapped and defeated. When we finally reached the sanctity of the woods we flopped to the ground, too tired to move. After a brief rest we roused ourselves and departed, hoping to put a safe distance between ourselves and that air base before dawn.

Daylight began brightening the landscape as we came to a busy highway where we could plainly distinguish people and vehicles moving about. A town was on our left. Ahead and to the right we saw a hilly region that appeared to be our safest destination. With no other choice we gritted our teeth and proceeded through the thoroughfare. Walking nonchalantly, looking straight ahead, we tried to appear at home and to look as though we knew exactly where we were going.

Our masquerade succeeded, even though we felt about as much at home as a couple of wild animals in similar circumstances. We would have presented a miserable picture had anyone observed us closely. We were wet, dirty and bearded. Our GI caps were pulled down over our ears, our lumpy packs bending our tired backs as we limped along with eyes facing rigidly forward.

No one challenged us; perhaps they were too sleepy to notice us at that early hour, or maybe they had reached the point where they were surprised at nothing. Maybe they were too preoccupied with their own problems of self preservation to bother with us since the fighting could not be too far ahead.

After being stopped by one blind street we climbed a steep trail that lead into the hills and took us away from the town. Reaching a summit we were able to look down into the valley and see many fortifications. Apparently this valley and town were going to be heavily defended.

We felt very lucky to be out of that area. Walking in broad daylight for the the first time, we surveyed the surrounding rugged terrain. It was the kind we had wished for, to hole up in and await the arrival of our front lines.

After we'd proceeded a few miles more away from the town we found what we thought was an ideal thicket. Nearby was a spring with clear water flowing out of a hillside. Feeling very satisfied with our situation we fell into the deep sleep of the exhausted.

In the afternoon we were awakened by the sound of breaking twigs. Squeezing each other's arm in mute signal we froze motionless. Turning our heads very slowly, we caught sight of an elderly couple collecting wood. They were only about a hundred feet away, breaking off the lower dead limbs from the saplings in which we were hiding. They worked all afternoon coming and going with their fagots. We were confident they wouldn't notice us and tried to rest, but with the continual cracking of twigs and the uncomfortable feeling their presence gave, we were unable to relax.

By the time they left our fatigue had reached the point where we simply had to sleep. We both knew that if we didn't get some sleep soon our judgment might become clouded. So early that evening we scouted the area and decided we would risk spending a night there.

After dark we took soap and a razor down to the spring. We sponged ourselves off, then lathered our long beards and shaved by feel in the darkness. We returned to our nest feeling considerably refreshed.

After persistent nagging I got Ken to consent to making a

fire. We chose a spot quite a distance away from our nest, and in the center of another thicket. I dug a small hole and placed a few twigs in it. While Ken covered me with a blanket, I lit a small fire. We were so accustomed to the darkness it seemed as though the fire's glare was a searchlight spotting us. We imagined people staring at us, not to mention the fire watchers who were surely triangulating our position.

Ken was unable to cover me sufficiently to keep some light from glaring out. My twigs would flare up, then go out. I spilled most of our precious cocoa, but finally got some lukewarm. I offered it to Ken. He refused. I knew then that he was really furious with me. It took something serious to make him refuse food, and warm food at that. I had to drink my cocoa alone. I should have enjoyed it. Ken asked me if it was worth all the trouble and risk. I had to admit it was not.

We went back to our nest and slept quite soundly all that night and far into the next morning.

Feeling relieved when the old couple did not return that morning we sneaked out for some daylight scouting, leaving our packs concealed. We were quite rested now, and without the weight of the packs, rather enjoyed investigating our surroundings. We crept from tree to tree, Indian-fashion, down to the spring. After seeing that the coast was clear we drank its sweet, pure water.

Returning to our thicket we walked confidently along a narrow dirt road. We came around a bend and found ourselves face to face with a middle-aged couple carrying a picnic basket. We stopped still for an instant, too startled to think or act intelligently, then we spun around and walked guiltily fast in the opposite direction. As soon as we'd rounded the bend we dived into a clump of bushes and lay quiet.

As the couple passed by us we could see the man looking apprehensively in all directions. We knew we had aroused their suspicion and they might soon have the whole town looking for us.

We rushed back to our nest and broke camp hurriedly. Fortunately it was a cloudy day and the friendly darkness came early, swallowing us up in its comforting embrace. Soon after darkness that evening it started raining again. Several times during the next days and nights we narrowly escaped detection. Our experiences and privations were beginning to tell on our minds and bodies. We both had contracted dysentery from bad water. We were tired of being continually wet. Our strength was being sapped from trying to negotiate the rugged terrain in pitch darkness. Living the life of hunted animals was taking its toll. We felt dazed and we started seeing mirages.

The weather cleared at last and the welcomed sun warmed and refreshed us. We found ourselves in a virgin forest and, with no other place to hide, we chose a brush heap where the remains of large tree tops were neatly stacked. Eager to rest, I wanted to simply crawl into the center of the heap and curl up. But despite his emaciated condition Ken would have none of that. So we spent two weary hours tearing down the heap, then restacking it, leaving a perfect little room inside.

Surveying our surroundings this appeared to be our best stopping place so far. On top of a large knoll with cleared forest in all directions, we could see anyone approaching while still inside our room, yet not risk being seen ourselves. We decided to stay.

The sun was warm enough for us to attempt drying our wet clothes. One of us would spread them out on the ground while the other stayed on lookout inside the heap.

At noon on our second day there the spearhead passed us. We had expected action when that occurred, but we had not expected all hell to break loose as it did. Bombers and fighters swarmed overhead. We heard bombs exploding close by and fifty-caliber guns rattled as fighters strafed nearby targets. One bomb fell within a hundred feet of us. Foot soldiers walked by near us. We couldn't see them but we could hear their rifles and shouts.

Martin and I, scared stiff as we hid in our brush heap, didn't know whether to be glad or sad. We were glad we had finally reached the fighting because that meant Americans and freedom. Yet we were now face to face with our most difficult problem, how to penetrate the American lines. We felt we were so near, yet so far, and wondered if we would have the strength and mental acuity to complete our escape. That afternoon we might have have sold out cheaply.

That evening the intensity of the struggles subsided somewhat, and we decided we had better clear out. We headed westward. We wanted to parallel the fighting from a safe distance until we were far enough behind the spearhead to find a quiet gap to worm our way through.

We could see and hear the conflict as we walked along. We stayed about one or two miles south of the main action. As we had expected, that appeared to be taking place along the east-west highway.

We were tired and weak, and seemed to fall more often, and needed to rest frequently. Several times one of us would catch the other before he fell down a bluff.

We saw a lot of German activity. Often we had to hide beside a road to wait for a column of tanks, trucks, or foot soldiers to pass before we could cross. Our practice was to lie quietly and listen carefully. Then when all was quiet we would hurriedly cross and get away from the road as fast as possible.

Despite our caution we were almost hit by bicycles twice, so silently did they glide along.

At dawn on the eleventh night of our escape we came out into a great open space. Realizing it was futile to try to find a forest we sought some other form of cover. We found a small, isolated barn, and became frantic when we found it was locked. It was getting quite light and we could see the area we were in was thickly populated. We tore off a board and squeezed inside. We were not alone; there were two sheep in the barn with us. We knew the owner of the sheep would have to feed and water them, so we reluctantly abandoned the idea of sleeping there.

We left hurriedly and ran up a trail until we came to a downward bluff. Looking down we saw we were standing on the rim of a deep quarry with a paved highway at its floor. As steep as the cliff was, it was our only way to go. Surprisingly, we got down the bluff without too much difficulty.

Boulders and slabs were strewn about on the floor of the quarry. We selected and crawled beneath a slab that was propped up about two feet by a boulder. We attempted to enclose ourselves by filling the sides with piles of smaller rocks.

That day was a most miserable one. A cold drizzle kept us wet and chilled all day. Our bed was hard and full of sharp pointed rocks. We soon became so cold we shivered constantly. To make matters worse the rim above us turned out to be a sort of promenade where people strolled and loitered all day, in spite of the bad weather. Their voices sounded as though they were standing right next to us. An SS officer conversed with his girl friend nearby and we heard every word they spoke.

The highway we hid beside was constantly busy. A column of bicycle troops passed by continually. All this left us feeling very insecure.

We ate the last of our food, then discarded everything else we were carrying except one blanket each and our emergency rations. When we started out that night we were determined to get through the lines to freedom.

We found a brook across the road. We washed, drank and filled our cans there. Then we waded a creek and started climbing a very steep hill. We fell several times, rolling and sliding until we caught a bush or tree to grab onto.

We made it to the top eventually and came out on a rather flat plateau. Again we could see the flashes of battle and hear explosions off to our right. We headed that way.

Two German trucks passed so close we were certain they saw us. We flattened ourselves in a fresh plowed furrow as one of the drivers stopped to investigate. After a few anxious moments he returned to his truck, then moved on. We were grateful to be able to do the same. Then we heard the babble of many voices and the jingle-jangle of equipment ahead. As we listened intently I was sure they were Americans. As they came nearer I was even more convinced. But I must have been delirious. We stayed hidden in a furrow close to the road as they came closer. After a few seconds I knew I had been wrong and they were German soldiers.

It was surprising to see Germans so jubilant and carefree. There were about 200 of them, and they passed within six feet of where we hid. We guessed they had just come from a battle and now had the exhilarated joyfulness of people who are surprised to find themselves still alive. After they had gone by we too moved on.

We could now detect a line of light artillery stretched along parallel to the battle. By watching and listening carefully we were able to spot each gun and choose a corridor between them. They were whamming away at our American troops along the road.

Once when we were picking our way between the guns we almost ran into a soldier. As we hurried away he started calling, "Hans! Hans!" in a youthful, frightened voice. He continued bleating like a lost sheep until we were out of hearing.

After a few hundred yards we came into an area beneath the

artillery that we considered to be no man's land. We spent about three hours under the screaming shells, trying to figure out where to go from there. Our side had by then spotted the guns which we had just passed and were opening up on them. We just made it through in time!

We could tell where the shells were coming from and where they were landing but not much else about what was going on. We had learned three nights before to time the difference between an artillery flash and its explosion. That gave us an accurate estimate of its distance from us.

All thoughts of the war going on around us suddenly left us when we ran across three sacks of potatoes lying in the field. We felt rich finding such a huge quantity of potatoes without having to dig for them, and stuffed our pockets.

Ahead, where we aimed to intersect, we could see a large fire with much activity in its vicinity. We wanted to reach the apparently quiet area just behind the fire. We crept along slowly, pausing every few steps in whispered consultation to G-2 the situation as best we could before we proceeded. We estimated the road was a hundred yards ahead. Shells screamed over our heads and whammed into their targets in the distance. There was a constant rattle of small arms fire. Our position was extremely precarious.

We were huddled together whispering when we were startled by the sound of a German voice. "Halt!" someone said, quietly but firmly. My insides seemed to drop as I fumbled for a suitable answer in German. Ken did not know that the word "halt" was the same in German as in English, except for a slightly different sound of the "A", and I had not thought to tell him! The "halt" we had heard was decidedly German!

Ken started talking fast in English, explaining who we were, where we had come from, and asking them not to shoot.

The answer that came back bewildered me completely. "Okay, boys, come on up and be recognized." The language was American but the accent was German. I was really perplexed. I quickly whispered my suspicions to Ken, adding that we had to do something fast. We eased forward cautiously, then one of us asked them if they were French. This time the response was decidedly American, accent and all. "Hell, naw, we're Americans."

By now we were within six feet of them and could see their

silhouettes. There were three figures, and we could see then that they were unmistakably, heartwarmingly American infantrymen.

We jumped into their foxhole and, laughing with giddy joy, we shook their hands and slapped their backs. We both were out of our minds with happiness. We repeated to each other, "We made it! We made it!" and kept on laughing and shaking hands.

The soldiers, now realizing we were senior officers, respectfully reminded us to pipe down, pointing out that we were on the very front of the front. They said they had just had a counterattack and we were damn lucky they hadn't shot first as was their usual custom. At first their admonitions fell on deaf ears. We were safe, we were home, we were free! It seemed nothing could harm us now. We hadn't talked above a whisper in twelve days and there was no shutting us up now. To accommodate them, though, we did quiet down.

I wrote down the mens' names while one of the soldiers called their company command post on his field phone to find out what to do with us. The three men were in Company I (the letter "I"). Third Battalion, Twenty Second Infantry Regiment, Fourth Division, Seventh Army; they were Staff Sergeant Fred Squilla and Private First Class (PFC) Joseph Schwartz; I regret that I did not get the name of the third soldier.

Before we left the foxhole the mystery of the German accent that had almost stopped my heart a few minutes earlier was solved. PFC Schwartz was German American and spoke with a strong accent. His "halt" had been spoken exactly as pronounced in German!

On instructions received over the field phone, one of the soldiers escorted us from the foxhole and to the company command post. Ken and I had not seen ground fighting at close hand before so our walk to the command post was very interesting. Ground war was totally different to the air war we had known.

We entered a village that had been shelled; most of its structures were still burning. Every few yards we were halted by an unseen sentry and our escort had to whisper the password.

After following a complex route we eventually arrived at the command post of Company I. It was located in the cellar of a house vacated only the previous afternoon by its fleeing occupants.

A strange sight greeted us when we entered. About a half-dozen soldiers appeared to be sleeping or dozing on the tile floor of what had been the kitchen of the house. The typically German furnishings were cluttered with military equipment. One man was lying on the floor with his eyes closed, making strange noises. We wondered aloud if the man had gone around the bend. First lieutenant Milton Schneider, the company executive officer, explained that he was now running the war in that sector, and the man was the company communications sergeant. The strange noises were the sergeant's signals over the field phone, which we could not see, to the men in the perimeter foxholes positioned around the town. The strange-sounding man was Sergeant Ernest Odykirk; his wire man was PFC George Scholten; also present was PFC William St.John, radio operator.

Lieutenant Schneider asked if we were hungry. Was he kidding? Our mouths were watering at the sight of a pile of fresh eggs in the kitchen. I had had exactly one fresh egg in the past year. He fixed us each a large bowl of boned chicken and five fried eggs, apologizing for what he thought was a meager ration. Talking as we gulped our feast, I know we must have sounded like lunatics, and surely we looked worse.

With our hunger sated, our happiness was boundless. We loved everybody and everything. We praised the Army, the USA, the President, and the U.S. Infantry, and particularly Company I.

Schneider gave us a brief resume of the Fourth Division. He was temporarily in command of Company I, as their commanding officer had just been killed. He said most of the personnel in the division had been replaced four times. He told us we were extremely fortunate not to have been shot, since the men those days tended to shoot first and challenge afterward. Furthermore, some Germans disguised as escaped American prisoners had been caught recently.

We had to be properly identified before we could be sent to the rear. Lieutenant Schneider called his regimental headquarters and in a few minutes an escort arrived. We thanked the lieutenant and his men for their wonderful hospitality, then were escorted to the regimental operations office in a nearby building. There, a Captain Roche satisfied himself that we were not spies. He treated us to a nice shot of cognac and was very hospitable. The cognac tasted good, but had little intoxicating effect on us because we were already drunk with happiness at being free. We gave him what intelligence we had gathered behind the German lines.

At about four a.m. a jeep picked us up and we departed from the front lines. Our driver zipped along at top speed on the narrow road to regimental rear.

I can't forget that dark, terrifying ride. We passed the remains of what we were told was a jeep that had hit a mine the night before, killing its four occupants. There wasn't enough of it left to tell what kind of vehicle it had been. I suspected our driver thought if he hit a mine going fast enough he would be able to pass over it before it exploded. Or perhaps he was racing with the dawn which was fast approaching. At any rate we were lucky to arrive at Twenty-Second Regiment Headquarters in one piece.

The staff of the Twenty-Second was extremely hospitable. It was commanded by Lieutenant Colonel J. F. Ruggles (West Point '31), with Lieutenant Colonel A.S.Teague as executive officer. They took us to a residence that had so recently been commandeered that its civilian occupants were still inside. We enjoyed the luxury of a bath and shave, then were given new field uniforms from top to bottom.

Things were moving too fast for our numbed minds to keep up, and several times Colonel Teague had to remind us to hurry! hurry! Their attitudes were the opposite of ours. For them, there was still a job to do, a war to win; they were strong, vigorous, eager warriors. For us the war was already over and all that remained was anti-climax and memories. We had fought our battles, achieved our goals, and in the process had drained our physical and mental resources, leaving a void.

That noon we had lunch with the commanding general of the Fourth Division and his staff.

When we tried to sleep in real beds that night at division rear at Bad Mergentheim, far back from the front, it was hopeless; the beds were much too soft.

All the next day the staff at division rear tried hard to welcome us back by trying to amuse and entertain us, but we couldn't respond. The height of enjoyment for us was simply to sit in a blissful stupor and soak in the blessed freedom!

CLASS OF SERVICE

This is a full-rate Telegram or Cable-gram unless its de-ferred character is in-dicated by a suitable symbol above or pre-ceding the address.

WESTERN UNION

A. N. WILLIAMS
PRESIDENT

SYMBOLS

DL = Day Letter

NL = Night Letter

LC = Deferred Cable

NLT = Cable Night Letter

Ship Radiogram

1201

(37)

The filing time shown in the date line on telegrams and day letters is STANDARD TIME at point of origin. Time of receipt is STANDARD TIME at point of destination

N156 23 GOVT=WUX WASHINGTON DC 30 428P 30 APR 5 39

=MRS KATHERINE R BURTON

=215 WEST 109 ST NYK:

=THE SECRETARY OF WAR DESIRES ME TO INFORM YOU THAT YOUR
HUSBAND LT/COL BURTON PAUL T RETURNED TO MILITARY CONTROL

16 APR 45=

16 45.

THE COMPANY WILL APPRECIATE SUGGESTIONS FROM ITS PATRONS CONCERNING ITS SERVICE

The Escape as reported by New York papers.

NEW YORK WORLD-TELEGRM, FRIDAY, APRIL 20, 1945.

Free

A. P. Photo.

Lt. Col. Paul T. Burton, commander of a bomber squadron who bailed out over Antwerp while on a mission, April 22, 1944, escaped from a German prison camp to the American lines. His wife and two children live with her mother, Mrs. Mary O'Shea, 215 W. 109th St.

AIR FORCE CHIEFS HELD FOR YEAR ESCAPE NAZIS

Captive U. S. General Marches with Men

CREGLINGEN, Germany, April 16 [Delayed] - (AP) — Two United States 8th and 9th air force commanders who had been prisoners in Germany almost a year stumbled into the American lines early this morning. They had escaped from a prison camp 12 days ago.

The officers are Col. Kenneth R. Martin of Kansas City, Mo., commander of the 354th Mustang fighter group, and Lt. Col. Paul T. Burton of New York City, commander of a bomber squadron in the 389th Liberator group. Both were in good health.

They escaped on April 4 as the Germans began evacuation of their camp in western Germany.

NEW YORK HERALD TRIBUNE.

New York Pilot Escapes Nazi Camp After a Year

Col. Paul Burton Reaches U.S. Lines Unharmed

CREGLINGEN, Germany, April 16 (Delayed) (AP).—Two American Air-Force officers who had been prisoners in Germany almost a year, reached the American lines early today, following their escape from a prison camp twelve days ago.

The officers are Colonel Kenneth R. Martin, of Kansas City, Mo., commander of the 354th Mustang Fighter Group, and Lieutenant Colonel Paul T. Burton, of 215 West 109th Street, New York, commander of a bomber squadron in the 389th Liberator group. Both were in good health.

Burton, whose parents live in Magnolia, Ark., was flying as a command pilot in a raid on Hamm April 22, 1944, when his plane was crippled by flak over Dortmund.

All the crew but three bailed out. He and the pilot and the bombardier bailed out over Antwerp and were captured. The other two, Captain Bill Stotter and Lieutenant Lester Gins, both of Cleveland, still are prisoners of the Germans.

Wife W...s..at News

"It must have been the prayers." . . Mrs. Katherine Burton said yesterday, amid tears, when told that her husband, Lieutenant Colonel Paul T. Burton, was safe. With their two children, Richard Travis, nine years old, and Donald, two, she lives with her mother, Mrs. Mary O'Shea, at 215 West 109th Street.

Colonel Burton, who is thirty-one, was born in Arkansas. An aviation enthusiast since his boyhood, he once had a flying school at the Flushing Airport, Queens. He helped organize the first bombing and gunnery school in Canada. A veteran of more than twenty bombing missions over Europe, he holds the Distinguished Flying Cross and the Air Medal, both with clusters.

Flees Nazi Prison Camp

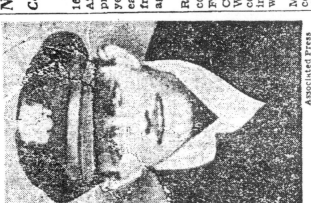

Associated Press

Lieut. Colonel Paul T. Burton

Newsclipping from <u>Stars and Stripes</u> Newspaper May 19, 1945.

Crashed Mustang Pilot Tells of Escape

Nazis Gave Him 3rd Degree in Hospital

By Andy Rooney
Stars and Stripes Staff Writer

PARIS, May 18—Col. Kenneth R. Martin, commander of the first Mustang group in the British Isles, whose plane went down in flames after crashing head on into an Me109, when both Martin and the German pilot refused to give way as they screamed toward each other with guns blazing, escaped before the German surrender and is now at USSTAF HQ waiting to return home.

When the Messerschmitt and the Mustang crashed both pilots were miraculously thrown free and escaped alive. Martin suffered a broken leg, a broken foot and a crushed left arm. He was taken to a German hospital together with the Luftwaffe pilot and while they both lay in beds only a short distance apart the nervy German flier broadcast a report of the aerial crash to a German audience. The broadcast was picked up by an Allied monitoring service and Martin's pilots back in England heard, for the first time, that he was alive.

As commander of a group of new-type planes operating against Germany, Martin had information German intelligence officers needed and he was put in solitary confinement for five weeks in an interrogation hospital where prisoners were treated and questioned simultaneously.

It was 12 days before they got around to setting Martin's badly mangled left

arm. In the operating room he was laid on a table and given a small dose of anesthetic. It was not enough to kill the pain but just enough to make him groggy. While the German doctor worked to adjust the bones in his arm, an interro-

Col. Kenneth R. Martin

gator standing over him hammered away with the same questions:

"How far can the plane fly?"

"How many groups will there be in England?"

"Where?"

The Germans used threats and pro-

mises of better treatment as the chief means of attempting to get information, Martin said.

"You knew they weren't getting the information they wanted and sometimes you wondered what they would do next and how much you could stand before telling them," Martin said.

After six weeks in the interrogation hospital Martin was moved to a hospital completely staffed with captured British doctors and medics.

After ten months in prison camps, Martin was moved, with 2,000 others, from Nuremberg in the direction of Moosburg to escape the approaching Allied armies.

At the end of the first day's march Martin and Lt. Col. Paul T. Burton, of New York, staged an escape attempt only to be caught.

That night the column stopped near a large barn. The two Americans lay quietly nearby and after everyone had settled down they edged away in the pitch black night, while the guards stood less than ten feet from them.

Using a compass Martin had kept hidden for ten months, the two traveled by night and slept during the day, eating the meager march rations and foraging at night for more food.

They came into American lines 12 nights later, having walked 75 miles through German territory.

Martin is 28 years old. His wife and two children live in Kansas City, Mo.

Appendix One

Glossary

(Kriegie vocabulary)
Note: Italicized words are from German.
Asterisked words are slang.

Abgeschlossen   Shot down, destroyed

Abort*   Latrine

Abwehr   Security Personnel

Alles im ordung   All in order

American Red Cross
    Supplier of food and clothing for
    POW'S

Amerikanisch   American

Appell   Roll call parade

Autobahn   Four-lane highway

A-1,A-2,A-3,A-4   American military functional groups

B-17, B-24   American four-engine heavy bombers

Barracks   Troop quarters

Bash* (or Food Bash)
                Act of overeating; food binge

BBC   British Broadcasting Corporation

Belaria   Town near Sagan; location of another POW camp

Block*   Barracks

Block Commander
                Barracks Commander

Blockbuster*   Very large bomb

Bolshevik   Communist

brace*   Standing at rigid (twanging*) attention (military jargon)

Burgermeister   Mayor

"C" Rations   Combat rations

cadre   Nucleus of trained personnel

camp*   Prison

CAVU   Ceiling and visibility unlimited

Center Camp*   One of the five segretated prisons of Stalag Luft III(others: North, South, East and West)

Chandelier *   Marker flares parachuted over target for night bombing

Chatter gun*   Machine gun

Coak-and-dagger*
                Undercover group, Intelligence

C.O. or CO   Commmanding Officer

Combine*   Organization of occupants of one
                    room

Compound*   POW camp or Lager

Company grade officer
                    Captain or Lieutenant

Contrail*   Aircraft vapor trail

Cooler*   Slang for punishment cell

"D" bars   High energy candy bars included in
                    "K"(emergency) rations

Detaining Power   Geneva Convention terminology.
                    in this case, Germany

Deutschland   Germany

D.P. *   Duty Pilot, code for block lookout
                    duty

Dulag Luft, or Dulag
                    German Air Force Interrogation
                    Center

ersatz   Substitute

Essen   Eat, food

Feldwebel   Sergeant

Ferret*   Member of *Abwehr*

Field grade officer
                    Major, Lieutenant Colonel, or
                    Colonel

Flak	Anti-aircraft artillery. (From German: *Flugziogabwehrkanonen*)
Flack alley *	Heavily defended industrial area of German Ruhr Valley
Flack House*	Red Cross rest and recuperation retreat
Flugzoigabwehrkanonen	Source of acronym, "Flak"
flap*	Uproar, panicky confusion
Fliegeralarm	Air raid alarm
Flieger	Flyer, aircraft
forts*	Flying Fortresses, B-17's
Forty-and-eight*	Train cars that can hold forty men or eight horses
FOODACO*	Food Account
Führer	Leader
G-two-ing*	Intelligence analyzing
Gefreidter	Private (soldier)
General	German General officer
Geneva Convention	1929 agreement for protection of prisoners of war
Gestapo	Geheime Staatspolizei, Nazi Political Police

GI*	"Government issue," also slang for American serviceman
GI'S*	Gastroenteristis
Goon*	German
Goon Baiting*	Creating problems for guards
Goon box, goon tower*	Guard tower
Gravy train*	Easy job
Gremlin*	Fictitious gnome believed responsible for malfunctions of aircraft or equipment
Group	Division of US Air Force Wing containing four Squadrons
Hauptmann	Captain
Halifax	British four-engine heavy bomber
Heat suit	Flight suit that could be electrically heated by plugging into aircraft's electrical system
Heavies	Heavy bombers; American B-17's and B-24's, British Lancasters and Halifaxes
Heer	Army
Herauf	Up!, Roust!
Herr	Master, sir
Himmel!	Heavens
Hitler Jugend	Hitler Youth

Hundfuhrer	Dog Master
International Red Cross	One of three neutral organizations whose representatives were permitted direct contact with POW's; the other two were the Swiss Legation in Berlin and the Swedish YMCA
IP	Initial Point, beginning of a bomb run to the target
Iron ration	Emergency ration
Jawohl	Yes sir, yes indeed
Jude	Jew
Jugend	Youth
"K" rations	Emergency rations
Kaputt	Out of order
Kein	No, not any, no one
Knickebrot	Miser bread, thin wafer, similar to rye
kohlrabi	Cabbage-turnip type vegetable
Kommandant	Commanding officer
Kommandantur	Command headquarters
K.P.	Kitchen police, or kitchen duty
Kriegie*	Slang for POW, from the German Kriegsgefangen
Kriegsmarine	Navy

Kuhler   Cooler, punishment cell

Kultur   Culture

Lager   Camp

Lagerführer   Camp Commander

Lancaster   British four-engine heavy bomber

Leutenant   Second Lieutenant

Luftwaffe   Air Force

Major   German Major (pronounced ma-yor)

Man of Confidence
                      Camp leader elected by enlisted
                      prisoners

Maschine kaput   Plane out of commission

May West*   Life Preserver

Mein Kampf   *My Struggle*, Hitler's autobiography

mess   Dining area

Mitte Lager   Center Camp

Mosquito   English twin-engine fighter-bomber

Nazi   Germany's National Socialist Party

NCO   Non-Commissioned Officer

Nein,nichts   No, don't

No-man's land   Unoccupied area between opposing
                      troops

Oberfeldwebel	Technical Sergeant
Obergefreidter	Private First Class, Lance Corporal
Obergrupenführer	*SS General*
Oberleutnant	First Lieutenant
Oberst	Colonel
Oberstleutnant	Lieutenant Colonel
O D	Olive drab color
Offizier	Officer
OKW	*Oberkommando Wehrmacht*, German Supreme Command
Old Man*	Senior Officer, Commanding Officer
Padre	Father, or Chaplain
Parole	Written Promise of a POW to fulfill stated conditions in exchange for certain privileges; usually carried threat of death if violated
P-47	American fighter aircraft
Pop-to*	To come to attention
Potato masher*	German hand gernade with long handle
POW	Prisoner of war
Protecting Power	Swiss Legation in Berlin
Prima	Excellent

Purge*	Group of POW's being transfered to a permanent camp
RAF	Royal Air Force †
RAAF	Royal Australian Air Force †
RCAF	Royal Canadian Air Force †
RNZAF	Royal New Zealand Air Force †
RSAAF	Royal South African Air Force †
Red Cross	International charitable organization
Reich	Government
Redoubt	Secret military withdrawal area
Revier	Sick-bay, hospital
Rundfunk	Broadcasting system
SAO	Senior American Officer
sack*	Bed
Sagan	Town in Lower Silesia, location of *Stalag Luft III*
Sanitäter	Medical orderly
*Schiesshaus**	Crude slang for abort
Section	Military staff functional organization
Senior officer	Highest ranking officer

† See end of Glossary for rank symbols with American equivalents

Siegfried Line	Line of fortifications between Germany and France at beginning of WWII
Slush fund*	Fund to obtain small luxuries
Spam	Canned meat
Spoof raid*	Diversionary air raid
Squadron	One of four operational forces in an air force Group
SS	*Schutzstaffel*, German Protective Echelon, elite corps of the *Nazi* Party
Stalag	Contraction of German Stammlager
Stalag Luft	Air Force permanent POW camp, from German *Stammlager Luftwaffe*
Stammlager	Permanent POW camp
Statsfeldwebel	Master Sergeant
Stroller*	A guard who walked along the fence between guard towers
Swedish YMCA	One of three neutral organizations whose representatives were permitted direct contact with POW's; the other two were the International Red Cross and the Swiss Legation in Berlin
Swiss Legation	Protecting Power; one of three neutral organizations whose representatives were permitted direct contact with POW's; the other two were the International Red Cross and the Swedish YMCA.
Tee	Tea (tee is pronounced "tay")

Terrorflieger	Terror flyer
Tiefflieger	Low-flying aircraft
Truppenlager	Soldiers camp, German guards' barracks
Unteroffizier	Corporal
USAAF or USAAC	Former names of U.S. Air Force: U.S. Army Air Forces, U. S. Army Air Corps
Vaterland	Native country, fatherland
Verboten	Forbidden
Vernicht	Kill
Vistula	River in Eastern Europe
Volkstrum	Senior Peoples Army
Voralarm	First alert
Vorlager	Front camp
Wehrmacht	armed forces
West Camp	One of five camps, or compounds, in *Stalag Luft III*
Westlager	West Camp
Wing	Part of an Air Force Division
Zahlmeister	Quartermaster,German rations issuer
Zahnpulver	Toothpowder

Appendix Two

AMERICAN/BRITISH RANK EQUIVALENTS

Abbreviation	Rank	USA Equivalent
F/O	Flight Officer, Flying Officer	Lieutenant
F/Lt	Flight Lieutenant	Captain
S/L	Squadron Leader	Major
W/C	Wing Commander	Lt. Colonel
G/C	Group Captain	Colonel

Appendix Three

NAMES MENTIONED